The International Handbook of Electronic Commerce

Jae K. Shim, Ph.D.
Anique A. Qureshi, Ph.D., CPA, CIA
Joel G. Siegel, Ph.D., CPA
Roberta M. Siegel

Glenlake Publishing Company, Ltd.
Chicago • London • New Delhi

AMACOM
American Management Association
New York • Atlanta • Boston • Chicago • Kansas City • San Francisco • Washington, D.C.
Brussels • Mexico City • Tokyo • Toronto

© 2000 The Glenlake Publishing Company, Ltd.
All rights reserved.
Printed in the United States of America

ISBN: 0-8144-0580-0

AMACOM
American Management Association
New York • Atlanta • Boston • Chicago • Kansas City •
San Francisco • Washington, D.C.
Brussels • Mexico City • Tokyo • Toronto

Printing number
10 9 8 7 6 5 4 3 2 1

Dedication

Shaheen Qureshi
Loving and Devoted Wife

Aqsa Qureshi
Wonderful Daughter

Acknowledgements

We wish to express our appreciation to our editor, Barbara Evans, for her outstanding editing work on this project. We very much appreciate her exceptional efforts.

Table of Contents

About the Authors

Jae K. Shim, Ph.D., is professor of business administration at California State University, Long Beach. Dr. Shim received his MBA and Ph.D. degrees from the University of California at Berkeley. For over 20 years a consultant on information systems development and computer applications, he is now president of the National Business Review Foundation, a management and computer consulting firm. Dr. Shim has more than 50 books to his credit and has published some 50 articles in professional journals, including the *Journal of Systems Management, Financial Management*, the *Journal of Operational Research, Omega, Data Management, Management Accounting, Simulation and Games, Long Range Planning*, the *Journal of Business Forecasting, Decision Sciences, Management Science*, and *Econometrica*.

In 1982 Dr. Shim received the Credit Research Foundation Outstanding Paper Award for one of his articles on financial modeling. He has also received a Ford Foundation Award, a Mellon Research Fellowship, and an Arthur Andersen Research Grant.

Anique Qureshi, Ph.D., CPA, CIA, is associate professor of accounting and information systems at Queens College of the City University of New York. He is an expert in computer applications, especially those related to the World Wide Web. Dr. Qureshi has written two books for Prentice-Hall and has contributed chapters to books published by both Prentice-Hall and McGraw-Hill. His articles have appeared in *Accounting Technology*, the *CPA Journal, Management Accounting*, the *National Public Accountant*, and *Internal Auditing*.

Joel G. Siegel, Ph.D., CPA, is a consultant to businesses on computer applications and professor of accounting, finance, and information systems, Queens College of the City University of New York. He was previously associated with Coopers and Lybrand, CPAs, and Arthur Andersen,

CPAs. He has served as consultant to numerous organizations including Citicorp, ITT, and the American Institute of Certified Public Accountants (AICPA). Dr. Siegel is the author of 60 books, published by Glenlake Publishing, the American Management Association, Prentice-Hall, Richard Irwin, McGraw-Hill, HarperCollins, John Wiley, Macmillan, Probus, International Publishing, Barron's, and AICPA. He has written over 200 articles on business topics, many on computer applications to business. His articles have appeared in such journals as *Computers in Accounting, Financial Executive, Financial Analysis Journal*, the *CPA Journal, National Public Accountant*, and *Practical Accountant*. In 1972, he received the Outstanding Educator of America Award. Dr. Siegel is listed in Who's Who Among Writers and Who's Who in the World. He formerly chaired the National Oversight Board.

Roberta M. Siegel is a computer consultant specializing in electronic commerce. Her computer expertise includes both hardware and software applications. Ms. Siegel was formerly affiliated with Lebensbaum and Russo, CPAs. She coauthored *The Accountant's Microcomputer Handbook* and *Selecting and Maintaining a Microcomputer*, both published by Prentice-Hall. She has also contributed chapters to several books. Ms. Siegel's articles have appeared in the *CPA Journal, Computers in Accounting, Prentice-Hall Corporation Service, New Accountant*, and *Personnel Management*.

What This Book Will do For You

Technology plays an increasingly vital role in business. Electronic commerce (e-commerce) improves efficiency and allows businesses to provide both value and convenience to customers. The World Wide Web (Web) allows retailers to reach not only customers but also suppliers; it provides another medium for them to expand internationally at a relatively low cost.

All types of businesses, not-for-profit entities, and governmental bodies are using the Web. The Internet is an integral part of most transactions. Selling over the Internet reaches international as well as domestic consumers.

Retailing on the Internet greatly benefits consumers. They can use search engines to find the lowest quoted prices on merchandise and services. With 3-D imaging, instead of just reading a description and looking at a photograph, a consumer can inspect the product from virtually any angle.

To remain competitive, businesses must maintain a presence on the Internet. Growth in commercial use of the Internet, rapid changes in technology, and the complexity of management today have combined to expand the duties of business managers. Managers must keep up to date with changes in technology.

This book—designed as a practical "how to" guide—covers all aspects of e-commerce to help managers implement it in their organization; it addresses such concerns as security. The techniques it covers can be adopted outright or modified to suit your own needs. Numerous examples illustrate practical applications. Checklists, exhibits, illustrations, and step-by-step instructions enhance the book's practicality. Common questions are answered. Our goal is to give managers an up-to-date compendium of current technologies and applications, taking into account new and emerging trends. Because e-commerce requires managers to be knowledgeable about both technology and its management, we have given special consideration to balancing these two needs.

We have tried to make this book easy to understand, comprehensive, and informative. We hope it will be a valuable reference that you can refer to every day.

Introduction

The importance of cyberspace to business is escalating rapidly. It's estimated that Web-related revenues will reach $1 trillion within the next year. Those using the Internet are disproportionately high income and well-educated consumers—a quite attractive pool of potential customers—and the current estimate is that there are 300 million of them worldwide. And within the next year, it's expected that about 40% of these regular Web users will be buying online.

About 25% of American small businesses have an Internet presence. It's estimated that 40% of all U.S. companies will sell merchandise online in 2000.

E-commerce—the purchase of goods and services over the Internet's World Wide Web—is a broad term. It encompasses all electronically conducted business activities, operations, and transaction processing. (The Internet is a global network of computers linked by high-speed data lines and wireless systems. The World Wide Web is a global hypertext system accessed by the Internet and navigated by clicking hyperlinks from one document to the next. Together they allow millions of communication devices like computers, using different hardware, operating systems, and software, to link to each other. An estimated 10 million computers in over 160 countries are connected to the Internet.) E-commerce transactions are controlled electronically from ordering to delivery.

E-commerce is important in such interrelated areas as business-to-business (estimated to reach $300 billion in 2000), customer-to-business, and intra-business, all relying on each other for supplies, distribution, services, and technology. E-commerce links companies, customers, suppliers, employees, and distributors.

E-commerce changes the way business is done. In some cases it replaces non-electronic ways of contracting, product and service delivery, and customer involvement; in other cases, it supplements them. To maximize its effectiveness, businesses must think about building infrastruc-

1

ture to share information, using intermediaries, and managing knowledge. The functional responsibilities of e-commerce include design, building, manufacturing, and controlling.

To do their jobs effectively and remain competitive, businesspeople as well as information technology staff must be familiar with online applications. Typical objectives of e-commerce include shorter manufacturing time, faster customer response, better service quality, cost reduction, and shorter product cycles. To accomplish these, managers must be aware of

- Recent developments in interactivity and real time transactions.
- Trends in hardware, software, and communications technology.
- How transactions are processed and secured through electronic web-based systems.

To be effective today managers and businesspeople must provide information over the Internet. This book is for them and for consumers who want their e-commerce activities to be more successful. In fact, e-commerce can improve the relationship between sellers and consumers. It simplifies the delivery of products, services, and information.

We hope this book will be of interest to all types of businesses of different sizes (small, medium-size, and large) in different industry groupings, whether they are manufacturers, wholesalers, retailers, or service-oriented businesses. We point out how to improve sales and cut the costs associated with e-commerce transactions. Consumers can learn from the book how best to use e-commerce to save money and be more efficient in buying products and services.

There are different definitions of e-commerce depending on your perspective:

- The business process viewpoint sees it as the use of technology to automate business transactions and workflow.
- The online viewpoint sees it as the facilitation of the purchase and sale of goods or services.
- The communications viewpoint sees it as the delivery of data, goods or services, computer network payments through telephone lines and other communication modes.

- From the service perspective, it's providing quality services and products to satisfy customers, both business and consumer, while reducing service costs and expediting delivery.

E-commerce should be of interest to business managers, marketers, accountants, financial executives, financial analysts, investors, creditors, lawyers, and consultants. Parties to e-commerce include:

- Manufacturers, wholesalers, and retailers
- Sellers of Internet commerce products like Oracle, Microsoft, and Netscape
- Financial institutions, including banks and insurance companies
- Government regulatory agencies
- Standard-setting organizations
- Industry associations

Because of digitization, the electronic marketplace requires no physical stores or market institutions. The electronic marketplace allows sellers to innovate the entire business process from manufacturing to customer service. In e-commerce sellers and buyers meet to trade products using digital processes. Sellers of goods or services that can be digitized or otherwise transferred electronically especially will find e-commerce a very quick and cost-effective way to reach consumers. Goods and services particularly suitable for e-commerce include software (via electronic downloading to the consumer), video, cable television, music albums, books (via electronic transmission), newspapers and magazines (in electronic format), information databases, education and job training, home banking, bulletin boards and chat rooms.

Users can interact with products by downloading business problem-solving software, exchanging personal settings, and e-mail. E-commerce may be used for such noncommercial functions as filing and paying taxes and other personal finance matters.

E-commerce includes:

- Data about goods or services, such as where to buy them, prices, warranties, quantities available, delivery terms, and laws that apply to the transaction. There are even online auctions like eBay, a giant virtual flea market. At the web site (www.ebay.com) companies and individuals trade goods, giving eBay a small transaction fee when the trade is affected.

- Corporate financial information.
- Production logistics.
- Project performance and data.
- Online searches for information.
- Personnel information.
- Warehousing data, including inventory-stocking levels.
- Online publishing of company information, such as reports, analyses, and documents.
- Subscription services.
- Electronic mail and messaging. About 75% of all online consumers use e-mail services, making it the most common form of e-commerce.
- Inventory management and distribution.
- Order tracking.
- Shipment and delivery tracking. Obtaining information to prepare a competitive bid.
- Production management.
- Tracking and monitoring sales.
- Product or service selection and delivery.
- Instant updates of pricing changes.
- Advertising and promotion of goods. For example, the new "virtual tag" technology allows consumers viewing multimedia advertisements online to order a product just by clicking the mouse on the advertisement. Among the goods and services being ordered via electronic catalogs are computer products, food, travel services, and apparel. Online advertising is expected to grow to $2.5 billion this year.
- Application engineering.
- Payments. A bill can be sent electronically to a customer, who then authorizes the bank by electronic check to transfer funds from the customer's account to the vendor's account. The customer's monthly electronic bank statements list the payments. With regard

to electronic money, CyberCash among others has a technology that allows a consumer to visit a CyberCash Web site, download an electronic "wallet" from the consumer's bank, and travel the Web spending electronic dollars at sites accepting Cyber Cash.

- Consumer searches for product and service information.

- Marketing research.

- Accumulating demographic data about customers.

- Customer service and support.

- Financial services, such as online investing in stocks.

- Distribution: Soft goods can simply be downloaded; hard goods can be set up for delivery.

Electronic data interchange (EDI) refers to the electronic purchase, receipt, and payment for inventory and supplies. EDI significantly reduces delivery time and related paper processing, thus reducing inventory and transaction costs. EDI software can be downloaded from the Internet for upgrades, program patches, and documentation.

Given its versatility, e-commerce thus

- Eliminates limitations of place and time.

- Improves information flow.

- Fosters better customer relations and better product distribution.

- Allows data continuity (data is created, altered, and distributed faster at lower cost).

- Reduces costs by allowing businesses to close stores; stock less merchandise at existing stores; minimize transaction costs by improving the linkage between vendors, purchasers, and intermediaries, eliminating duplication; and better share information.

- Stimulates sales and improves the revenue base by providing new markets, new information-oriented products and services, better channels of service delivery, and closer interaction with customers.

- Reduces order processing time and inventory levels.

- Improves how business transactions are processed, resulting in better performance, better customer satisfaction, better management decisions, higher quality, enhanced efficiency, and better interaction.

- Provides business efficiencies, such as upgrading technology, transferring content, transactional processing and payment, production processes, improved communication, more accurate transactions, better promotion and advertising, low-cost technological infrastructure, less obsolescence, enhanced sharing of information, and improved service.

- Allows for better internal integration of business operations (e.g., improved interaction among departments within the company), resulting in better coordination of decentralized decision making and for better external integration (linkage to the outside) through a network of companies, contractors, suppliers, and government agencies.

- Provides the opportunity for a business to move toward a virtual value chain and to two-way interactive communication.

In implementing e-commerce, managers must think about the consumer's role, the mechanism, and the nature of various applications. Implementation will require automating processes, using pilot projects, using data warehouses, and planning for growth and expansion.

An example of an e-commerce application is what Microsoft has done with the Microsoft Shopping Network (MSN). Microsoft formulated a business model enabling content providers to establish the fees and keep most of the revenues, about 60-75%, resulting from their content. Microsoft's take is 20% of advertising revenues and a 5% commission on merchandise sold over MSN but delivered by other methods.

Telecommunications companies like wireless, satellite and land-based, or cable-TV are building the e-commerce communications infrastructure (information superhighway). Their work and Internet transmission speed (bandwidth), quality, and reliability must also be taken into account.

Internet service providers (ISPs) are the entities that provide the basic connection to the Internet. These are expected to generate $50 billion in annual revenues in 2000. The national, regional, and local ISPs provide custom web site design, marketing, and other services besides hosting e-commerce services. Some ISPs offer "turnkey" e-commerce products in a single-ready-to-use package including hardware, software, payment processing and communications. They can provide for connection, catalog maintenance, order and credit card processing, as well as other services. You have to decide, though, what information stays on your company computers and what will reside with the ISP. How is information with the ISP to be controlled and secured?

You may have to think about whether to outsource some or all of your e-commerce functions. The following chapters will give you some guidance.

Chapter 1
WHAT E-COMMERCE IS
ALL ABOUT

This chapter introduces the benefits and drawbacks of e-commerce in terms of costs, implementation, competition, public policy and governmental issues, legal concerns, management strategies, organizational aspects, business processes, networking, the Internet, Intranets and Extranets, marketing, advertising, business and commercial use, customer support, electronic payments and fund transfers, and future developments.

Preliminary Considerations

Advantages

The short-term and long-term advantages of e-commerce include:

- Lower transaction costs
- Less paperwork for transactions like ordering, billing, and customer service
- More customer feedback
- More opportunities for satisfying customer needs
- Improved monitoring of consumer satisfaction.
- Ease of business with the existing customer base.
- New markets composed of new customers
- Ability to customize business activities and solutions for large customers.

9

- Enhancement of the company's image
- Simplified communication
- Creation of business value using gathering, organizing, selecting, synthesizing, and distribution—any point in the value chain—to adapt sales, marketing, outbound and inbound logistics, and manufacturing processes to give better value.

Although online business transactions have much potential, there are some drawbacks, including inadequate online payment instruments, poor security, and insufficient directories. A further disadvantage is that it's not easy to foster trust between businesses and consumers because there is no personal contact in accessing a Web site.

Public Policy and Legal Issues

Among the public policy issues arising in e-commerce applications are pricing for services, privacy, and access. For instance:

- What should be the proper cost to access information?
- How should global data traffic be monitored to protect information privacy?
- What government regulations are needed to prevent online fraud and violations of privacy? Some governmental restrictions associated with e-commerce relate to export of encryption hardware and software. However, it probably would not be advisable for the government or even a trusted independent party to have a master encryption key.

Among the legal issues related to e-commerce are company privacy, customer confidentiality, export controls on cryptographic products, and taxation.

Cost Control

E-commerce reduces operating costs by improving coordination and communication in manufacturing, sales, and distribution. Further cost reductions that enhance competitive position may also ensue from better operating efficiencies and downsizing.

Used as a communications medium the Internet may lower costs; for instance, issuing purchase orders in electronic form can eliminate rekeying of certain information.

Digital products like software can actually be delivered over the Internet, eliminating the need for packaging and printed documentation. Product upgrades may be automatically transmitted to the customer. Online electronic catalogs save time and eliminate the costs of printing and mailing.

Before undertaking any e-commerce, do a cost-benefit analysis. Ask yourself how long a payback period you'll need to recoup your initial investment—although this may be difficult to determine for some time after you begin e-commerce. The long term is more important than the short term. Some benefits to be sought include more accurate information, more efficiency, and better customer service.

Competition

You can improve your competitive position with e-commerce by offering more options and features, adapting to variability in customer demand, providing more and better products and services, shortening the product life cycle, and eliminating geographic boundaries.

Starting Up and Making Changes

A pilot study can identify potential problems beforehand. Once implementation is complete, almost all the problems will be identified.

E-commerce may require your company to make such changes as product innovations, total quality management (TQM), reengineering, and time compression. To achieve both internal objectives and customer satisfaction, TQM demands flexibility in responding to customer needs as well as quality improvement. Reengineering may require redesigning the company's organizational structure and processes to improve quality and reduce time and cost. Time should be reduced at every point from design to delivery and beyond to servicing. Flexibility in manufacturing can allow for mass customization to satisfy unique customer needs.

Management Strategies

The impact of e-commerce on areas like pricing, type of product or service offered, consumer interfaces, distribution, and sales will affect management tactics. E-commerce can benefit your company's bottom line through growth in the customer base, greater efficiencies, and information-based products leading to changes in management processes or strategies, both short term and long term, and even organizational structure. You must determine how much to spend on e-commerce technology and what products or services, new or old, should be offered. You must analyze how to reach and service the most desirable customers. Keep in mind in making these decisions your company's unique situation as well as the overall business environment.

Clearly, then, as manager you must keep up with what trends are emerging in technology, changing customer tastes, and new competition. This is how you identify and deal with your outside threats.

You thus must specify the objectives your company wants to achieve through e-commerce. To do this you must:

1. Formulate a strategy for e-commerce, taking into account corporate difficulties, management objectives, and company strengths.

2. Think about how technology can be integrated into high-value-added areas like sales and marketing, customer relationships, and distribution.

3. Identify, measure, and plan how to minimize the risks associated with e-commerce. Emphasize projects that have a high rate of return. Ask how customer value will not only be added but also clearly communicated.

The direction and success of your company's e-commerce will depend on your strategy.

Organizational Aspects

E-commerce allows businesses and individuals to share information. With e-commerce, new businesses can open with minimal investment in infrastructure. But implementing e-commerce may call for changes in corporate infrastructure, business processes, and daily business practices. These may affect organizational structure, information, and communications.

How to manage organizational changes to achieve more efficiencies is a key consideration. Companies must respond to changing market conditions by optimizing process design and being open to innovations in structure. That means you need reliable performance measures.

Web pages must be properly maintained. Information technology may be useful as a tool in support, operations, business policy and strategy, and reengineering.

The production infrastructure must concentrate on products, whether the products are physical merchandise or information. The distribution infrastructure supports the transfer of products or services from company to customers. The services infrastructure integrates support functions like security, customer support, and payment processing.

Work flow and process analyses are good ways to start making the organizational framework more efficient and effective. Make sure operating units are using a common data platform to coordinate and communicate to accomplish your overall business goals.

Business-to-business transactions for such services as banking and EDI are less costly over the Internet than was over private networks. The lower costs also allow small businesses to use electronic processes. Business-to-business (inter-organizational) commerce offers the following business applications:

- *Distribution control.* E-commerce improves how shipping documents—purchase orders, shipping notices, bills of lading, and claims—are transmitted. It also enhances the timeliness and accuracy of the data in these documents.

- *Inventory management.* E-commerce takes less time between order and shipment. Inventory information is transmitted instantly. There is better tracking and therefore better audit of documents. As a result, inventories can be reduced, inventory turns over faster, and stocking of merchandise is better.

- *Supplier relationships.* E-commerce makes it possible to reduce both the number of your suppliers and the cost of ordering from them. Fewer staff are needed to process purchase orders, further reducing cycle time.

- *Payment management.* By linking businesses with suppliers and distributors, e-commerce enables electronic transmission of payments, which implies more accurate computation of invoices, faster invoice processing, and lower transaction costs.

- *Channel management.* In e-commerce changes in conditions and circumstances are communicated faster among trading associates. You can post on an electronic bulletin board such data as prices, quantities available, service terms, and technical specifications. Electronic linking of manufacturing information with global distributors and resellers lowers manhours and time along with sharing more reliable data.

You can link a point-of-sale terminal to a central distribution center through the use of scanners, bar code systems, and satellite communications networks. Such systems lower inventory costs, inventory stocking time, and manufacturing costs; improve service, inventory management, and inventory control; add to sales growth; reduce delivery costs; lower the price structure; and reduce selling costs.

Most documents between e-commerce trading partners stay in electronic form from point of origin to receipt. EDI thus reduces cost, processing time and mistakes.

Intraorganizational e-commerce has as its objective helping the business to provide high customer value by carefully monitoring the integration of functions within the company. Among the functions it monitors are:

- *Sales force effectiveness and efficiency.* E-commerce improves data flow between the manufacturing and selling functions and between sellers and buyers. Integration of the sales function with other parts of the organization provides better data for making decisions, as about competitive markets. This makes it easier to set corporate strategy. More reliable information is collected faster, allowing for better evaluation.

- *Management-employee communication.* Management can communicate with staff through bulletin boards, videoconferencing, and electronic mail. Technology thus can provide employees with more timely information so they can do their jobs better.

- *Electronic publishing.* E-commerce helps a business to improve publications like product or service descriptions or catalogs, personnel policies, and production guidelines.

Intranets make it possible to publish and access key corporate data affecting the business itself, such as data related to research and development, capital and human resources, project status, internal memos and documents, internal reports and analyses, salesperson performance statistics, order tracking, or shipping dates.

Consumer-to-business e-commerce relates to how customers become aware of the goods or services you offer. Merchandise in your electronic catalog can be bought with electronic cash or other secure payment mechanisms. Information may be downloaded free or for a fee. E-commerce has advantages over factory ordering because it eliminates intermediary steps so the producer can maintain less inventory. Lower distribution costs can mean lower selling prices.

E-commerce allows consumers to communicate with each other, as in industry news groups or ISP chat rooms. It also facilitates investment services through online brokerage and personal finance services.

Security

Information safety is essential for the integrity of the entire system. We must be on guard against security breaches and fraud. That is why security problems must be identified, detected, controlled, and counteracted promptly. How good is the security of Web sites and transactions? Is industrial espionage something to worry about? Security issues to be monitored include:

• The hosting environment

• Unauthorized access, by level

• Methods of recording electronic transactions

• How electronic payments are processed and approved

• How on-line balances are verified

• How electronic audit confirmations are tracked

Security measures include firewalls guarding company information from outside invasion and transaction validation. To assure security with the payment services infrastructure, information going over the network must be encrypted and authenticated. *Encryption* makes data content indecipherable to anyone except the one who is to receive it. Soon sharing digital certificates with encryption algorithms will emerge. *Authentication* assures that customers are who they say they are.

Standards are being developed quickly. They include Secure Socket Layer (SSL) for safeguarding information transferred over the Web as well as Secure Multipurpose Internet Mail Extension (SMIME) and Pretty Good Privacy (PGP) for safeguarding e-mail messages. There are many options for securing communications on the Internet, such as public key cryptography, which is constantly being improved.

You must insist on access control. Improper access to published work may be prevented by (1) restricting changes to electronic files, and (2) restricting access to documents or to the Web server.

ISPs control Web server access and the data the user wants to access. Some ISPs provide complete, unrestricted access to the data on their servers; others restrict access. As an example, users may log on to a file transfer protocol (FTP) server as an "anonymous user" (one who has no account set up beforehand); that user can access only specified information.

Control over server access may be the first protection level for stored information. Server access may vary from fully uncontrolled access to partly controlled access to certain information on the server to fully controlled access. Access control may be established through authentication techniques (e.g., log-in names) and user identification.

You must decide at what computing and networking level to have security measures:

- Application level (e.g., security protocols for the Web and e-mail). The application layer applies to how the user uses the network. Application protocols include:

  - *Hypertext transfer protocol* (HTTP) for the World Wide Web

  - *File transfer protocol* (FTP) to transfer files

  - *Simple network management protocol* (SNMP) to control network devices

  - *Simple mail transfer protocol* (SMTP) for retrieval of messages

  - *Domain naming service* (DNS) for converting numeric IP addresses into names

  - *Post Office Protocol* (POP) for e-mail message retrieval

  - *Internet mail extensions* (MIME) for e-mail. MIME makes it possible to use multiple media types with e-mail.

    There are new protocols to prioritize traffic and assist with reserve bandwidth. A protocol for standardized mail receipts is being developed.

- Session level.

- Transport layer.

- Lower levels in the network.

Access will be denied to unauthorized users of a server or to specified information on a server. However, access control does not prevent copies from being made after the first protection layer is passed.

A second control level consists of measures related to the electronic files. For instance, the protocol Secured Electronic Transaction (SET) ties together and safeguards credit card information at the network, seller, and buyer levels.

Beyond this Intel's Common Data Security Architecture (CDSA) and Crypto API have layered security services that facilitate the sharing of encryption algorithms and digital certificates between applications. CDSA is directed toward cross-platform applications. Crypto API is for applications involving Microsoft Windows 95 and Microsoft Windows NT. Ultimately the two programs will probably interoperate.

In consumer-to-business transactions trust in e-commerce may be brought about in various ways, such as digital signatures and digital certificates. A difficulty is keeping a handle on multiple digital certificates in varying formats. Certificate authorities are in the early learning stages.

Developers of security products have concentrated on single or relatively few applications. Cryptography has been most popular.

Business Processes

E-commerce allows for greater diversity in such business activities as fulfillment, settlement, and workflow. The business processes most closely associated with e-commerce are data sharing, ordering, payment, information transfer, and customer service and support. The e-commerce cycle for the seller is (1) providing information, (2) getting the customer, (3) filling the order, and (4) providing customer support and service. The e-commerce cycle for the buyer is (1) identifying a need, (2) finding a source, (3) evaluating the good or service for possible acquisition, (4) buying the item, and (5) using the item, with periodic servicing. Potential customers trying to get information about products or services engage in Web surfing and Web searches. Customers scrutinize Web advertisements; they typically pay for items with credit card or digital cash. The front-end processes associated with the Web will influence your company's back-end processes.

Purchasing cards and electronic payment systems will be integrated with business processes. In this connection, the role of intermediaries will vary.

Within your business there should be integration of such things as the electronic receipt and filling of orders, manufacturing instructions received electronically, electronic billing and shipping, and inventory records to create the capability for immediate electronic transmission and information retrieval.

Electronic messaging is an important element in workflow or collaborative computing systems (groupware). Groupware takes nonelectronic methods and puts them into an electronic platform to make business processes more efficient.

One question to be considered is how e-commerce will alter company processes. For example, digital cash is a recent type of financial instrument that will modify banking processes, particularly in the personnel area due to new staffing requirements and job responsibilities. Banks will need fewer tellers and clerical staff but more employees knowledgeable about information systems and processing, especially security specialists.

E-commerce benefits information integration and coordination—the smooth interaction of customers, suppliers, and staff to handle business-related problems, provide innovative products and services, and improve ways of doing things.

Infrastructure

E-commerce depends on a series of infrastructures, among them:

- The Internet
- Private company networks
- Cable TV
- Wireless
- Telecommunication networks

The infrastructure of information distribution and messaging includes e-mail, EDI, and HTTP. The infrastructure of multimedia content applications include JAVA, HTML, and the Web.

The Internet infrastructure is decentralized. Improvement in business applications infrastructure for easier access and use, along with better security, is highly likely with enhancements in digital certificates, electronic payments, and public keys.

Financial institutions and banks provide for electronic funds transfers nationally and internationally over private networks; and in the short term they will probably not be on the Internet. However, these financial institutions are starting gateways between their services and the Internet for business applications; they are extending their infrastructures to attain a larger customer base.

Some firms like DigiCash and CyberCash are attempting to develop their own Internet-based linkage between sellers and buyers. These infra-structures are also linked directly to financial systems via partnerships and with banks or through vendors like CyberCash. At present these Internet-based systems operate independently. The future will see alliances between developers, software concerns, and financial institu-tions.

Digital cash is treated for electronic purposes as real cash. Digital cash has infrastructure difficulties when each bank has its own electronic cash tokens that are incompatible with those of other banks, creating problems for merchants.

The incompatibility of digital cash systems will continue as a diffi-culty in consumer-to-business dealings for a while, but it will not neces-sarily be a difficulty in business-to-business dealings. A uniform means of transmitting financial and buying information is EDI. The main prob-lem with EDI is the setup time. Some companies serving as intermedi-aries, such as Nets Inc., make financial transactions between sellers and purchasers easier.

Public key systems and digital certificates do not have a pre-existing trust network as do existing financial infrastructures. We can see what is required for verifying and distributing digital certificates. Business enti-ties like VeriSign, Nortel, and CyberTrust are issuing digital certificates to companies and individuals. In the future there will be a hierarchy of certificate authorities, both domestically and overseas. However, there is no assurance that their certificates will be interoperable. Thus there may be more than one public key algorithm.

When public key pairs are issued, some problems may surface. The one who secures the private key is the user. The key pair will be revoked if the key is lost, stolen, or compromised in some way. The efficient infra-structure for this is still being developed. It's not yet clear whether the contemplated hierarchy of certificate authorities can be expanded to han-dle literally millions of key pairs and digital certificates as EC becomes more widely used.

Networks

The information superhighway combines many types of network trans-port, such as satellite-based, modem-based PC, air-based wireless, and telephone. A message from one location to another, which may include text, numbers, video, audio, and pictures, might travel across many dif-ferent kinds of interconnected transport networks, provided by the mobile radio and satellite networks of wireless companies, the telephone lines of telecommunication businesses, the coaxial cables and direct broadcast satellite (DBS) networks of cable television companies, computer networks both private (e.g., Prodigy, America Online), and public (the Internet).

The Web is the mechanism by which content such as product data may be created and published in a network server, which is in effect a distribution center. A business or person may develop content in the Hyper Text Markup Language (HTML) and have it published on a Web server.

E-commerce has affected local area networks (LANs) and client/server computing. New computer intelligent networks provide a multitude of value-added services:

- *Value-added networks* (VANs) between business partners are privately maintained and dedicated to EDI.

- *Virtual private networks* (VPNs) are corporate networks.

- *Asynchronous transfer mode* (ATM), a new network technology, integrates voice with video and data networking from a wide area network (WAN) to the desktop.

- *Integrated Services Digital Network* (ISDN) provides fast access to the Internet using telephone wires. ISDN's efficient data communication links bypass the digital-to-analog conversion (modem function) typically required for translating a digital signal from a PC to an analog signal used over telephone lines. With ISDN, the user's computer is connected to the Post Office Protocol (POP) using data rates that are in most cases either 128 Kbps or 64 Kbps. ISDN integrates image, data, and voice within one network. With ISDN single service networks may be changed into broadband communications networks able to provide a full assortment of services. Yet although the benefits of ISDN are numerous, there is much difficulty in consumer usage.

E-commerce improves transactions among parties over interconnected networks. Information-based transactions result in better ways of doing business. Virtually any type of work can be digitized and saved for use in digital format. This makes it easier and faster to reproduce work, modify it, and deliver it to the public. Networking allows copies of digitized work to be sent to a host of receivers.

Technical standards assure compatibility over networks. For example, certain current standards of video and electricity distribution restrict global use of certain products or services.

Terminal equipment is the gateway to business transactions, information services, and digitally compressed channels. Certain hardware and software tools furnish an interface with various networks and terminals that are private communications equipment attached to a network. Subscriber terminal equipment has the following three elements:

- Networking hardware, consisting of wiring closets, hubs, and digital switches or routers

- Computer-oriented telephony

- Cable TV set-top boxes

Businesses need stable network operation with maximum uptime and support for applications. Consumers are more interested in speed and reliability.

Over a network everything is in digital form in ones and zeros. A packet is information grouped for transmission on a digital network. The packet is a sequence of bits that includes not only the data itself but also control information to transfer the data.

The response time of a network depends on bandwidth, which affects the speed at which data can be sent or received. Response time is restricted by the speed of the connection to the Internet. There are many high bandwidth internetworks (networks of networks). The Internet itself is composed of very high-speed backbone links.

In connecting internetworks, routers and digital switches are of value. Routers are equipment devices connecting LANs within a company with the WANs of network providers. Routers provide access to distributed computing resources and allow for communication between widely separated networks. Two major router companies are Bay Networks and Cisco. These companies manufacture equipment linking data communications networks through the Internet.

Protocols

A protocol specifies how a network will function. Protocols dictate how the network will be accessed, how an application is broken down into a packet for transmission, and which electrical signals constitute data on the network cable.

Protocol suites (stacks) determine how data will be exchanged among layers above or below it. Protocol suites are structured in distinct layers to facilitate substitution between protocols without affecting network functioning.

What if you need to retrieve files (e.g., worksheets) from someone else's computer? An FTP may be used to transfer files between that person's PC and the ISP file server. Files may be transferred (uploaded or downloaded) individually or in batches (listing of files), depending on the software used.

The Internet Protocol (IP) provides address space for internetworks. It also handles packet routine over it. A recent version of the Internet protocol furnishes greater multimedia options, additional security, and more network device addresses.

Transmission Control Protocol/Internet Protocol (TCP/IP) protocols form the basis of the Internet. These protocols subdivide information into packets for transfer in the network. They in turn use numerous protocols that define network media. Point-to-point protocol governs TCP/IP transmissions using serial modem connections. The TCP/IP protocol suite is also widely used for Intranets, which share information within a company.

The Resource Reservation Protocol (RSVP) reserves bandwidth for multimedia transmissions like videoconferencing. The same protocol may be used for priority e-mail and for FTP for file transfers and EDI messages. However, it will take some time before many Internet routers support RSVP, although routers to support RSVP are available.

The Address Resolution Protocol (ARP) aids network equipment to determine an IP address.

Application protocols are crucial to carrying out business on the Internet.

Telnet and Usenet

Telnet resembles an FTP program in the sense that users connect to a host computer using their identification number and password. (Anonymous FTP is a server that accepts anonymous logins so even a user who does not have an account with the host computer can still log in, view, and download information. However, uploading is restricted to authorized users.) Telnet users access their office computers from any location. Further, a remote user can log in to the library Telnet system and electronic bulletin boards to obtain information. Telnet is very cost-efficient.

UseNet refers to discussion groups (newsgroups) that distribute messages around the globe.

Messaging

After content is created and saved on a server, messaging information methods distribute that content over the network. Messaging and information distribution includes translators to analyze and interpret as well as transform information formats. "Middleware" is the messaging software between the end-user and the Web server.

Messaging vehicles allow the communication of structured (formatted) and unstructured (nonformatted) information. In formatted document messaging, we have automated interchange of standardized and acceptable messages for applications over telephone lines; it can include sales invoices, shipping reports, and purchase requisitions. Nonformatted messaging vehicles include e-mail, fax, and form-based systems like Lotus Notes. It's best when messaging software works with many types of communications devices, such as wireless communicators, set-top boxes, personal computers, and workstations; networks, whether wireless, fiber optics, satellites, twisted pair, or cable; and interfaces, including virtual reality, graphics, and characters.

The Internet

The Internet is the superstructure that connects heterogeneous computer networks worldwide—heterogeneous meaning dissimilar operating systems and content. The content on the Internet resides in independent high-capacity computers referred to as servers. These servers are linked to regional networks that connect to the essential high-speed/high-bandwidth long-distance wires that are the "backbone" of the Internet. There are various network or primary access points (NAPs) on the backbone. NAPs are the entry and exit ramps on the superhighway.

The Internet has a hierarchical framework consisting of a bottom layer of regional and individual networks and a top layer of high-speed backbones. Many host computers connect users to the Internet.

Much information can be obtained and processed using the Internet. It creates the opportunity for a global decentralized market and introduction of new products and services. The Internet can be used for interactive multimedia communication with customers without restrictions in time and place. But because there are constant changes on the Internet, a company must always be ready for change.

In the Internet, there is distributed computing: host and client computers operate independently. A client machine usually establishes a connection to a host (the server) and makes a service request, such as downloading a file.

LANs connect to the Internet via routers. Routers direct information traffic. The structure of WANs is formed by routers and dedicated long-distance wires.

To be successful doing business on the Internet, your company must make a significant initial investment. Your company can catch up with the Internet only by purchasing quicker servers and better links to the network, and by using the system more efficiently. Seek faster and better routers. Take advantage of new technological developments like IP switching.

Yet the Internet has lowered the cost of e-commerce because you can use it (1) as a communications medium by converting corporate data into digital form, or (2) to replace other networks.

The strength of the Internet as a communications medium for e-commerce is in how traffic is managed or routed and the open interconnection of disparate networks.

The World Wide Web

The most known and visible interface to the Internet is the World Wide Web. The Web is based on a set of codes, HTML, and on HTTP technology. A Web browser is software running on a client machine. Web browser software lets you connect with servers to access HTML documents and Web pages, as well as to follow linkage among document pages. The Web browser on your system examines HTML to ascertain how graphics and text will be shown.

Web server software manages information at the Web site, controls access to that information, and answers questions from browsers. HTTP determines how a file (document) is transmitted between you and the server. HTTP sends out HTML files (Web pages) upon a browser's request.

The Web is a system of servers that are interconnected and provide data (including text, graphics, audio, and video) via browsers. A user of a Web browser becomes a client and is able to connect to any Web server providing content.

Advantages of the Web over other data channels are its multimedia ability and interfacing with Web servers as well as to gopher-a menu-based program used as an adjunct for finding files, definitions, and resources—UseNet, e-mail, etc. On the Web you can also move from one place to another by using hypertext links.

Web searches filter, organize, and process search data. Filtering is conducted by search intermediaries in two steps—selection and presentation. A filter is a proxy server that retrieves a document and removes such things as unwanted advertising banners and "junk" e-mail. The filter can be used to select documents from incoming messages and can rank the importance of each message based on specified selection criteria (for example, a message from an advertiser can be assigned a zero).

Search engines navigate the virtual marketplace. They are the easiest way to find particular information. Search engines include Lycos, Yahoo, InfoSeek, and AltaVista. If you're researching a given topic, visit different search engines as well as web sites that may have meaningful links.

Software agents are self-learning programs that you can instruct to carry out certain functions. Arthur Andersen, for instance, has a software agent that accesses information from different Web-based audio CD dealers to get the lowest price for an item. Software agents can do comparison-shopping for you.

Intelligent agents screen, absorb, and assimilate information on the Web. These are software packets roaming the Internet to find relevant business information. Intelligent agents (also called *digital butlers*) do boring mechanical functions such as scheduling meetings. They contain heuristics, which are rational procedures using broad guidelines in decision making. Intelligent agents exercise reasonable judgment and learn from their experience in screening and classifying data.

The Web allows for two-way, many-to-many communication. Online services provide "chat rooms" for discussion of stated topics and knowledge sharing.

On a distributed computer network, each connected computer may perform as either a server or a client. A PC connected to the Internet can host a Web site or send a file rather than just visiting a Web site or downloading files. Information stored in one database may be used for different purposes.

Web sites provide product and service information. Your Web site and e-mail should be designed to tailor information to customers or clients rather than broader demographic groups. As more bandwidth is available, users will spend more time on Web sites and less time accessing them because shorter access times will allow more complex graphics to be shown on Web sites.

Web pages serve as sales assistants providing product information. *Web storefronts* enhance interaction with customers. When a customer asks for a product, your databases are queried, the best prices are provided, and delivery is scheduled as soon as the order is placed.

The *virtual shopping basket* allows electronic shoppers (e-shoppers) to combine their purchases from a site. The shopping cart can hold items bought from different merchants in a single electronic shopping mall, which may contain merchants form different countries. The electronic mall consists of sellers assembled in one electronic domain; stores need not be located next to each other on a list but should be linked in a rational manner. In other words, similar stores such as bookstores are listed on the same page. In effect, web store proximity is based on similarity of subject or use.

A customer who orders an item is transferred to a secure area where the browser communicates with a secure server to receive credit card information. Always make sure the browser is secure whether you're shopping or selling on the Web.

The various stages in the shopping process in e-commerce are:

1. *Search.* You look at different sites for competing merchandise, comparing features, availability, price, and delivery times.

2. *Purchase.* You put the item in your virtual shopping cart and pay for it with electronic money (E-money) or credit card.

3. *Delivery.* You can track the order and delivery schedule.

4. *Post-purchase.* The vendor gives you on-line support; you can raise questions by e-mail about the product or the bill.

You'll notice that many companies improve customer support and also lower costs by placing frequently asked questions (FAQ) and answers in a document or searchable database on the Web.

Internet Providers

Internet providers include America Online, Microsoft Network, and Prodigy. They provide a full range of services for accessing the Internet for either a fixed or a variable fee, depending on the time you spend online.

Internet access providers (IAPs) do not offer their own content but rather provide a vehicle by which users travel to the Internet to obtain the desired information. IAPs include online services, cable or telephone companies, national independents, and regional and local providers.

Internet service providers (ISPs) furnish a variety of technologies and services, including:

- Internet access for both businesses and the public.

- Payment mechanisms for online purchases (examples are CyberCash and First Virtual).

- Network management, providing access for other service providers, and systems integration. An example is Policy Studies Inc. (PSI) technologies.

- Client and server software to navigate online. Examples are Quarter Deck, Netscape, Net Manage, and Microsoft.

Most online services provide indirect access to the Internet. With indirect access users first connect to the online service company's network of servers before being routed through that company's Internet gateway. The provider may limit the user's access to certain Internet features.

Indirect access is more costly and slower than direct access but may be more suitable for those who rarely access the Internet. Most online services are directed toward individual consumers rather than businesses. Aside from transmitting electronic mail, ISPs usually do not interface with the Internet.

Since the Internet is a network of networks, it has both strong and weak links. Consumers should search for the most beneficial ISP, one that provides quality transmission, good service, and sound technical support, and is readily accessible from locations domestic and international. For private networks, traffic can be switched between carriers as it's transmitted over the Internet, so one ISP's assurance of service does not cover the entire Internet.

There are differences between an Internet access provider like Netcom or AT&T Worldnet and a full service provider like America Online, among them degree of control, metered or flat pricing arrangements, and open or closed architecture.

ISPs are beginning to provide their own end-to-end networks over the U.S. separately from the Internet but linked to it as needed. These networks are very suitable for business. They speed business traffic with minimal effect from high levels of consumer traffic on the Internet.

Private commercial networks make it easier for companies to set up virtual private networks (VPNs). VPNs are much more secure than private corporate networks that use leased lines. Overall, private commercial networks can also be cheaper than leased lines even when additional rates are charged. VPNs have an additional benefit in that they are connected to the Internet, so there is communication with other business partners and customers.

Outside the United States Internet access is structured differently. There are a significant number of backbone and mid-level networks in foreign countries. As an example many western European nations have national networks attached to the European backbone. Many local access lines and backbones are handled by national telephone companies. In general, Internet access outside the United States is less efficient, slower, and of poorer quality. Therefore, traffic between two European countries is often routed through the U.S. backbone.

Intermediaries

Intermediaries, an important element in online commerce, can serve different functions. Some intermediaries are agents between parties to an agreement or transaction. They are the electronic brokers between seller and buyer.

Intermediaries guide consumers. Web sites are directed at both the public at large and businesses. Some intermediaries or brokers provide sites allowing buyers and sellers to transact business, make bids, or exchange information, with the intermediaries facilitating the transaction. The intermediary assures that the contractual terms are carried out.

Intermediaries are mostly associated with the financial sector; they include mutual funds, insurance companies, banks, and venture capitalists. Other intermediaries are traders, mediators, brokers, and agents.

An online intermediary may act in more than one role. The major types are:

- Financial intermediaries, such as Quicken
- Web server providers, including those who design Web pages
- Information access providers, such as Microsoft Explorer and Netscape Navigator
- Network access providers, such as Prodigy and America Online
- Information rating services, such as *Consumer Reports*

- Providers of equipment including network cards (3 COM), routers (Cisco), servers (Sun Microsystems), and clients (Dell Computer)
- Information directory providers, such as Yahoo and Info Seek
- Payment/transaction facilitators, such as Mastercard and Visa

Intermediaries:

- Inform potential customers of bargain prices for products or services.
- Obtain merchandise that is otherwise difficult to find.
- Provide information on the potential uses of products.
- Monitor special arrangements.
- Evaluate changes in market conditions.

Intermediaries can help resolve incompatibilities between suppliers and manufacturers. They can also help control and monitor access to company records and data. This is a viable option if your company wants to share data without installing additional security measures for outside users.

Cyberintermediaries (intermediaries engaged in e-commerce) act as data sources for software agents. An example is Nets Inc.

Cyberintermediaries are needed because the Internet can be unstructured, complex, and sophisticated. It's not always easy to find what you want on the Net with even the best search engines, but intermediaries can help you. They cut through the maze of information to get the information you want quickly. Cyberintermediaries are very experienced and knowledgeable. Some present sites recommended by their staff, such as "What's New" and "What's Hot."

Some intermediaries use keyword matching for searches, but keyword searches may bring up irrelevant information. Other intermediaries organize their databases by categories. An example is Yahoo's subject listing. These typically provide more reliable information on a particular topic. Some search intermediaries provide predetermined lists of Web sites to searchers. However, when searched data is mixed with advertising, a question of objectivity arises.

Information filtering places a filtering program between a content server and user. The program uses criteria referred to as "profiles" or "scripts." The profiles are updated regularly.

Internet intermediaries assure product availability, quality, distribution, and suitability for the customer's needs. However, the less the intermediaries are associated with online transactions, the lower the costs and the greater the efficiency. It's best to minimize the number of intermediary steps in consummating a market transaction.

With online retail intermediaries, a vendor describes its product or service online, a buyer places an order, the vendor may adjust the product or service as requested by the buyer to meet his needs, and the product or service is delivered.

Intermediaries may not only process information but add value to it. Information-based products may run the gamut from simple to very complicated. An example of a simple situation is filling an order for a finished item. An example of a very sophisticated situation is customized production of a highly complicated technological item like a robot.

In the noncomplicated case a customer order can be processed via online intermediaries to a retail store for delivery. In a complicated situation, intermediaries may have software enabling a consumer to view and select the robot by computer. The software provides information to the robot manufacturer about production, stocking, and distribution requirements.

As far as online retailing is concerned, intermediaries package and sell information through computer networks. An example is online catalogs or an electronic mall in which many products or services are listed for sale. Consumers browse through an enormous product database. An intermediary like CUC International electronically transfers the customer's order to the manufacturer, wholesaler, or retailer, who then ships the goods to the customer. The lower costs of the electronic selling process are passed on to consumers in the form of lower prices.

Electronic brokerage is an intermediary that facilitates services. An example is making an information product compatible with the computers of different customers by providing a common interface without adjusting either the product's initial interface or its applications. This is an important contribution because the electronic broker is helping achieve standardization.

In terms of e-commerce, intermediation is being achieved by software agents that possess "intelligence" in that they can react to external conditions.

Some consider e-commerce as a production mechanism that converts data from digital inputs into value-added outputs via intermediaries. With online trading, for example, value is added by ratio and directional analysis of information on securities by prospective investors.

Intranets and Extranets

Intranets are localized internal company computer networks limiting access with Internet technology. They allow for information sharing within a company. An Intranet can only be used by authorized employees or other parties associated with the corporation. An Intranet is like an internal Web; it uses Internet technology and protocols. An *extranet* is the sharing of intranets.

Commercial Applications

E-commerce, whether in information, goods and services, or online payments with electronic money, has changed the way companies do business. A transaction occurs when a product or service is transferred over an interface linking the manufacturer (server) and the customer (client). When sales transactions take place electronically, there are different ways to access the information, arrange it, and use it. E-commerce uses computer technology to enhance business processes, data exchange, and customer interaction. E-commerce includes transactions that support revenue generation, including generating demand for a product or service, providing sales support and customer service, and aiding communications between the parties. Industries affected by e-commerce include manufacturing, service, telecommunications, banking, and entertainment. Table 1-1 presents the e-commerce mechanisms necessary for buying and selling a product.

Table 1.1. E-Commerce Mechanisms in Buying and Selling a Product

Function	Mechanism
Obtain data about a product (Buyer)	Web page
Look at catalogs for features and prices (Buyer)	Online catalogs
Request the product (Buyer)	e-mail
Generate and send order (Buyer)	e-mail, Web page
Receive order (Vendor)	EDI
Prioritize order (Vendor)	Online database
Determine availability (Vendor)	Online database
Make delivery arrangements (Vendor)	e-mail, Online database
Produce invoice (Vendor)	Online database
Confirm receipt (Vendor)	e-mail
Send invoice (Vendor)	e-mail
Receive invoice (Buyer)	EDI
Schedule payment (Buyer)	EDI, Online database
Send payment (Buyer)	EDI, Online database
Receive payment (Vendor)	Electronic funds transfer

Corporate structure should be suitable for exchanging information.

There should be interaction between departments and individuals. That is why information technology can be the impetus for reorganizing some businesses.

Customer information should be distributed to interested parties within the organization from marketing staff through product designers, manufacturing staff, and engineers, to credit analysts. The managers who must make operational and strategic decisions should be flexible to take advantage of opportunities.

Industry.net has formulated a very significant online database for business and industry. Its WWW address is *http://www.industry.net*. Industry.net and AMP connect customers so they may look at product specifications and download CAD files to make their own designs. The data may be customized to the user's needs.

Many companies have electronic business centers to exchange information about products and services. There are files containing such information as product descriptions, manufacturing data, and supplier information. There is much interactivity at business sites, videoconferencing and Internet telephony.

There should be standardized communication and sharing of databases between business partners. By using digital information for commercial activities, e-commerce makes it easier for groups to cooperate, among them:

- Retailers sharing information with customers to improve relations.
- Joint ventures between companies to design and construct new products.
- Joint corporate efforts to provide services.
- Departments within a firm sharing data such as marketing survey results or profiles on competition.

An Example: An employee can go to the Web site of a furniture manufacturer or distributor and chooses a file cabinet that meets his needs in terms of size, type of lock, number of drawers, and color. Using e-mail the employee asks his manager for permission to buy it, perhaps attaching the Web page describing the cabinet. After approving it, the manager e-mails the request to purchasing. Purchasing copies the information into its database and sends the supplier an electronic order, perhaps via EDI. After the supplier receives the order, a software program automatically places it into the database of pending orders to determine whether it's in stock and whether the buyer's credit rating is good, and then arranges for delivery. The same software program might transmit a shipping order electronically to the warehouse and prepare the invoice. Where there is a shipping agent involved, the warehouse will instruct the shipper by e-mail. After the equipment is received, the buyer's accounts payable section notifies the bank by e-mail to electronically make payment to the supplier.

Marketing Applications

The many marketing applications of e-commerce include:

- Providing marketing channels.
- Testing pricing strategies.
- Providing post-sale customer support.
- Rendering satisfactory customer service and support.
- Targeting specific audiences.
- Providing detailed product and service information to potential customers.
- Enhancing customer relationships.
- Fostering and communicating product differentiation.
- Test marketing.
- Engaging in market research.
- Establishing a customer base.

Your marketing plan should consider demographics, customer background, and psychological implications. Marketing considerations include pull vs. push information flow, segmentation, customer profiling, and fostering two-way interactive communications. Web-based marketers must interact actively with customers to determine their views and concerns and should try to customize products, if possible, to customer preferences. Web pages act as a sales assistant, guiding consumers in their buying decisions.

An important part of customer support is getting the opinions of customers. Customer surveys may be transmitted via e-mail or on the Web site. On the Web, users leave an electronic trail of where they come from, what they did at the site, and whether they bought anything, so that advertisers and online personnel can determine who and how many have accessed the site. Customer data can be cross-referenced for advertising and other business purposes.

After marketers determine from consumer surveys, focus groups, and test marketing who wants which products and why, the seller can match the product with the customer category using demographic segmentation.

Before a sale can be made, the seller must give potential customers as much information as possible about its wares in the form of promotion, advertising, and marketing data. Information is communicated to potential customers so they can make informed decisions. Based on their responses, the seller may modify the pricing and/or the physical features of the product.

Search activities are important in marketing a product or service. A simple search may be just to obtain price information if you are already familiar with product quality. Online searches may be performed either sequentially or simultaneously. A sequential search is surfing through different web stores. A simultaneous search is doing a price search using a price database. Information obtained from the many stores accessed in a the search include:

- Price
- Vendor name and address
- Brand names available
- Product features and specifications, such as size, fabric, and color
- Sales terms
- Quality
- Performance benchmarks
- Type of care
- Safety records
- Third-party evaluations
- Warranties
- Availability of demos, samples, or shareware.

The search may also reveal the reputation of the seller (including any complaints against it by regulatory bodies) and prior sales records.

Customers may use search engines and intelligent software agents to obtain information they need at minimal cost. Intelligent agents are programmed by the user to conduct particular tasks. For example, some agents search information over a network. Most Web page databases search services are generated by sending intelligent agents to search for user preferences. Intelligent agents can also view incoming e-mail messages, appraise them, put them in a priority order, and reply to them.

The *search market* refers to the space in which search processes are carried out. The *search service* is the intermediary facilitating the search process. Intermediaries collect, classify, process, store, and analyze information. Intermediaries get information packages from sellers and digest and organize them for the benefit of buyers. (Intermediaries can also help manage quality and service disputes between seller and buyer.)

The search engine sends out intelligent programs to gather data about Web documents. The search should be carried out quickly, comprehensively, informatively, and efficiently. Analyze the results for quality and value.

Search information should consider what is available on company Web pages, indexes, and databases. Web pages are a primary source, carrying more detailed information. Web pages should offer the expertise and knowledge of a trained sales person, furnishing data on product features and specifications, differences from competing products, and recommendations. Indexes and databases are a secondary source, with more condensed information collected by information brokers. Information brokers are experienced in appraising and classifying information into different categories.

A search may be done by *keyword* or *topic*. The accessed information should be relevant to the buying decision. A keyword search is simple, providing access to the complete database, but it often results in numerous irrelevant links or documents. A non-interactive selection of subjects may be based on preselected criteria, as is the case with Yahoo and Lycos. Search services differ in content scope and selection mechanisms.

Consumers obtain a list of sites that meet their search criteria but the relevant information must be downloaded or accessed by visiting the Web site. Accessing the information involves connecting and retrieving. There are a series of filtering processes in the search process to make the information manageable and meaningful.

The profile of customers influences Web content, promotions, and product customization. Customization is made easier by data warehousing and mining to comprehend customer tastes and requirements. This approach facilitates micro-segmenting of the market, resulting in greater customization. Customer profiles may be formulated based on customer browsing, buying habits, requests for service and support, and requests for technical advice. What do customers want to buy, what are their preferences, what are their characteristics, what do they like or dislike, what services offerings do they want, what are the customers' tastes and habits, what is their browsing behavior? Watch for changes in customer buying patterns and brand loyalties; Industry.net and AMP Connect collect information about customer searches and data requests.

Advertising

Advertising content will change with the type of product. Advertising for *search goods* (a product whose quality can be learned before consumption) should be informative—such as a product description. *Experience products* are consumed before their quality can be determined, like automobiles, software, and household items.

For complex products that are difficult for customers to appraise, detailed product information is not enough. Advertising for experience goods must be more persuasive than informative. It's a good idea with experience goods to provide warranties, samples, or free trials. Giving products away signals your confidence in their quality. Free products also relieve consumer uncertainty. An example is shareware programs. Many shareware programs are licensed to larger entities that incorporate them into commercial software or operating systems. These include compression and anti-virus software. A free product may have a significant long-term effect as a barrier to entry or in discouraging competition.

About 10% of those surfing the Web click on advertisements. Interactivity is a cornerstone of Internet advertising. Customer participation in advertising is important. There should be an interactive online advertisement between seller and buyer so each gets relevant information at the seller's Web site. Make your advertisements active, not passive.

The Internet is good for targeting advertising to specific consumers, taking into account their needs and tastes, product features, technologies of processing data, and the means to convey the information. You can identify key words of interest to potential customers to focus your ads. However, because intrusive advertising like mass e-mail messages is not welcomed by consumers, it can be counter-productive.

Digital products are more difficult to describe in advertising. Consumers cannot try them out first. Any product data presented must therefore assure the buyer of quality without giving away any information without getting paid for it.

A possible solution to resolving any consumer quality uncertainty is to offer guarantees or a refund. This allows consumers the opportunity to try out the product. However, there are difficulties of doing this for digital products, including the possibility that digital information may be fully consumed when viewed by consumers. Unlike a physical product, the return of a digital product typically does not prevent the customer from using the product in the future. Further, the return of a product or its purchase price may result in prohibitive transaction costs. In fact, the transaction cost may be more than the product cost, as with microproducts. You may want to assess a charge for printed material, technical support, or customer service to prevent abuse.

Banner ads and e-mail solicitations on Web pages are the electronic equivalent to conventional advertising. These advertisers are pushing products to potential customers whether or not they are interested. This advertising approach is targeted and very customized. Pushing products on the Internet is based on a broadcast medium. Push software is particularly popular on an intranet because it lessens the amount of traffic and provides timely, relevant and useful information. There are problems with banner ads, such as delayed downloading, which frustrate Web users. However, many potential customers will accept banner ads to avoid paying for contents.

A very useful method of advertising is the "pull" approach where potential customers are pulled by the information on Web storefronts and advertisements. Customers then come to the merchant. Information advertising is attractive when there is enough product differentiation and potential customers find it difficult to make the choice that best satisfies their preferences. The seller must convince the consumer that competing products are not a good fit. The consumer may be willing to pay a higher price if he is convinced the product is of higher quality.

Internet advertisers want to pay based on how many people visit their site rather than the number of banners displayed elsewhere. In a common arrangement potential customers must click on the ad and connect to the advertising site before the advertiser will pay the search engine provider.

A new entrant into a particular market must match the advertising policies and expenditures of competitors. This may require a significant initial budget. A Web storefront is not just for marketing but also for customer service, manufacturing, and sales.

Because the Internet is a two-way communication arrangement, the purpose of advertising should change from simply sending product data to an interactive conversation between buyers and sellers designed to satisfy the buyers' wants. Buyer participation will help you formulate useful advertising content.

Other forms of e-commerce advertising include:

- Soliciting and exchanging web links or listing from search services.
- E-mail updates.
- Using Web site visitor information to create mailing lists.
- Endorsing and reviewing products and services on newsgroups.

In formulating an advertising strategy, keep in mind that:

- Advertisements are just one important element in the entire marketing plan.
- Advertisements should concentrate on your company's image and reputation as well as its brands.
- Advertisements must be visually appealing to viewers, persuading them to buy now.
- Advertisements should offer potential customers something valuable and relevant.

Electronic advertising can also refer visitors to the Web sites of retailers who stock the product. Information provided about the local retail establishments may include location, directions to get there, telephone number, hours of operation, return policy, and warranties.

Consumers obtain information by examining different catalogs and then making their own comparisons. This can be facilitated if catalog organization and approach as well as the form of product information have some uniformity, making it easier to accumulate information about goods and services, and to use software agents to search different catalogs. In the future, more work will be done to make catalogs standardized and intertwined; see, for instance, the Web site CommerceNet. Resellers may collect data (e.g., product specifications) from various manufacturers' catalogs to present to prospective purchasers.

CD-ROMs are an inexpensive and efficient alternative to print catalogs. They add multimedia capability, including photos, motion, and sound, to product presentations. CD-ROMs are also interactive. Some CD-ROM catalogs allow for online ordering.

Another good vehicle to communicate information about your products or services in addition to the usual advertising media is through networked communities like newsgroupings, bulletin boards, chat rooms, and multi-party conferencing.

The Federal Trade Commission's (FTC) Bureau of Consumer Protection appraises advertising activities for fairness and reasonableness and takes action if false advertising is found.

Retailing

Commerce on the Internet is especially suitable not only for digital products but also for commodity-like products that you do not need to touch, smell, or try on. The Internet may also be used to link different aspects of the sales cycle, giving rise to new services and channels, as when sales are linked to online catalogs and order forms.

Interactivity between online retailers and consumers surfing the Net enables the retailer to obtain consumer preferences in price, service, and quality. The best design for a user interface will make goods available for sale appear nearer to customers. Make it easy for consumers to find your site, and then find their way through your pages. How will the product actually look, perform, or function?

Retailers like the Web for its lower costs, innovation, access, and reach. Setting up a Web storefront is a major aspect of EC advertising activities, especially for multimedia and video products. The consumer interfaces can include graphics, text, simulation, virtual reality, and 3-D images. Virtual retailing should be faster, have higher quality, and be less expensive than actual shopping.

If you are to be successful in e-commerce, your online technology must be complemented with supportive operational and managerial strategies. The software framework you need incorporates product and service content, Web server with retailer services, checking and authorizing transactions, payment settlement, and filling and delivering the order. Try to leverage any brand names you sell. Emphasize the quality and value of your products and services. You must constantly revise, enhance, improve, and repackage products.

Consumers may place electronic orders for your products and services through client/server applications, the Web itself, or e-mail. If forms-based e-mail on the Internet is not used, a CGI script may be written to process ASCII-text messages and have ordering data put into a database. Workflow software may be used internally to move customer orders, facilitating the merger of the electronic exchange of orders and the retailer's internal processes.

In online retailing, there are two types of prices, *access pricing* and *product pricing*. Access pricing is what is charged someone who wants to shop at a particular place. This is the fee charged by the Internet access provider.

Online retail sales may be encouraged in a number of ways including trade-in allowances, price discounts, and rebates. You can entice consumers to download a file by offering a discounted price, providing a free add-on product, giving an additional service contract, and giving "points," as toward a hotel stay. Retailers want to encourage a customer to buy today, not wait till later. A sale can be accelerated through short-term promotions, such as coupons expiring within a month.

Formulate an online merchandising strategy that takes into account what to sell and how to sell it, pricing, timing of product introduction, shipping mechanism, supply/demand relationship, product mix and integration, customer demographics, consumer behavior, product development, safety issues, and quality. To do that you must identify desired customer segments, consumer profile, and how to make a desirable package of products. Fortunately, online retailing is without the constraints of space and time. These are the factors to take into account:

- Type of goods appropriate for online selling
- Prices customers are willing to pay based on quantity, quality, features, packaging, and conveniences
- Steps the buyer must take to shop
- How customers will pay for online purchases
- Type of location and site appraisal
- Market segmentation
- How to penetrate the market to attract most customers
- Inventory management
- Image enhancement
- Managing human resources
- Advertising and promotion
- Necessary software interfaces
- Policies and procedures

- Retail organization
- Decision support
- Pricing
- Quality of customer service

In setting your retail strategy think about

- Where to find new customers
- How to establish a long-term relationship with them
- What kind of customer you want
- How you will present your product
- How you might modify your marketing approach based on customer feedback
- How to deal with customer complaints
- How to determine customer needs and what influences them to buy an item
- How you will make the sale

You will also need a postpurchase plan incorporating customer service and support to deal with such issues as product defects, merchandise returns, and customer complaints.

Some retailers are only online. Amazon.com, the bookseller located in Seattle, Washington, has no actual stores.

Some companies have inventory that is only digital. For example, a company offering commercial software packages stores its inventory in the computer system that receives and processes its orders from the Web. Some companies have hardware components (e.g., electronic connectors) in their Web-based catalog. This avoids the need for an EDI-based buy order and confirmation.

Vendors are constantly evaluating their technological solutions to reduce costs for delivery, manufacturing, and staffing so that they can become more efficient manufacturers of products.

Products

Products available on the Web may be classified as soft goods ("bitable," information) and hard goods (nonbitable, tangible). Bitable goods are those that can be delivered via the Net, like software, information, and certain types of money. Nonbitable goods like clothing and furniture must have physical delivery. Both categories of products can be sold in e-commerce.

Not just software but many other products may be digitized (made bitable), including paper-based information vehicles like magazines or newspapers, online content, and audio products. A fully digital business is much more than conventional e-commerce. It requires modifications of communications infrastructure and systems of electronic payments, among other things.

Products may also be classified as commodity or noncommodity goods. Commodity goods are those customers do not have to visualize, try on, smell, taste, or touch before placing an order. Bitable commodity goods are the best ones for e-commerce. Noncommodity goods may be reduced to commodity goods in the minds of consumers if, based on their experiences, they are comfortable ordering them; a typical example might be ordering slacks of a certain size from L.L. Bean or Land's End.

Electronic information can be stated in and stored as computer bits, which means the product is more versatile as new media are developed. As an example, catalog information in a database can be presented electronically through the Web, but it can also be printed in customized catalogs directed at a specific market or delivered on a multimedia CD-ROM. Such catalogs may be used for dealings among businesses as well as between businesses and consumers.

The Internet and e-mail make available such information about products and services as:

- Answers to often asked consumer questions
- Technical information about product features, characteristics, and applications
- Updated information and software updates that may be downloaded
- Revisions to previously sold software

Customer questions should be encouraged and answered because they provide feedback on how customers think.

A seller who relies on distributors or intermediaries for product information and distribution will share advertising plans, product development, and product release schedules because such sharing is mutually beneficial. Sellers can use both e-mail and a Web site to make information available about their goods and services, though the Web site can provide a lot more information.

Finance on the Web

E-commerce allows for fund transfers and electronic payments between buyers and sellers. Banks are now faced with digital currency and electronic checks. Software allows for connection to both credit card and banking networks; thus banks are expanding their private networks to interface with the Internet.

Consumers in e-commerce can use credit cards, digital cash, electronic checks, and microcash (when less than $1 is involved). In doing online business, the buyer remits an electronic payment (digital cash or electronic check) and some payment information to the seller. The account is settled when the seller substantiates the payment information.

E-commerce can be used not only for billing and payment but also for escrow, managing cash, financial data and reporting, foreign currency exchange, and investment services. You can now be assured of security in transactions and safety in such online payment instruments as electronic checks and digital cash. An electronic check is a debit-payment including the payer's name, payee's name, identity of the payer's financial institution, the payer's account number, and check amount. When the electronic check is offered, the payer signs it digitally. The payee also signs the electronic check digitally before it's deposited. For safety purposes, public key cryptography is associated with electronic checks. An example of electronic checks is the NetCheque system.

Electronic currency is in the form of electronic bank notes. The notes are identified by serial number and denomination with a digital signature of the issuing bank. To make use of electronic bank notes customer and merchant both establish E-cash accounts at the issuing bank. Security safeguards assure that the same bank note is not presented for payment twice. The issuing bank keeps an online database of issued bank notes and compares it with notes presented for payment. A match means the transaction has been settled. The match must exist before the bank accepts the note for payment. In E-cash transactions the payee does not know the payer's identity unless it's provided voluntarily. The issuing bank may or may not keep track of the identity of the recipient of electronic bank notes.

This anonymous digital money is the electronic cash exemplified by DigiCash and NetCash. DigiCash's E-cash is extremely anonymous because the issuing bank, the merchant, and any third parties to the transaction do not know the payer's identity. Blind signatures allow issuers to digitally sign bank notes without being aware of their serial numbers. The consumer's software randomly selects the serial number of the bank note. The bank note is then encrypted and sent to the issuer, who gives it a blind digital signature and returns the encrypted bank note to the consumer. The consumer can then decrypt the original encryption without destroying the signature of the issuer The issuer accepts the bank note when it substantiates its own signature. With blind signatures, the issuer does not know who receives the bank notes The homepage for E-cash is *http://www.digicash.com*. There is much less security with NetCash because the parties cannot collude to hide the payer's identity.

Web server software can handle payment transactions. Most on-line payments are made by credit cards, with the final payment stage performed conventionally. Because credit card data is transferred over secure Web browsers and servers, there is virtually no risk of interception while in transit over the Internet. But Visa and Mastercard have developed a Secure Electronic Transfer (SET) specification standard using public key cryptography, digital signatures, and digital certificates.

How does SET work? A cardholder obtains from a card-issuing bank a certificate that is a digital analog of a credit card but does not include the account number and expiration date. The issuer digitally signs the certificate; the signature assures the validity of the credit card. The seller obtains a similar merchant certificate, also digitally signed by its financial institution. The seller is not informed of the credit card number or expiration date. Because possible misuse of credit card data at the merchant site is thus eliminated, SET transactions are more secure than typical credit card transactions. Thus the integrity of the system is assured.

Electronic money is not restricted to the Internet-based payment systems. Off-line electronic payment as through *smart cards* is also possible. A smart card is a device, usually a plastic card about the size of a credit card, containing a chip. The chip is a microprocessor with memory elements. Smart cards are prepaid or stored-value cards. Once the value has been used up, more can be added. Smart cards are becoming common in metropolitan transit systems. Besides the card itself, a smart card scheme includes a card-accepting terminal and software to handle smart card transactions.

Some physical products will be made into smart products that permit digital interfaces for monitoring and control purposes. Smart cards can be used to make purchases in e-commerce. For example, Mondex International is developing a smart card to be used with a digital cash system. In Europe, a study is being undertaken to use smart cards as a medium of exchange for the European currency unit (ECU).

The personal ATM, a countertop device, allows for downloading money to the consumer's smart card. Mayes Microcomputer Products' Smart Card modem lets consumers use telephone lines to update personal smart cards. Verifone has come up with an inexpensive smart card terminal for retailers that can be used with a smart card reader attached to a personal computer.

Other devices besides the smart card that consumers can use include the *balance reader* and the *electronic wallet*. The balance reader is a small electronic device to read the balance on the card. The wallet is a more sophisticated balance reader. The wallet can hold a substantial amount of electronic money for transfer to the card as needed. The wallet also allows the transfer of money among cards.

The wallet should be kept in a secure place. The smart card can be carried by the consumer with much less risk because it only has a limited amount of money.

Pilot projects are being reviewed examining micropayments. Some systems being tested are M. Sirbu's Net Bill System and Digital Equipment Corporation's Millicent System. CyberCash's CyberCoin software has a system supporting microtransactions. Funds are drawn from a customer's bank account. CyberCash has alliances with banks such as First Union.

Cybermediaries such as Click Share process microtransactions for companies. Click Share tracks fees assessed from electronic publishers located at their site. Future cybermediaries will most likely not limit clients to one Web site, even though consolidation at a site can be attractive from a marketing perspective.

Customer Service and Support

An initial sale may be the beginning of a long relationship. A seller's relationship with a buyer often continues after sale in the form of customer service and support. Perhaps the seller may be able to improve its products and services based on feedback it receives from customers.

The Internet offers several ways to provide customer support. If you have a Web server, you can answer customer questions using a Web browser. Such questions may be directed toward support staff. Questions that are often asked may be included in a separate file. Such a list might be distributed by e-mail, the Web, and UseNet news. If your Web site does not accept questions, give consumers an e-mail address for corresponding with your support staff.

Convergence

Content convergence enables digitized data to be processed, transmitted, sorted, searched, enhanced, condensed, encrypted, converted, and copied at low cost. It improves browsing and publishing activities. This type of convergence helps businesses use networked databases and electronic publishing to improve data processing and decision making on both a business and an individual basis. There is better accumulation of information, processing and modifying of data, and distribution. Content convergence aids the network and computer infrastructure, improving business processes and workflow integration and coordination.

The convergence of information-access devices has helped *transmission convergence*. Transmission convergence compresses and stores digitized data for travel through telephone, cable, or wireless systems. The convergence of communication equipment provides pipelines to transmit video, image, voice, and data using the same line. Convergence over a single line facilitates the connection of computers, peripherals, and electronic devices. It enhances multimedia and image applications. It speeds network access and provides consumers with new, low-cost delivery channels.

Digital convergence is reshaping telecommunication services. Digital convergence involves internetworking, distributed computing, and multimedia.

Electronic Data Interchange

Electronic data interchange (EDI) is computer-to-computer communication of standard business transactions in a standard format. In other words, EDI enables companies to exchange business documents in a standardized fashion over the Internet (or networks) either through Web-based forms for recording EDI transactions with a services company on the Internet, or by e-mail for EDI transmission to business partners.

There are ever more new EDI products and standards over time, and continuing integration of EDI with other software. A seller can use EDI to instruct carriers to ship merchandise to customers who have ordered goods. Customers, suppliers, and distributors use e-mail to check the status of deliveries. Customers, for instance, may access the Web to see the delivery status of products entrusted to United Parcel Service or Federal Express.

Private network EDI is used by large companies when buying goods but smaller businesses are deterred from using EDI because of high setup costs. Over the Internet, EDI is more reasonable, especially in a VAN.

Integrated with just-in-time production EDI allows suppliers to deliver parts directly to the manufacturing floor, reducing storage and handling costs and introducing warehousing efficiencies as less inventory is needed.

EDI is effective in category management: satisfying customer wants by having on hand the right product in the right amount at the right price. Products are categorized into logical groupings rather than promoted singly. Products selling best in a category are emphasized.

Some companies are providing Web-based EC server software linking to EDI systems. Some intermediaries like Nets Inc. are integrating EDI-based back-end processing with Web browsing of online catalogs.

EDI facilitates the sending and receiving of documents in a uniform electronic form between entities and/or individuals. Examples are sales invoices and purchase orders.

Electronic Mail

E-mail is an important aspect of e-commerce. In addition to actual text messaging being exchanged, e-mail is often used to transfer files. Multipurpose Internet Mail Extension (MIME) expands the capabilities of e-mail messaging to include sound clips, video, and graphics. MIME facilitates the secure transferring of different kinds of transactions on the Internet. A standard to secure multi-part e-mail including that for EDI documents is S/MIME, such as the Templar software from Premenos.

VANS often employ e-mail to transfer EDI information between associated companies. HTML documents can of course be sent via e-mail since they are essentially text files. They may be viewed on a simplified Web browser or even an e-mail program having help applications.

Work is being done to acknowledge receipt of a message when using e-mail over the Internet. The protocol to achieve this is being analyzed. S/MIME and digital signatures make e-mail more appropriate for handling information transfer over the Internet.

The nature of E-mail is changing. Historically, most e-mail was in ASCII and therefore limited to traditional characters. Today, special files can be attached to e-mail as *.DOC file (for word documents), *.XLS file (Excel documents), etc. Many mailers are MIME-compliant, providing for a much wider set of attachments. MIME also allows for easy reading after decompression and encryption. The process remains heterogeneous, however, with frequently read files presenting major problems to most users.

E-mail unfortunately lacks directory service, and security is not guaranteed. However, security and directory service are being improved with the newer protocols.

The Future

The future of e-commerce is very bright. The future will show more custom catalogs derived from corporate databases. A possible e-commerce future application might be notifying computer software, referred to as a mobile agent, to search online catalogs of suppliers of a product to find the one the buyer wants and have the mobile agent present comparatively priced products in a spreadsheet. Look for new digital products and services, too, as well as new electronic payment systems.

As transmission speed improves, CD-ROM and disk-based sales will be common online. Paper-based products will be converted to or replaced by digital counterparts using images, sound, and graphics.

Some experimental technologies related to the infrastructure are undergoing review. Some limited scale technologies have yet to be tested on a large scale. But expect better technology in the future.

Work is being done on protocols so Internet users can reserve bandwidth for applications, and on prioritizing traffic. The future will see more developments in satellite access, cable modems, digital subscriber lines (DSL), and asynchronous transfer mode (ATM). E-commerce will move beyond computers to point-of-sale terminals, automatic teller machines, television, and other devices linked to smart cards.

In business-to-business dealings, there will be additional supplier and partnering arrangements that will improve transaction processing. Electronic partnering will include Internet trading partners, browser-based trading partners, direct connect trading partners, and VAN trading partners. Companies will integrate EDI and the Internet.

Conclusion

In looking at e-commerce, you have to take into account the structure of your business and its operations, your competition, and the characteristics of your industry. E-commerce allows for a good integration between the Internet, computerized corporate practices, and digital data.

Chapter 2
THE WORLD WIDE WEB
AND E-COMMERCE

It seems ironic that technology spawned from the military and political minds wrapped up in the Cold War may be the single greatest advance in the business world in the 20th century. Originally designed as a channel through which the Unites States government could share post-apocalyptic information, the Internet and its spin-off network the World Wide Web have become an integral part of day-to-day business around the world. Since the National Science Foundation (NSF) lifted its ban on commercial use of the Internet in 1991, this advanced computer network has rapidly become crucially important to today's business world.

As the Internet and the Web have become much more user-friendly, the resulting explosion in their popularity has spurred the development of a radically new method of conducting business. The revolution of e-commerce has completely reshaped the business world's approach to consumer interaction and the business transaction. As more businesses and consumers turn to the Internet and the Web for their day-to-day business, e-commerce will certainly prove to be much more than a passing fad.

How It All Began

The Internet has its roots in the Cold War of the early 1960s and the perceived need for a decentralized computer network that would enable the United States government to maintain open lines of communication in a post-nuclear apocalyptic society.

Researchers felt that even a decentralized computer network with multiple computer nodes connected via a backbone of high-traffic telephone lines would present too many targets for the Soviet Union to take

51

out in a nuclear war. This network, the ARPANET, would survive through its nodes even if several of them were destroyed. From this initial concept, it's not difficult to foresee the numerous ways a similar computer network connecting businesses and consumers would be invaluable to business communication and sales.

By the end of the 1960s advances in the ARPANET would spawn what has become the Internet. The new system was designed as a crude newswire to handle the transfer of news articles between nodes. 1972 proved to be a monumental year for the new technology. In that one year, the first computer-to-computer chat took place, the first electronic mail program was developed, and the first public demonstration of ARPANET using Internet protocols took place in San Francisco (Mayr, 1998). The following year the system went international as nodes were set up in Europe.

Over the next decade advances in technology enabled business to begin to take advantage of the Internet. The development of electronic data interchange (EDI) allowed manufacturers, suppliers, and sellers to communicate via proprietary networks. EDI was the first case of business using the Internet to open up better lines of interoffice communication. Business was now online. In time over 100,000 companies developed EDI to some level (Booker, 1996).

While EDI empowered business partners to share information on sales, inventory, shipping, and other project information, developing these proprietary networks proved tremendously expensive, so they were therefore only cost-effective for the largest of companies. However, this was all about to change.

In 1984 the NSF, which was the administrator of the nation's network backbone, developed a new network separate from the Internet. The new NSFNET backbone was the beginning of what would become the World Wide Web. By 1990 the first relays between a commercial electronic mail carrier and the Internet had taken place.

That year, 1990, proved to be another landmark year. "The World" became the first commercial provider of dial-up access. Later that year the first remotely operated machine was hooked to the Internet. The "Internet Toaster" was the ancestor of the server-based system that now supports the Web (Zakon, 1998).

Despite these tremendous developments, the NSF still maintained complete control of the two fledgling networks. Until 1991, the NSF had implemented a ban on commercial Internet use. Lifting the ban was like opening the flood gates. The Internet was now ready for the revolution.

Developing separately from the Internet, the NSFNET backbone created a new network over which computers could communicate. In 1991 Tim Berner-Lee developed a new set of protocols, including http, URL, and html, designed to run on the NSFNET backbone. It was these protocols that created the interface for today's World Wide Web. By 1993 the World Wide Web was growing 341,634% annually; estimates have placed the current number of registered domains worldwide at over 7 million.

In 1993 came the first mainstream Web browser software, Mosaic. The Web was now poised for today's rich content that makes it so dynamic. The advent of Web protocols and the browser enabled the Web to separate itself from the Internet because of the rich graphical interface that was now possible on the Web. Corporations had an exciting new medium in which to display their corporate messages as well as achieve a level of consumer interactivity never before possible.

Not long after the advent of the Internet, and later the Web, network administrators began to fear that traffic was approaching self-destructive levels. The Internet was originally designed to handle the transfer of two articles per day between nodes; data traffic quickly began to push the limit of the new networks (Winstein, 1996). The same year that Berner-Lee developed the Web protocols, NSFNET upgraded the congested backbone to new T-3 bundled telephone lines. With the new backbone in place the Internet and the Web were now ready for the unprecedented growth of the second half of the 1990s. The backbone was now in place to handle the individual dial-up access that has expanded the Internet and the Web from a handful of large corporations and university researchers to the individual consumers, businesses, and computer enthusiasts.

The Internet and Web Access

In 1990 The World became the first provider of commercial dial-up access. This was one of the biggest steps in bringing the Internet and the World Wide Web to the forefront of business. Until individual consumers and businesses were able to access these networks, the Internet and the Web had no commercial value.

In 1995 several new dial-up companies began providing access to the Internet and the Web. America OnLine, CompuServe, and Prodigy quickly developed the infrastructure to bring the Internet and the Web to the masses. These companies positioned themselves as the telephone companies of the Internet and the Web. The rise of these ISPs and their ability to provide affordable access to the Internet and the Web may have been the single biggest step to the commercialization of these networks.

The Web and E-Commerce

With the World Wide Web in the homes and businesses of tens of millions of people worldwide, businesses now have a new and exciting method of conveying their corporate messages. Forward-thinking companies were quick to take advantage of the unique advantages that the World Wide Web presented. They began to shift resources away from traditional advertising methods into Web campaigns. Here was a totally revolutionary way to achieve a level of interactivity and intimacy with consumers that marketers had never before dreamed possible. Instead of trying to capture the attention of potential consumers as with radio, television, and newspaper advertisements, here was a system in which consumers were actually seeking out product and service information.

Companies no longer had to sit and hope that consumers would follow an advertisement to the store. They could now present corporate information to consumers at the point of sale. Consumers exposed to an advertisement could immediately make a purchase. Fortune 500 companies quickly began to compile Web budgets; most were spending between $840,000 to $1.5 million just to get their Web sites up and running. Many Fortune 500 companies continue to spend as much as several hundred thousand dollars per year to maintain and market their Web sites (*Internet World,* 1996).

As the Web continued to grow, Web sites became more than just online brochures. Companies quickly began to build not only sites with appealing graphic content and informative copy, but sites that implemented secured credit systems to accept online purchases and integrated entire databases to compile consumer information and manage products online. The new point-of-purchase situation that was created with the Web enabled sellers to generate revenue from additional sources. Manufacturers could sell directly to consumers, smaller domestic companies could sell internationally, and entire niches of new businesses began to pop up almost daily. This new method of e-commerce quickly made the Web become an even more powerful business resource.

However, with this new way to shop for products came new challenges for businesses. First and foremost, how were consumers going to pay for their purchases? Second, given experiences with individuals gaining uninvited access to computer networks (see Levin, pp10-11) security issues emerged as it became apparent that large amounts of money would be changing hands daily over the new networks. Finally, businesses needed to address the subtle challenges of e-commerce, such as the need for new methods of organizing products online and for maximizing consumer convenience, as well as for completely new marketing strategies and techniques.

As companies began to sell on the Internet in ever increasing volumes, it became increasingly important to integrate into it a monetary system that would be compatible with this new medium. Although a myriad of currency systems quickly popped up, credit card processing via the Web soon came to dominate e-commerce (Lang, 1999). As a result, many of the initial online currency systems have vanished. However, there are still several alternatives to paying with credit cards. These few viable payment methods, while not as popular as credit transactions, remain an important means to giving consumers and sellers flexibility in e-commerce.

Online check systems and online cyberbank accounts are two of the most popular alternatives to credit card payments. Systems like the Online Check System and CyberCash enable the consumer to send an electronic check directly from the consumer's bank account much as a consumer would write a traditional check in a mall. Other services like CyBank and CyberCents allow consumers to set up online bank accounts to disburse payments for products and services over the Web. These online accounts are set up through deposits from the consumer's credit card.

While these systems may provide important payment options they require sellers to implement these systems in their online store, which in some cases may increase initial e-commerce set-up costs. Additionally, online bank accounts like those offered by CyBank and CyberCents may present a perceived dual security issue in the minds of potential consumers. With the negative portrayal of Web security in the media, potential consumers may be fearful of storing their money and conducting business transactions online. With credit card processing and CyberCash systems there is only a single security issue.

Despite the advantages presented by a CyberCash system, straight credit transactions using the consumer's credit card of choice has been the most popular method for purchasing products and services online. These systems are easy for the seller to set up; they do not require any special purchasing systems other than encrypting Web transactions.

Credit card transactions enjoy another distinct advantage over these other systems that is particularly important to Web consumers. Credit companies, in the rare event of fraud or system malfunction, will tradi-

tionally reimburse all or at least part of a consumer's purchase (Lang, 1999). This is an advantage that electronic checking and online account systems often cannot match.

Types of E-Commerce

There are three distinct general classes of e-commerce applications: interorganizational (business-to-business), intraorganizational (within a business) and customer-to-business. E-commerce facilitates the following interorganizational applications:

1. *Supplier management.* Electronic applications help companies reduce the number of suppliers and facilitate business partnerships by reducing purchase order (PO) processing costs and cycle times. They also increase the number of POs that can be processed by fewer people.

2. *Inventory management.* Electronic applications shorten the order-ship-bill cycle.

3. *Distribution management.* Electronic applications facilitate the transmission of shipping documents such bills of lading, purchase orders, advance-ship notices, and manifest claims. They allow for better resource management by ensuring that the data in the documents is more accurate.

4. *Channel management.* Electronic applications quickly disseminate information to trading partners about changing operational conditions. By electronically linking production-related information with international distributor and reseller networks, companies can eliminate thousands of labor hours and share accurate information.

5. *Payment management.* Electronic applications link companies with suppliers and distributors so that payments can be sent and received electronically. Electronic payment reduces clerical error, increases the speed at which companies compute invoices, and lowers transaction costs.

The purpose of intraorganizational applications is to help a company maintain the relationships that are critical to delivering superior customer value. How do you do this? By integrating various functions in the organization. Intraorganizational e-commerce facilitates business applications

like workgroup communications, electronic publishing, and sales force productivity.

In consumer-to-business transactions, customers can learn about products through electronic publishing, buy products with electronic cash and other secure payment systems, and even have information goods delivered over the network. From the consumer's perspective, e-commerce facilitates social interaction, personal financial management, buying goods and getting information.

Consumers consistently demand greater convenience and lower prices. E-commerce facilitates orders by eliminating many intermediary steps, thereby lowering inventory and distribution costs, thus leading to lower prices for consumers.

Intermediaries are the economic agents that stand between the parties to a transaction, the buyers and sellers, and perform functions necessary to fulfilling the contract . Most firms in the financial service sector, including banks, insurance companies, mutual funds, and venture capital firms, are intermediaries. The results again are more efficient production and distribution and lower prices. Whether strict, general, or electronic interpretations are adopted, intermediaries clearly comprise a significant portion of the online economy. Therefore, understanding the forces that give rise to the demand for intermediaries, as well as the characteristics and structure of intermediate online markets, is crucial to understanding electronic markets in general.

How The Internet Affects Certain Industries

The Internet is affecting all businesses in similar ways. Every industry, for example, has suddenly become part of a global network where all companies are equally easy to reach. However, even though the forces affecting them are the same, the consequences for each industry are very different.

Financial Services

Universal access to information is hitting the financial services industry hard. This is a classic example of how the Internet can open up an existing infrastructure. In the past, stock brokers justified their high fees by pointing to the quality of their advice; now knowledgeable amateurs as well as industry experts can trade stock for no charge in popular sites like the Motley Fool. Investors can get advice and market information from many sources other than full-service brokers, so they are less willing to pay a premium just to trade. Assets worth $111 billion are already managed online; that figure will rise to $474 billion by 2001. The challenge here is to survive on thin margins, or find some way to add value.

There are currently some 140 banks on the Web from 26 different countries.

Travel and Airlines

Travel agents are another group that thrived on exclusive access to information. Now over 100 airlines have created Web sites, and a number are not only taking queries but are actually selling tickets online. Most travelers would still rather use travel agents than check every airline and figure out how to work the flight-booking services on commercial online services, especially since using an agent costs them nothing. However, the Internet is giving the airlines an opportunity to eliminate the middleman and cut the cost in two ways. The first is by selling seats on their own Web sites, or together on Sabre's Travelocity, American Airlines' booking service. The second, led by Northwest and Continental, is by cutting the fees they pay to online travel agencies to 5%, because customers find and book by themselves on the net, so the costs are far lower than in the physical world. However, online sales still make up less than 1% of total airline ticket sales, and as long as the airlines are prohibited by law from offering online bookers a price advantage, most independent travelers will prefer a quick call to their travel agent.

Retailing

The advantage of online shops are that their costs are lower and they are less constrained for space than their physical counterparts. Yet less than a third of online marketers are making money today. The reason is that most of their offerings are distinctly unimpressive. Even big mail-order retailers like J. C. Penney and J. Crew offer only a small fraction of their print catalog online and the items they offer are hard to find, slow to download, and hard to see on-screen. Building an online shopping site that is attractive to buyers takes longer and costs more than most retailers thought.

Perhaps one of the best examples of retail marketing on the Web comes from Van den Bergh Foods, better known as Ragu. Hundreds of recipes and an online soap opera fill this site! Interflora is another great example of how a Web site can add value to existing services.

Music

Unlike the book industry, the music industry is controlled by just a few labels. Therefore they have the power to stifle any online venture that offers serious competition. Several online music stores have had trouble getting record companies' permission to offer album samples, and their prices are typically only a little lower than those of physical music stores. As a result, most are losing money. Still, good online music stores like Firefly are showing their sites built around a thriving community of music fans. They have the potential to outdo their physical competitors like Amazon, which beats it book-trade rivals. However, it could be slow going. Online music sales will increase to $186 million by 2000.

Books

This market is no longer a one-horse race featuring Amazon. America's two largest booksellers, Barnes & Noble and Borders, have now opened sites online. Optimists think online book sales will reach 8% of the market by 2000. Pessimists think there will be a struggle for just the bottom 1% to 2%.

Cars

It seems like a foolish idea to buy a car on the Internet, but more customers are shifting to online shopping instead of spending a long afternoon with a salesman. Customers report prices up to 10% lower than their best face-to face negotiation. The reason is that it costs a dealer only about $25 to respond to an Auto-By-Tel lead, instead of hundreds of dollars to advertise and sell a car the conventional way. Chrysler, which puts its Internet sales in 1996 at just 1.5% of the total, thinks that the figure will be increased by 25% in 2000.

Manufacturers are thrilled by this trend. They generally consider dealers a necessary evil, just as airlines do travel agents. But a creative dealership, which can set up its own Web site, can also use the Internet to expand its franchise.

Advertising and Marketing

Although these two industries are not strictly in the category of e-commerce themselves, they are being profoundly changed by it. The Internet is an interactive medium, completely customizable for each viewer—unlike any previous advertising vehicle before. In today's world, reaching 12 people by telephone is easy. Reaching 12 million people by taking an ad during the Superbowl is also easy. However, reaching the people between is hard. The best tool, direct mail, is expensive and inefficient.

The Internet makes it easier both to target potentially interested consumers and to communicate with them. Another advantage of an Internet ad is immediate response. It provides a direct link to the advertiser's site, offering interested consumers an easy way to get more information or to buy. Total Internet advertising revenues were just $267 million in 1996, compared with $33 million spent in America alone on television advertising. However, the possibility is huge. The biggest Internet service provider, America Online, has 16 million subscribers (and adding even more). It has more viewers than any cable television network or newspaper, and all but the world's most popular magazine. The market may be too new for advertisers to be sure they'll get their money's worth, but it's only a matter of time.

Advantages of E-commerce

24 Hours A Day / 7 Days A Week Availability

Keeping a retail establishment open 24 hours a day and 7 days a week can be very costly. In a normal retail store there are certain variable costs, the largest being the cost of labor. High turnover rates for employees working the "graveyard" shift can make it seem more costly.

Depending on your business, another consideration may be security. Cameras and bullet-proof glass can be a significant expense. Armed security can be a very costly variable expense. Expenses like electricity can add up.

Of course, one reason most businesses don't stay open around the clock is diminishing returns. At certain times of the day, it may cost more than the business can make to stay open. Businesses are turning away from the questionable profit of the few customers that want to shop after normal business hours.

E-commerce is a great way to get the business of these off-peak shoppers. For a very small amount of money, a company can have its "cyber-shop" open 24 hours a day and 7 days a week.

Savings on Customer Service Staff

In the past when customers had questions about a product, especially one bought by mail, the customer had to call the company. In a company selling a variety of products, it can be difficult if not impossible for customer service staff to know every detail about every product the company sells.

To best serve the customer, a detailed description of each product can be put on the Web page, with details like price, dimensions, test results, pictures, and even Virtual Reality files that let the customer look in the object in three dimensions.

Savings on Telephone Operators and Salespeople

Every customer who makes a purchase online is one less customer using the company's telephone operators and salespeople. The more customers use e-commerce to buy products, the less need for telephone operators and salespeople. While doing away with these employees entirely is not practical, a reduction in their number can reduce variable selling and administrative expenses.

Instant Update of Catalogs and Prices

When prices change frequently, printed catalogs can be inaccurate before they reach the customer. This problem can be eliminated by e-commerce. When a price change is needed, a simple change of the Web page will correct it. This saves money on catalog printing.

With printed catalogs, too, if a product is added to or taken out of inventory, the business must wait for the next catalog printing before customers will know about it. With Web-based commerce, products can instantly be added or deleted.

Product Targeting

Product targeting can be accomplished actively or passively on the Internet.

Active Targeting

One way to target products to particular customers is to ask them what interests them. For example, in order to shop on some Web sites you must first get a cybershopping cart. To do that, you must create an account. As part of the account creation, you are asked questions that will allow for the Web site to target products to you.

For example, after-market car parts retailers like Jegs and Summit will ask shoppers what cars they own. The company can then target products made for those cars as customers shop online.

In addition, obtaining a customer's e-mail number makes it possible to reach them directly with advertisements. For example, when a new product is added to the inventory, potentially interested customers (based on past buying history) can be contacted via e-mail. And e-mails are often free.

There are two disadvantages to active targeting. One is that the system requires the user to enter the information. If this process is too long or has too many questions, the customer may be discouraged from shopping at the site.

Another disadvantage is the questionable reliability of the responses. With the news stories lately creating concerns about individual privacy in the information age, some customers may purposely give inaccurate responses.

Passive Targeting

Another form of targeting is passive targeting. This does not rely on the customer filling out a questionnaire or opening an account; the process is transparent to the user. Here is how it works:

A customer goes to a site that sells bicycle equipment. He buys mountain bike tires and mountain biking shoes and looks at mountain bike pedals. It can be assumed that this customer owns a mountain bike. The information about the items he purchased and the items he looked at can be stored on the user's computer in what is known as a "cookie." The next time the user goes to the site, the site looks for cookies and reads the information from them. It sees that the person browsing the site is interested in mountain biking. Now the Web page can suggest to the user products of possible interest. It can also target advertisements to the user, from either the company or third parties.

Better Overhead and Inventory Control

Using Internet-based purchasing, inventory control can be made simple. When a shipment is received, the quantity is entered into a computer database. As customers order the products and the products are shipped, the computer can track how much of the products are in stock. It not only warns about inventory but also gives an hour-by-hour picture of what's moving and what isn't.

Worldwide Visibility

With the Internet reaching all corners of the world, it's economically possible for even the smallest business to engage in global trade. Also, small companies can now advertise globally for a very small price.

An Attractive Option for the Physically Challenged

Online shopping not only appeals to those who don't actually shop, it also appeals to some people who wouldn't otherwise be able to shop easily, among them the mobility-challenged.

Disadvantages of E-Commerce

Credit Card Fraud

Credit card numbers can be stolen by the disgruntled or criminal employee who has legitimate as well as illegitimate access to the company e-commerce system. These employees can either use the credit card numbers to purchase goods for themselves or sell the numbers to others. This can put the company at great liability.

It is also possible for a consumer to give a number for a credit card that does not belong to him. With current technologies, it's very difficult, if not impossible, to verify that the person at the keyboard is the legitimate card owner. Credit card theft is a great concern when doing business overseas. There is a much higher rate of stolen credit card number usage overseas, particularly in Eastern Europe (Radosevich, 1999). Developments in electronic signatures are likely to reduce fraud in e-commerce.

Products that Don't Show Well

An e-commerce company usually has very descriptive Web pages that can include dimensions, pictures, specifications, and even virtual reality clips of the products for sale. Yet there are items that are very difficult to sell effectively over the Internet. One example is diamonds. It's impossible to show the beauty of a diamond on the Internet. In instances like this, e-commerce may not be practical.

Limits to the Market

Although the number of people on the Internet is increasing at an amazing rate, the simple fact is that not everyone is on the Internet. Stores like

Amazon.com that operate strictly on the Internet are missing the non-Internet user. Some are not on the Internet by choice; others may not be on the Internet because of geographical or governmental restrictions.

Small Companies Unprepared for Global Selling

Even though the smallest businesses can put up a Web site and start engaging in e-commerce around the globe, they may not have the experience or knowledge that worldwide trade requires. To begin with, doing business worldwide means having a Web page that considers cultural differences. US Web designers like Web pages with black backgrounds, yet black has a sinister connotation in many other countries (Radosevich, 1999).

Another problem with worldwide commerce is the variety of currencies. Most small companies are set up to handle only U.S. dollars. The easiest way around the problem is to accept credit cards, since conversion rates and other hassles are handled by the credit card company. However, you need to be prepared for the possibility of fraud, as we've mentioned. (Radosevich, 1999)

Finally, getting the product to the overseas customer may be a chore in itself. For a small company that sells a relatively small product, an international shipping company like DHL may be the easiest solution. These companies will deal with the logistical problems. Larger items may require other shipping means.

E-Commerce Strategy

Successful e-commerce business strategies must address an entirely new set of challenges. As with all new business ventures, intense research is vital to success. Research will not only uncover what it takes to get started, but will also reveal potential markets. Because of the access the Web offers to potential consumers across various geographic and demographic sectors, niche e-commerce systems have been particularly successful. While it's not necessarily a prerequisite, developing a product for a niche market will give any potential e-commerce project an immediate advantage.

In addition to uncovering niche markets, research will also give potential Web entrepreneurs the information to implement the systems they need for successful e-commerce. These include encryption of transmissions, shopping cart or product database features, and types of payment to accept. Implementing effective and convenient product management systems as well as encrypting any confidential transactions will result in increased sales. It's equally important to choose the best method for buyers to purchase products. Peter Lang (1999; Internet Marketing Center) recommends that any e-commerce purchasing system be based on credit card transactions.

With strong back-end systems in place, you next need a good HTML interface to the consumer. Appearances matter. Often the Web site will be the first contact your business will have with a consumer. Because the HTML interface is what makes the first impression, you need a clean, professional appearance that is easy to read and move through.

While a good HTML interface is crucial, it may be completely ineffective if consumers are not coming to it. To overcome this, you must take an aggressive, tireless approach to marketing the your e-commerce site. Search engine listing and relisting, conducting banner and link exchanges, issuing press releases, and mass electronic mail campaigns will generate the exposure that is vital to the success of any e-commerce site. Value-added features like pre- and post-sales support, testimonials, and personalized customer support are essential (Lang, 1999). Other features that increase sales are multi-lingual capabilities, contests, and multiple options for ordering (e.g., facsimile or 800 numbers). It's especially important to allow consumers to order in multiple ways as many consumers are still leery of providing credit information over the Web. Providing multiple options for ordering will bring you orders from consumers who would not have otherwise made a purchase over the Web.

Online Security

With personal credit and other confidential information being transferred across networks, security is naturally a major concern of both businesses and consumers. To be viable, your e-commerce system must address it. Businesses now protect themselves and their consumers by encrypting transmissions of credit information and other confidential data. Secure Server Lockout system as well as firewall systems to protect online accounting, billing, and product management and e-mail databases help protect both seller and consumer. Be sure your system secures certification from the site host and publicizes your site as secure.

Consumers may also be taking an active role in insuring the security of their transmissions. *ZDNet Online Magazine* urges consumers to buy only from secured sites, and educate themselves on each site's privacy policies. Watchdog organizations like the Truste have been formed to police the privacy policies of e-commerce sites. Savvy consumers provide only the information required to process the order, and always order with credit cards.

Ordering via credit card, as opposed to alternative payment methods, provides an extra layer of security as credit card companies reimburse consumers for e-commerce fraud (Lang, 1999). The Office of the United States Attorney General actually recommends that consumers use an 800-number to place orders rather than ordering online. Finally, consumers educate themselves about online scams through nonprofit groups like the US Consumer Gateway, the FTC, and the Internet Fraud Watch.

E-commerce and the Future

In 1998 e-commerce revenue exceeded $32 million (IDC, 1998). Forecasters are expecting the e-commerce industry to top $3 trillion dollars by 2003 (Forrester Research Group, 1998). The future of e-commerce is so attractive to business that by the end of 2000 56% of all US firms are expected to have some level of e-commerce system in place (Financial Executives Institute, 1999).

These e-commerce projections are staggering. However, even as more businesses begin to take advantage of this seemingly fail-proof gold rush, less than 5% of all e-commerce enterprises are expected to actually generate a profit in their first 12 to 18 months of operation. While this may be a sobering thought, lower overhead, decreased capital investment requirements, and the ability to sell globally will continue to make e-commerce attractive.

Declining Web development costs, advanced security, better product management, and inventory, sales, and accounting systems integration will in fact pull more businesses to e-commerce into the future. As e-commerce sites enjoy increasing success, competitors will have to move to e-commerce or lose market share. In fact, e-commerce has become so important that stocks of companies that have been slow to adopt it have lagged on Wall Street. Market analysts are demanding to know what plans companies are making for incorporating e-commerce systems.

From a consumer standpoint, decreasing hardware and dial-up costs, as well as dramatically increased connection speeds, will make buying on the Web increasingly attractive. E-commerce offer consumers increased selection, convenience, and in many cases better deals as it becomes easier for manufacturers to sell directly to the consumer, thus eliminating the costs of wholesalers and retailers.

Connectivity improvements and the development of new proprietary business networks promise to have a dramatic effect on the future of e-commerce. The implementation of cable lines and modems as well as the DSL technology recently offered by companies like Pacific Bell have led to a tremendous increase in the speeds with which people can connect to the Web. These increased connection speeds have made it easier for buyers to browse e-commerce sites, and for sellers to process orders faster.

The new proprietary networks are based on EDI. The new eXtensible Markup Language (XML) promises to bring to small businesses the same opportunities formerly available only to the largest companies via EDI. Small businesses—sellers, wholesalers, and manufacturers—will be able to share proprietary information using the Web backbone without the cost of setting up their own proprietary networks. Sharing information electronically will enable e-commerce systems to run much more efficiently.

According to *InternetWorld OnLine Magazine* the next great areas of e-commerce expansion will be in financial and institutional services, travel, entertainment and sports, and groceries, with 7 million households expected to be purchasing grocery products online in 2002.

Summary

Businesses consider the Internet and the World Wide Web an invaluable advertising and marketing medium. Moreover IBM recently announced that its e-commerce revenue is now topping $1 billion per month (*www.nua.ie.com*, 1999), and Dell Computer recently announced a single e-commerce transaction of $7 million (*www.nua.ie.com*, 1999). In addition to comprising an ever-increasing portion of total sales, e-commerce sites are beginning to integrate inventory, accounting, and fulfillment. As transactions are made, sales are automated, inventory and accounts updated, and orders processed through to fulfillment.

As business moves into the next millennium, and e-commerce becomes a multitrillion-dollar economy, more operations and traditional business software platforms will become integrated with the Web platform. Advances in connectivity and the downward trend in computer prices will bring more people worldwide onto the Internet and the Web.

In the next millennium, e-commerce may become the way that international business is conducted. A global economy developed over the World Wide Web is very likely to become the future of business.

References and Sources

Booker, Ellis. "Web Will Replace EDI Nets," *Web Week*, Vol.2, No. 7. Mecklermedia Corp., 1996.

Www.domainnames.com. NetNames, Ltd., 1999.

Eldridge, Earle. "Web Can Aid Deaf Shoppers E-Mail Helps Buyer, Seller Communicate," *USA Today*, April 27, 1999.

Florida Attorney General. *http://www.legal.firm.edu/consumer/tips/internet.html*, 1998.

Financial Executives Institute, Duke University. *http://www.nua.ie.com*, 1999.

Giga Information Group. *http://www.nau.ie.com*, 1999.

IBM (press release), *http://www.nu.ie.com*, 1999.

Internet World Online Magazine, at *http://www.internetworld.com/print/monthly/1996/09/Webwatch.html*, 1999.

Internet World Online Magazine. at *http://www.internetworld.com/daily/stats/1998/05/2103-ecommerce.html*.

Lang, Peter. "How to Beat Credit Card Fraud," at *http://www.sellitontheWeb.com/ezine/howto004.shtml*, 1999.

Lang, Peter. "The Internet Marketing Center," at *http://www.sellitontheWeb.com/ezine/opinion030.shtml*.

Mayr, David. "An Internet Timeline," at *http://members@magnet.at/dmayr/history.htm*, 1998.

Radosevich, Lynda, "Going global overnight," *InfoWorld*, Apr 19, 1999.

Winstein, Laura. Electronic mail post: net.explodes.txt, 1996.

Zakon, Robert 'Hobbes.' "The Hobbes Internet Timeline, v.4.1," at *http://info.isoc.guest/zakon/Internet/History/HIT.html*, 1998.

ZDNet Online Magazine. "6 Security for Buying on the Web," at *http://zdnet.com/zdtv/callforhelp/projects/story/0,3650,2232583,00.html*.

Chapter 3
THE INTERNET AND
THE ACCESS
PROVIDER INDUSTRY

Whether you're a seasoned Internet user who has been online for years or you have yet to send your first e-mail message, a key aspect of the Internet that you should understand is the role of the Internet Service Provider, better know by the acronym ISP.

As the name implies, an ISP provides your physical connection to the Internet. To understand the importance of the ISP and its role in the grand scheme of the Internet, think of the driveway leading from your front door down to the street in front of your house. Your ISP is the driveway connecting your home or business to the Internet.

Then consider the vast network of streets, thoroughfares, local freeways, and major interstate highways spreading from your street across the landscape. That is the rest of the Internet, which connects everyone and everything attached to it. From your "driveway," you can travel anywhere you want to go.

But just as there are limits on how fast you can drive the roads based on their size, their quality, and traffic conditions, your ISP affects how fast you travel on the Internet. And as anyone who begins to use the Internet soon learns, once the novelty of the medium wears off, the speed of your Internet connection quickly becomes a vital concern. Business users also have strategic, and increasingly mission-critical, reliability, scalability, and security concerns as well.

Internet Basics

It's useful at this point to think about the makeup of the Internet. A web of high-speed fiber optic cables buried underground connects the major metropolitan areas of the United States. These huge bundles of cables are called the *backbones* of the Internet; they are principally owned by large telecommunications companies like Worldcom and AT&T. Fiber optic cables strung under the major oceans of the world connect the United States to similar networks in every major country and continent. Networks of progressively smaller cable bundles connect smaller cities and regions to the high-speed backbones. This is how the term World Wide Web originated. At each physical intersection of this web there are special computers called routers and switches receiving packets of digital data, reading the "addresses" on each packet, and routing them on to their destinations.

To see how this works, consider the transfer of a Web page to your computer over the Internet. You send a request for the page by clicking on a special word, phrase, or graphic on your computer screen; this contains a link to the Web page you want. A packet of data requesting the page travels from your computer to your ISP. Your ISP's router reads the address and sends your packet on to the next router on the way to its destination. The packet speeds along from router to router, point to point, until it arrives at a computer called a server located at the address on your packet. The server then sends the Web page you requested back to you in the same way.[1] (*Infoworld*, 1997) How fast you can connect to your ISP and how your ISP connects to the backbones of the Internet is the key to understanding the ISP market.

The Need for Speed

According to Forrester Research, the number of online accounts will grow from 28.7 million in 1999 to 77.6 million in 2002. At the same time, many people will use the Internet for videoconferencing, telephony, telecommuting, and online gaming (*PC World*, 1999). As more and more companies and individuals embrace the Internet, each ISP's ability to handle the ever-larger volumes of traffic will be challenged. How your ISP handles the increased demand for speed and volume will determine whether it survives or is gobbled up by the competition. ISPs have to supply you with a fast connection to their networks, and then they

---

[1] Available at <*http://www.infoworld.com/cgi-bin/displayArchive.pl?/97/18/e01-18.71.htm*>

need a fast connection from their network to the high-speed backbones of the Internet. We'll discuss the computer-to-ISP connection first.

Referred to in the ISP industry as "the last mile." the connection from your computer to the ISP can be fast or slow. The six most common connections today are discussed in terms of prices, speeds, pros, and cons. Most connections can download information to your computer faster than they can receive information uploaded from you. Connection speed is measured in thousands of bits-per-second (Kbps) and millions of bits-per-second (Mbps).

Dial-up: Using a 56Kbps modem and a phone line, your maximum performance range using telephone dial-up service is from 56Kbps downloading to 33.6Kbps uploading. Typical monthly cost is $20. Today, dial-up access is cheap, easy to install, and available everywhere. It's slow, however, and it ties up a phone line. Still, it's recommended for people who can't get other types of connections and for notebook-using travelers. Travelers can dial into their ISP via modem from anywhere.

ISDN: Integrated Services Digital Network is a local phone company service; at 128Kbps, it's about twice as fast as a dial-up connection (see *http://www.isdn.ocn.com/general/index/html#whatisISDN*). It costs between $50 and $130 a month and is more complicated to set up than dial-up. The speed is relatively slow, although ISDN is widely available. ISDN is recommended for the home business user who needs better than dial-up speed, but can't get other faster connections (*PC World*, 1999).

Satellite: The next fastest connection is by satellite, which is available to anyone with a view of the southern sky. At 400Kbps download speed it's about three times as fast as ISDN. However, to upload, you must use a ground-based connection, i.e., a standard telephone modem, at 33.6-56Kbps. The satellite sends high-speed data in only one direction. The cost is about $50 for 100 hours, and installation is complex. This connection is recommended for business and home users who can't get other high-speed connections, especially in rural areas.

Cable: Where available, cable is currently the least expensive way to get a continuous high-speed connection to the Internet. At 1 to 5Mbps downloading and 33.6Kbps to 2.5Mbps uploading, it's very fast, and you stay connected to the Internet continuously. At $30 to $65 per month it's relatively cheap. However it's not yet widely available and you have no choice of your ISP: You must use your cable provider. Since most businesses aren't wired for cable today, home users will benefit the most from this service.

Frame relay/T1/T3: The current methods of connecting to the Internet for medium and large size businesses are frame relay and T1/T3 connections. These connections are widespread business-oriented services that come with speed guarantees and quick repair service. Upload and download speeds reach 45Mbps because you're paying for a fiber optic cable connection much closer to the Internet backbones than other connection types. The cost, $300 to $3000 per month limits this connection to serious business users.

DSL: Digital Subscriber Line connection is another high-speed route to the Internet that's coming into the marketplace. Although availability is limited, analysts project up to 1,000 percent growth for both cable and DSL over the next few years.

Using the standard copper telephone wire already in your home or office, DSL converts it to a high-speed digital data carrier. With upload and download speeds of up to 8Mbps, it converts your ordinary telephone line into a fast connection that's always on. The cost is high, however, ranging from $50 to $1,200 per month. DSL will be used by small offices that can't afford frame relay/T1 connections, and for home users who can't get cable (*PC World*, 1999).

Future Connection Technology

A new type of Internet connection called Broadband wireless is just being introduced. Two companies, Teligent in Virginia and Winstar in New York plan to use wireless radio frequencies instead of congested copper phone lines to traverse the last mile. They place a small dish on the roof of your building and transmit voice and data to a local central office connected to your ISP. Designed primarily for urban areas, this arrangement is much cheaper than laying underground fiber optic cable; it also provides connection speeds of up to 622Mbps.

Sprint planned to role out a new connection service called ION®, or Integrated On-Demand Network, in mid-1999 to deliver voice, data, and video at speeds up to 620Mbps. Businesses and home users alike will be able to buy an ION hub at a local retailer for $200 to $300 and connect it to a standard phone jack. Then by connecting your computer to the ION hub via a standard Ethernet network card in your computer, you'll have a persistent high-speed Internet connection, a video conferencing option, local calling with caller ID, and virtually unlimited long distance calling, all with service and support from Sprint (*PC World*, 1999).

US Internet Service Providers

The advent of the Internet has spawned an explosion of ISPs worldwide. There are now more than 7,000 individual ISP's in the United States alone (see *http://thelist.internet.com*). While the ISP market is still growing briskly, it's expected that once growth begins to slow, many local and regional ISPs will merge or be acquired by larger, better capitalized ISPs, because as technology advances, many small ISPs won't be able to upgrade their networks and equipment fast enough to retain their customer bases. However, there will always be a niche for ISPs that cater to markets either too small or too distant from major cities to be economically attractive to the major ISPs.

Currently, the ISP market is divided into three tiers: large national ISPs, midsize regional ISPs, and small regional and local ISPs. I will concentrate here on national and some large regional ISPs. In any case, the vast majority of ISPs are small companies that contract with larger ISPs for access to their networks and backbones. The pro for using a smaller ISP is the potential for more direct contact and service support. The con is that they're further from the Internet backbones, and therefore data has farther to travel through more switches and routers on its way to the Internet. They may also not offer the value-added Internet services that larger, business-oriented providers can.

Large national ISPs like AT&T and Worldcom boast of direct access to their own fiber optic networks and the benefits of contracting with a large provider that can offer businesses value-added services and fast physical networks.

When choosing an ISP, consider how much service your company will need in the future as well as the present. An ISP Finder service available on *PC World Online* at *http://www.pcworld.com/top400* allows you to fill in the type of service you require and your telephone area code to bring up a list of your local ISPs. Contained below is a sampling of the product and service offerings of the largest national ISPs. Large regional ISPs offer many of the same services but have to contract with larger ISPs for network access.

America Online http://www.aol.com

America Online (AOL) is the largest Internet service provider in the world. With over 14 million subscribers, mostly individuals, it easily dwarfs its next largest competitor. AOL makes it easy to get started on the Internet, but it's not well suited for businesses, though if simple e-mail and World Wide Web access is all you need, it may suffice. Its network speeds are the slowest of the major ISPs (*PC World*, 1999, p. 128).

AT&T http://www.ipservices.att.com/products/index.html

AT&T is now one of the largest ISPs in the U.S. with a customer base of more than 3 million corporate and consumer users. AT&T has been rated consistently as one of the top ISPs by Inverse Network Technology, which performs monthly tests of the 13 top national ISPs in the U.S., measuring call-success rate, download time, and other service metrics.

AT&T claims to offer the world's premier single-source, global remote access service, enabling users to easily access the Internet, Intranets and Extranets from nearly 60 countries by simply selecting a local calling AT&T number.

The span of AT&T's world-class networking capabilities now extends to more than 850 cities with more than 2,000 local points of presence, giving AT&T the ability to provide national, regional, and global connectivity to businesses in nearly 60 countries. AT&T Solutions Group gives customers the broadest possible range of managed-network services, advanced IP solutions, and custom network outsourcing.

AT&T WorldNet® Virtual Private Network Service combines the best of the Internet technologies with the advantages of private networking. It has created a single, end-to-end, state-of-the-art solution with security features that allows controlled access to employees, business partners, and customers. Using a high-performance IP backbone, AT&T offers a platform that lets you create Intranets and Extranets and provide remote access to LANs.

Earthlink/Sprint http://www.earthlink.net

EarthLink Sprint TotalAccess is committed to delivering all the access, service, and tools you need to get the most out of the Internet. With high-speed local access from more than 1,200 locations nationwide, it's in your neighborhood. Sprint offers fast, nationwide 56K Internet access from more than 1,200 local dial-up numbers, as well as Sprint's Integrated Online Network, and an extensive array of business connection services.

MCI WorldCom http://www.us.uu.net/about/

UUNET, the Internet services division of MCI WorldCom, is a global leader in Internet communications solutions, offering a comprehensive range of Internet services to business customers worldwide. Providing Internet access, web hosting, remote access, and other value-added services, UUNET offers service in 114 countries to more than 70,000 businesses, and owns and operates a global network in thousands of cities throughout North America, Europe, and Asia Pacific.

UUNET offers a complete line of high-quality, high-performance Internet, Intranet, and Extranet solutions. Customers can choose from in-house deployment to end-to-end, fully- managed Internet services backed by excellent technical resources, people, and experience.

UUNET's product portfolio contains cost-effective IP-based services, including:

- Internet access: Dial-up and dedicated access from 56 Kbps to OC-3 speeds and wholesale Internet access for Internet and online service providers

- Other communications services, including Internet fax services and multicast-based services (currently available only in the USA)

Value-added Internet services available include: virtual private networking (VPNs); remote access; managed security, and hosting and e-commerce, including core hosting, e-commerce solutions, extended enterprise, co-location, integrated application, and custom and complex hosting.

To ensure seamless service, UUNET offers businesses a comprehensive range of customized programs including end-user billing support, customer premise equipment (CPE) purchasing/leasing options, help desk support, and end-user implementation services.

UUNET's Network Operations Centers and technical support staff offer customers individualized support for their business-critical Internet solutions and provide network monitoring 24 hours per day, 365 days per year. UUNET's field integration teams develop unique solutions by working with customers to evaluate applications and business requirements. For more information, see *www.us.uu.net/about/*.

IBM Internet Connection http://www.ibm.net

IBM offers three service levels for businesses to access the Internet:

Business Dial Service: This connection, available in many countries allows a business to use services like the Web, e-mail, and newsgroups. Connection speeds are 56Kbps and ISDN. IBM supplies an integrated Internet Access Kit, which includes your choice of Internet browser software plus 12MB of e-mail storage space; your e-mail addresses can be customized to be meaningful. 10MB of personal Web storage space is available for an additional monthly charge.

There are over 1,300 IBM Global Network dial-in numbers in 52 countries. For a $1.00 surcharge per hour you can also access over 600 ISDN connection numbers worldwide. Toll-based 1-800 access numbers are available in the US and Canada for roaming access at $6.00 an hour. IBM has a free 24hr/7day a week toll-free technical help desk.

LAN Internetworking Service: The next level of Internet connection from IBM is the LAN Internetworking Service, which comes with firewall security. This is important if you're connecting your business LAN to the Internet via a single connection.

Leased Line Service (Frame relay, T1/T3): Direct Leased Line Internet access provides open two-way traffic between your site and the Internet. No security is available, though you may implement any Internet security protocol on your own. Currently, e-mail and newsgroup support are not available through the leased line service, but again you may implement their own software.

IBM can be contacted at *www.ibm.net* for ISP service information, or at *www.ibm.com/services* about e-commerce consulting services.

Mindspring.com
http://business.mindspring.com/access/index.html

Mindspring offers small business packages that make communicating with employees, establishing a website, accessing the World Wide Web administratively simple.

ISDN FastPack, offered along with Eicon Technology and Nortel Networks, provides digital Internet access. The ISDN FastPack single channel line is ideal if you need faster Internet access. It's faster than traditional phone lines and analog modems, with fewer errors when sending or receiving files because there is no telephone line interference or distortion. Data transfers at speeds up to 128 Kbps; there are two lines in one, for voice data fax, or video.

LAN on Demand, offered in cooperation with Toshiba and Nortel Networks, allows small businesses to connect all of their computers to the Internet with a single ISDN line, and router. Simple to set up and maintain and backed by a top-notch tech support team, LAN on Demand is ideal for businesses that need Internet access but can't afford an expensive dedicated connection.

The ISDN router MindSpring recommends has a built-in DHCP server so it can be used to network several computers if they aren't already connected, or it can be added to an existing network. Once the router's on the network, any Internet application (such as a web browser, mail client or news reader) that makes a call for information on the Internet causes the router to connect to your MindSpring account to handle the request. Because of the speed of ISDN, the router can connect in a matter of seconds.

DirectConnect: Since MindSpring acquired Netcom, a national ISP with a complete line of business services, it offers premium dedicated access options to its business customers, from ISDN to high-speed T1 leased lines. DirectConnect is designed to give you a dedicated port, which only you can use, giving your business a direct, full-time connection to the Internet.

The DirectConnect product line is supported by an expansive high-speed network and high-quality, responsive support, backed by an industry-leading Service Level Agreement (SLA) that guarantees a 99.5% uptime. The six DirectConnect solutions all include 24x7 toll-free technical support, e-mail and Web hosting, file transfer, multimedia presentation and video conferencing. MindSpring will also order your line from the local telephone carrier, register domain names and IP addresses, provide domain name services (DNS), and configure and test equipment you buy from MindSpring.

Concentric Network http://www.concentric.net

Concentric Network offers a full range of always-on access solutions with services ranging from 144Kbps IDSL to full OC-3 connections, with the capacity to grow as bandwidth needs expand.

DSL Services: ConcentricDSL provides high-speed Internet access over standard telephone lines, at prices lower than comparable ISDN service. At speeds ranging from 144Kbps to 1.5Mbps, ConcentricDSL is an excellent access solution for small business, Small Office/Home Office (SOHO), telecommuting, or high-speed personal Internet connectivity. All speeds operate at the same speed in both directions, except for the 1.5Mbps/384Kbps ADSL service, which offers faster 1.5Mbps speed on download.

ConcentricWireless provides high-speed Internet access to businesses in the Bay Area at speeds far faster than ISDN but without many of the distance limitations of DSL and at a fraction of the cost of T1 services.

At speeds ranging from 384Kbps to 1.5Mbps, ConcentricWireless offers business-class Internet access with the ideal combination of speed, availability, and reliability. A unique wireless distribution system provides sustained speeds up to 1.5 Mbps—50 times faster than analog modems using ordinary telephone lines and 10 times faster than an ISDN line. ConcentricWireless is competitively priced with ISDN and DSL and costs significantly less than T-1 services.

Dedicated Access Services: Concentric's Dedicated Access Services allow your enterprise to communicate internally without the cost of point-to-point dedicated circuits and without the security risks and poor performance associated with carrying wide-area-network and Extranet traffic over the Internet. At speeds ranging from 56 Kbps through OC-3 (155 Mbps) over Concentric's private IP network connect enterprises are connected to remote offices, business partners, and the Internet via a high-capacity, nationwide backbone rigorously engineered for business-critical operations.

A staff of technical experts monitors network performance 24 hours a day, 365 days a year from the Network Operations Center (NOC). They will handle everything to get a business up and running including primary Domain Name Service (DNS), CPE configuration, onsite installation, and end-to-end circuit testing, to ensure successful implementation.

Major US Regional ISPs

Regional ISPs offer many of the same network and connection services that the national ISPs do. With direct "last mile" access to their phone customers, all the Baby Bells have become major players in the ISP market. They offer a wide range of services and work with phone customers to customize networking connections. An added plus to using a phone company as your ISP is that usually all your services can be integrated into one bill, simplifying payment and accounting. Regional ISPs (see *PC World,* 1999, p. 128) include:

Ameritech (Midwest US region) *http://www.ameritech.net*: A nimble performer, clearly the Midwest choice, Ameritech excels at everything—except support quality and ease-of-use.

SBC/Pacific Bell Internet Services (Southwest US Region) *http://public.pacbell.net/business.html*: The Pacbell ISP may be hard to set up but its performance is great, the best after AT&T's.

BellSouth (Southern US region) *http://www.bellsouth.net*: Good performance makes Bell South preferable to its main competitor in the South, Cybergate.

RCN (Northeast US region) *http://www.rcn.com*: Here you get solid, all-around service, especially if you want to upgrade to new high-speed technologies.

Rocky Mountain Internet (Rocky Mountain region) *http://www.rmi.net*: Support hours are limited, but reliable service gives Rocky Mountain the edge over US West in this coverage area.

The Future of the ISP Market

As the Internet continues its fast-paced growth, the ISP is growing right along with it. However, industry consolidation has already begun; small ISPs are being taken over by larger ISPs desiring larger customer bases and increased revenues. The largest long distance company, AT&T, not long ago bought two of the largest cable companies, Tele-Communications, Inc. and Media One, Inc., giving it access to nearly 60% of homes with cable. AT&T intends to be the market leader in Internet access for both consumers and businesses.

Because the technology of the Internet is in constant transition, we recommend that you choose an ISP with whom you have cultivated a business relationship. As your company and its needs grow, the ISP should be able to scale up its connection speeds and bandwidth without disrupting your enterprise. Outsourcing some or all of your information technology needs to your ISP will allow you to focus your internal resources on the products or services that you do best, while your ISP keeps you current and supplied with the best, most competitive technology the ever-changing Information Age has to offer.

Appendix 3.1
Common Services, Features, and Definitions related to the Internet Service Provider Market

Asynchronous Transfer Mode (ATM)—technology combines the reliability of circuit switching with the efficiency of packet switching, producing the optimal way to deliver diverse traffic: data, image, voice, and video. Through simplified packet-switching techniques, ATM segments packets into 53-byte cells, each containing a 48-byte information field and a 5-byte header. The header identifies cells belonging to the same virtual channel for appropriate routing. ATM speeds the cells over the public network, makes quick connections, and accurately reassembles the transmission at its destination. ATM provides cost-effective access for companies requiring higher speeds than DS1 leased lines (1.544 Mbps) but not the full speed of DS3 leased lines (45 Mbps). Unlike DS3 lines, ATM has no distance-based pricing component (*see* public.pacbell.net/business.html).

Decryption—The process of converting encrypted data back into its original form so it can be understood. For more information see Encryption.

Dedicated Line—*See* Leased Line

Dial-up service—Offers up to 56Kbps telephone modem access; must be dialed into and connected each time it's used.

E-commerce—the buying and selling of goods and services on the Internet, especially the World Wide Web. This term and e-business are often used interchangeably. E-commerce can be divided into:

- E-tailing or virtual storefronts sites with online catalogs, sometimes gathered into a virtual "mall"
- Gathering and use of demographic data through Web contacts
- Electronic Data Interchange (EDI), the business-to-business exchange of data
- E-mail and fax media used for reaching prospects and established customers (for example, with newsletters)
- Business-to-business buying and selling
- Security of business transactions

Electronic commerce—*See* e-commerce.

Encryption—The conversion of data into a form, called a cipher, that cannot be easily intercepted by anyone unauthorized. The use of encryption and decryption is as old as the art of communication. In wartime, a cipher, often incorrectly called a code, can be employed to keep the enemy from learning the contents of transmissions. (Technically, a code represents a signal without the intent of keeping it secret; examples are Morse code and ASCII.) Simple ciphers include the substitution of letters for numbers, the rotation of letters in the alphabet, and the scrambling of voice signals by inverting sideband frequencies. More complex ciphers work according to sophisticated computer *algorithms* that rearrange the data bits in digital signals.

The correct decryption key is required to easily recover the contents of an encrypted signal,. The key is an algorithm that undoes the work of the encryption algorithm. Alternatively, a computer can be used to break the cipher. The more complex the encryption algorithm, the more difficult it becomes to eavesdrop on communications without the key.

Encryption and decryption are especially important in *wireless* communications because wireless circuits are easier to "tap" than their hardwired counterparts. Nevertheless, encryption and decryption are a good idea for any kind of sensitive transaction, such as a credit-card purchase online, or discussion of a company secret. In general the stronger the cipher—the harder it is for unauthorized people to break it - the better. However, as the strength of encryption and decryption increases, so does the cost.

Extranet—A private network using the Internet protocols and the public telecommunication system to securely share part of a business's information or operations with suppliers, vendors, partners, customers, or other businesses. An Extranet is that part of a company's Intranet that is extended to users outside the company. An Extranet requires security and privacy, which are effected by firewall server management, digital certificates or similar means of user authentication, encryption of messages, and virtual private networks (VPNs) that tunnel through the public network (see *www.whatis.com/*).

Firewall—A set of related programs at a network gateway server that protects a private network from members of other networks. (The term also implies the security policy used with the programs.) An enterprise with an Intranet that allows its workers access to the wider Internet installs a firewall to prevent outsiders from accessing its private data and for controlling what outside resources its own users have access to.

Basically, a firewall, working closely with a router program, filters all network packets to determine whether to forward them toward their destination. A firewall also includes or works with a proxy server that makes network requests on behalf of workstation users. A firewall is often installed in a computer separate from the rest of the network so that no incoming request can get directly at private network resources.

There are a number of firewall screening methods. A simple one is to make sure requests come from acceptable (previously identified) domain names and IP addresses. For mobile users, firewalls allow remote access to the private network only by the use of secure logon procedures and authentication certificates. Features include logging and reporting, automatic alarms at given thresholds of attack, and a graphical user interface for controlling the firewall (see *www.whatis.com/firewall.htm*).

Internet Protocol (IP)—Rules for handling the address part of each data packet transmitted from one computer to another on the Internet. Each computer (or host) on the Internet has a unique address containing four sets of numbers separated by periods (for example, 199.0.0.2). Each file you request (for example, a page from someone's Web site) is identified in part by a domain name that maps to the Internet address of its computer. The file is in turn sent to you at your Internet address by the IPs at the other end of the exchange (see *www.jyu.fi/~eerwall/ip.htm*). The IP and the Transmission Control Protocol (TCP), which manages the assembly and reassembly of data into packets, form a program, TCP/IP that each computer on the Internet uses to communicate with any other computer.

Intranet—A network of networks that is contained within an enterprise. It may consist of many interlinked *local area networks* and also use leased *lines* in the *wide area network*. Typically, an Intranet includes connections through one or more *gateway* computers to the outside Internet. The main purpose of an Intranet is to share company information and computing resources among employees. It can also be used to facilitate working in groups and for teleconferences.

An Intranet uses TCP/IP, HTTP, and other Internet protocols and in general looks like a private version of the Internet. With tunneling, companies can send private messages from the Intranet through the public network.

Typically, larger enterprises allow users within their Intranet to access the public Internet through firewall servers that can screen messages in both directions to maintain company security. The part of an Intranet that is accessible to customers, partners, suppliers, or others outside the company is called an *Extranet* (see *www.whatis.com*).

Leased Line—A telephone line, sometimes called a leased line, that has been leased for private use; usually contrasted with a switched line or dial-up line. Typically, large companies lease lines from a telephone carrier like AT&T to interconnect different geographic locations of their company. The alternative is to buy and maintain their own lines or, increasingly perhaps, to use public switched lines with secure message protocols (*see* tunneling.)

Point-of-presence (POP)—An access point to the Internet. A POP necessarily has a unique Internet (IP) address. Your independent service provider (ISP) or online service provider (OSP) has a POP. POPs are sometimes used as one measure of the size and growth of an ISP or OSP. A POP may actually reside in rented space owned by a telecommunications carrier like AT&T. A POP usually includes routers, digital/analog call aggregators, servers, and frequently frame relay or ATM switches (see *www.whatis.com/pointofp.htm*).

Protocol—A set of rules for communicating on the Internet.

Remote Access—The ability to get access to a computer or a network from a distance. People at branch offices, telecommuters, and people who are travelling may need remote access to an employer's network (see *www.whatis.com*).

Secure communications—Password protection and data encryption measures used to keep communications private on the public Internet.

Tunneling—Using the Internet as part of a private secure network. The "tunnel" is the path that a company message or file might travel through the Internet. The *Point-to-Point Tunneling Protocol* (PPTP) has been proposed to make it possible to create a virtual private network through tunnels so that companies would no longer need their own leased lines for wide-area communication but could securely use the public networks.

PPTP, sponsored by Microsoft and other companies, and Layer 2 Forwarding, proposed by Cisco Systems, are among the main proposals for a new Internet Engineering Task Force (IETF) standard. With PPTP, which is an extension of the Internet's Point-to-Point Protocol (PPP), any user of a PC with PPP client support will be able to use an ISP to connect securely to a server elsewhere in your company (see *www. whatis.com/tunnelin.htm*).

Virtual Hosting—Provision of a Web server and other services so that companies or individuals don't have to purchase and maintain their own host with a line to the Internet. A virtual hosting provider is sometimes called a Web or Internet "space provider." Some companies providing this service simply call it "hosting." Typically, virtual hosting provides a customer who wants a Web site with: domain name registration assistance, multiple domain names that map to the registered domain name, an allocation of file storage and directory setup for the Web site files (HTML and graphic image files), e-mail addresses, and, optionally, Web site creation services. The customer (the Web site owner) needs only a File Transfer Protocol (FTP) program for exchanging files with the virtual host (see *www.whatis.com/index.htm*).

Virtual Private Network (VPN)—A private data network that uses the public telecommunication infrastructure, maintaining privacy through a tunneling protocol and security procedures. The idea of the VPN is to give the company the same capabilities as a system of owned or leased lines at much lower cost. Phone companies provide secure shared resources for voice messages; a VPN allows the same secure sharing of public resources for data. Companies today can use private virtual network for both Extranets and wide-area Intranets.

On a VPN data is encrypted, sent through the public network, and decrypted at the receiving end. For more security not only the data but also the originating and receiving network addresses are encrypted.. Although there is no standard protocol yet, Microsoft, 3Com, and several other companies have proposed one, the Point-to-Point Tunneling Protocol (PPTP). Microsoft has built PPTP into its Windows NT server. VPN and security software would usually be installed on a company's firewall server (see *www.whatis.com/index.htm*).

REFERENCES

"Boosting Bandwidth", *Infoworld*, May 5, 1997, Vol. 19, Issue 18, available at *http://infoworld.com/cgi-bin/displayArchive.pl?/97/18/e01-18.71.htm.*

Furger, Roberta, "Good Providers: The Best National and Regional ISPs," *PC World*, March 1999.

"Managing your ISP," Infoworld, April 21, 1997, Vol. 19, Issue 16, available at *http://infoworld.com/cgi-bin/displayArchive.pl?/97/16/e01-16.55.htm.*

McCracken, Harry, "Bandwidth On Demand," *PC World*, March 1999.

Navarrete, Angela, "Future Internet," PC World, March 1999.

PC World, March 1999, p. 164.

"The U.S. Internet Service Provider (ISP) Market Will Add Nearly $4.5 Billion of Revenues Annually over the Next Three Years, According to IDC", available at *http://smartmoney.com/smt/news/pr/index.cfm? story=pr-19990419-001030-1011.*

Whatis.com, available at *http://www.whatis.com/index.htm.*

Chapter 4
INTRANETS AND
EXTRANETS

Intranets are becoming more and more common in corporate America. The Internet technology they use gives ready access to external data—in effect, they are internal Web sites. An Intranet is easy to install and flexible (what is developed for one platform may be used for others). In an Intranet, one protocol connects all users to the Web server, run on standard protocols supported by any computer.

An *Extranet* is an extended Intranet creating virtual private networks between companies, business partners, and clients. It allows intranets to interact. Security provides the appropriate level of access to users. The key point is that all three "nets"—Inter-, Intra-, and Extra- —use the same technology. The only difference is who has access to what. The goal is to have access to what you need no matter where you are at any time of the day or night. No matter where you are when you log in, things should work the same way.

Corporate managers must understand how Intranet structure and organization relates to accounting, tax, audit, and security issues. Managers, customers, employees, stockholders, potential investors, creditors, loan officers, government representatives (SEC, IRS), and other interested parties can access the information in a company through Web browsers (interfaces) like Netscape and Internet Explorer. Management may set up an Intranet to improve operating efficiencies and productivity and to reduce operating costs (e.g., distribution expenses), time, and errors.

Of course, keeping information current on an Intranet takes time and resources. Proper controls must be established to guard against unauthorized access to the company's data. One security device is to use firewalls (barriers) to prevent misuse of the Intranet by outsiders who might otherwise be able to alter accounting and financial information, steal property, or obtain confidential data. Add-on security tools are available to restrict users from performing certain acts or viewing restricted information.

Intranet Benefits

Information system (IS) and functional department managers quickly saw the power of this new communications medium as a resource to be leveraged within the corporation. A Forrester Research study found that two-thirds of large companies already had or are contemplating Intranet business applications; they identified the Intranet as a powerful tool to make information more readily available both within and outside the company.

With businesses under significant pressure to empower employees and to better leverage internal information resources, Intranets furnish a very effective communications platform, one that is both timely and extensive. A basic Intranet can be set up in days yet can eventually act as an information hub for the whole company, its remote offices, partners, suppliers, customers, investors, creditors, consultants, regulatory agencies, and other interested parties.

Intranets provide:

- Easy navigation (internal home page provides links to information)
- An integrated distributed computing strategy (localized Web servers reside near the content author)
- Rapid prototyping (can be measured in days or even hours in some cases)
- Accessibility via most computing platforms
- Scalability: you can start small and build as you need to
- Extensible to many media types (video, audio, interactive applications)
- Tie-ins to "legacy" information sources (existing databases, word processing documents, or groupware databases)

Thus, among Intranet benefits are these features:

- An Intranet is inexpensive to start, requiring minimal investment in infrastructure.

- Open platform architecture allows for large and increasing numbers of add-on applications.

- A distributed computing strategy uses computing resources more effectively.

- An Intranet is much more timely and less expensive than traditional information (paper) delivery.

More Effective Publication

One of the key drivers in the adoption curve is that Intranets allow businesses to evolve from a calendar or schedule-based publishing strategy to one that is event-driven or needs-based. In the past, businesses published an employee handbook once a year, whether or not policies changed to coincide with that publication date. Traditionally, even though these handbooks may have been outdated as soon as they arrived on the users' desks, they would not be updated for another year.

An Intranet allows information to be updated instantly. If the company adds a new mutual fund to the 401K program for instance, the benefits page can reflect that immediately, and the home page can have a brief announcement about the change. Then when employees refer to the 401K program, they have the new information at their fingertips.

Marketing

The traditional publication model includes a multistep process: creation of content, migration of content to desktop publishing environment, production of draft, revision, final draft production, duplication, and distribution. Intranets dramatically reduce the costs and time for content development, duplication, distribution, and usage.

The Intranet publishing model skips many of the traditional steps. As the information is centrally stored and always presumed to be current, the company will not have to retrieve "old" information from employees, thus saving updating expenses.

If the corporate LAN environment can support Intranet activities (and most can), the information technology (IT) infrastructure is already in place. Further, most popular Intranet Web servers can run on platforms most companies already use (Intel 80486 or Pentium class computers, Apple Macintosh, Novell NetWare, etc.), so that little if any new infrastructure is required.

Organizations estimate that the traditional model may entail physical duplication and distribution costs of as high as $15 per employee in addition to the content development or testing costs. An organization with 10,000 employees may find cost savings of moving to an Intranet policy for a single application alone—the employee policies and benefits manual—of $150,000. This savings does not even take into account the additional value of making information more easily available to staff, thus improving their productivity and morale.

Practical Applications

The uses of Intranets by companies are unlimited. Companies can:

- Furnish outside CPAs with accounting, audit, and tax information.
- Provide marketing and sales information to current and prospective customers or clients.
- Provide information to field salespeople and managers at different branches (e.g., sales and profit reports, product tracking, transaction analysis).
- Furnish resource needs and reports to suppliers.
- Communicate corporate information to employees, such as company policies and forms, operating instructions, job descriptions, time sheets, human resource data and documents, business plans, newsletters, marketing manuals, phone directories, schedules, and performance reports.
- Support employee training and development.
- Transfer information to government agencies (e.g., Department of Commerce, SEC, IRS).
- Furnish current and prospective investors with profitability, growth, and market value statistics.
- Provide lenders and creditors with liquidity and solvency data.
- Provide project, proposal, and scheduling data to other companies participating in joint ventures.
- Issue press releases and product/service announcements.
- Give legal information to outside attorneys in litigation matters.
- Provide trade associations with input for surveys.

- Access and search databases and rearrange information.
- Furnish information to outside consultants (e.g., investment management advisors, pension planners).
- Provide insurance companies with information to draft or modify insurance coverage.
- Allow for collaboration by letting users access drafts of a specific project document interactively and add annotations and comments. For example, Ford's Intranet links design engineers in the U.S., Europe, and Asia.
- Furnish economic statistics about a company to economic advisors.
- Facilitate database queries and document requests.
- Provide spreadsheets, database reports, tables, checklists, and graphs to interested parties.
- Display e-mail.

Site maps (e.g., table of contents) should be included so users may easily navigate from each note (element) and should be visible through frames or panels.

For quick response time, there should be a direct connection to the server. Web browsers may be used to achieve cross-platform viewing and applications if a wide variety of desktops are used within the company. Web technology (e.g., Web servers) allows each desktop having a Web browser to access corporate information over the existing network. Therefore, employees in different divisions of the company located in different geographic areas (e.g., buildings) can access and use centralized and/or scattered information (cross section).

The major element in an Intranet is the Web server software which runs on a central computer and serves as a clearinghouse for all information. Web servers for the Intranet are available from many vendors including:

- CompuServe (800-848-8199): Spry Web Server for Windows NT.
- IBM (800-426-2255): Internet Connection Server for MVS.
- Lotus (800-828-7086): InterNotes Web Publisher.
- Microsoft (800-426-9400): Internet Information Server (comes with Microsoft's NT Server).

- Netscape (415-528-2555): Fast Track and Commerce Server for Windows NT.

- Quarterdeck (800-683-6696): Web Server and Web Star for Windows 95/NT.

Microsoft's Windows NT Server has higher security and makes it easier to upgrade to more powerful hardware as application needs increase.

No matter what your operating system (Windows, UNIX, Macintosh), many Intranet tools are available, and there are many Intranet tool vendors like Illustra Information Technologies (*http://www.illustra.com*; (510) 652-8000) and Spider Technologies (*http://www.w3spider.com*; (415) 969-7149). Frontier Technologies' Intranet Genie is a tool that includes a fairly secure Web server, HTML authoring instructions and guidelines (discussed below), Web browser, and e-mail functions *(http://www.frontiertech.com; (800) 929-3054)*.

Setting Up the Intranet

Hypertext Markup Language (HTML)

Hypertext markup language (HTML) should be used in developing Intranets because it is an easier graphical user interface (GUI) to program than Windows environments like Microsoft Windows. HTML is good for integrating database applications and information systems. It facilitates the use of hyper links and search engines, making it easy to share identical information among different responsibility segments of the company. Intranet data usually goes from back-end sources (e.g., mainframe host) to the Web server to users (e.g., customers) in HTML format.

Common Gateway Interface (CGI)

The majority of Web applications connect users to databases through a mechanism in the Web server referred to as the common gateway interface (CGI). Most CGI programs are written in Tool Command Language (TCL) or Pert (a scripting language). However, because these languages involve printing a source code of the Web server, there is a control and security threat. Other deficiencies are relative slowness in applications, nonexistence or inadequate debuggers, and maintenance problems. Consider other languages for the CGI, such as C or C++.

The following should be kept in mind:

1. You need code management tools to enable different participants in a corporate project or activity to communicate. You also need tools for database design, modeling, and debugging. The following Web sites, among others, can give you helpful information:

   (a) Basic HTTP:
   http://www.w3.org/hypertext/www/protocols/http/http2.html

   (b) HTML Browser List:
   http://www.w30rg/hypertext/www/clients.html

   (c) Web Server Comparison Chart:
   http://www.proper.com/www/seners-chart.html

   (d) HTML Specs from the WWW Consortium:
   http://www.w3.org/hypertext/www/markup/markup.html

   (e) Introduction to CGI:
   http://hoo.hoo.ncsa.uiuc.edu/docs/cgi:/overview.html

2. Set up your system so that it can accommodate many servers and browsers. Do not commit to a particular server or browser, because new technological developments require flexibility.

3. Make sure your HTML user interface is separate from the database and application logic.

Intranet applications are scaleable—they can start small and grow. This allows many businesses to try out an Intranet pilot, publishing a limited amount of content on a single platform, and evaluate the results. If the pilot looks promising, additional content can be migrated to the server.

Content

You must decide if data should be made available via a Web server, e-mail, or some other means. If the data are of general import, such as company travel guidelines or mileage reimbursement, they can be posted on a Web server so that when employees and travel agents, among others, require this information, they can click on Travel Guidelines from the human resources page and get the most current information.

Many businesses find building Web interfaces to legacy information a key application. With tools like Purveyor's Data Wizard, HTML Transit, and WebDBC, end users can build simple point and click access to legacy information without any programming, allowing nontechnical users to look at customer records, product information, inventory, technical problem tracking, call reports, etc. You can also quickly set up such things as seminar or training registration forms for short-term usage, loading the registrants' information into an easily manipulated database.

Conversely, interoffice e-mail may be more appropriate for "interrupt-driven," time-sensitive information, especially for a focused group of recipients. "Our most important customer is coming in March 2, so please attend the briefing at 9 a.m." In this case, the Web server can be used as an extended information resource: "Before the meeting, check the internal Web server link for Current Customers for updated information about this account."

Enhancements

Intranets can provide efficient access to other external information resources including group mailing lists, threaded discussion groups, and stock/bond quotes. Oft-accessed information can be aggregated at the firewall and efficiently dispersed within the company, thus reducing external bandwidth and connectivity requirements.

Multithreaded discussion group software or conferencing applications can run on the same platform as the Intranet application, providing further chances to discuss company issues and the content that resides on the server.

Intranets and Groupware

Intranets and groupware are not mutually exclusive. Many companies find that groupware (work flow, collaborative computing, etc.) is appropriate for certain focused applications, while Intranets are suitable for migrating existing content to online delivery. Others find a powerful combination in groupware and a Web server (an example is the Lotus InterNotes engine for publishing Notes databases on the Web).

Ultimately, each application strategy has its merits. Beyond this, Intranet applications and Web servers make an excellent foundation for Web-based groupware, allowing businesses to employ a Web-centric Intranet system strategy and leverage the nearly ubiquitous Web browser and the powerful navigational aids provided by HTML.

Intranets and Corporate Finance

Intranets should be used for corporate real-time decision support. The true competitiveness of a firm is determined by the ability of its management to make accurate, timely decisions that improve profitability and long-term prospects. To make these decisions, an organization must know about customers, products, and suppliers, the availability of its assets, the status of its commitments, and the profitability of its activities.

While most companies have sophisticated transaction systems that collect operational data, the information that managers need for decision-making and performance measurement purposes is less readily available. How can the tremendous amounts of corporate financial data be transformed into useful information? Firms need to access certain information with which to make smart decisions without the clutter of data. Why? Because to respond to an emerging business situation means sifting through large amounts of data from business units or product lines. To do this properly, firms are increasingly using online analytical processing (OLAP).

Analyzing the data is not the only problem. Data accuracy, timeliness, and accessibility are also important. Managers facing increasing pressure to make profitable decisions faster need to be free of the constraints of time and space to access data from their office, home, or the road, at all hours of the day and night. The next generation of Intranet applications will have to provide access to the full range of corporate data to make strategic decisions. This might require software "intelligent agents" that pull together information from a variety of relational and legacy systems at regular intervals to construct an integrated view of business activities. These agents would present the data in a consistent, easily accessible format to whoever needs it (see Figure 4.1 on page 96).

This section looks at how companies can use the Intranet to deal with all their financial information and the role it plays in financial information management.

These are the kinds of business problems managers face, and the benefits once the Intranet solution is applied:

Business Problems:
• Non-integrated islands of valuable information

• Non-integrated financial and accounting applications

• Lack of analysis tools and decision support for management

Figure 4.1: Distributed Computing Environment

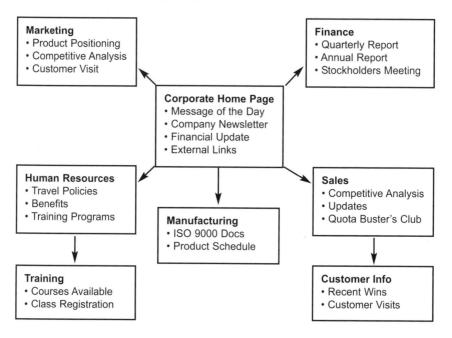

Solution:
- Fully integrated Web-based enterprise-wide financial and accounting infrastructure

Benefits:
- Integrated information across business functions

- Improved data analysis and decision support

- Better decisions

- Cost savings from increased efficiency

The competitive business environment is forcing firms to reengineer financial management processes. General ledger systems and spreadsheets alone are inadequate when voluminous data is spread across the world, when corporate structures change because of mergers and acquisitions, and when timely and reliable consolidations, budgets, and forecasts are essential.

A definition of exactly what goes into financial systems is necessary to establish the setting. Financial systems encompass business processes, procedures, controls, and data dedicated to the operation and maintenance of corporate financial objectives. They incorporate reporting and analyzing financial data, simplifying budgeting and forecasting, supporting better planning and control of the consolidation of actual results, answering ad hoc requests efficiently, and improving cost control and performance measurement.

The use of financial systems is often triggered by events with financial consequences, such as receipt of appropriations or other resources, acquisition of goods or services, payments or collections, recognition of guarantees, benefits to be provided, potential liabilities, or other reportable financial activities. Financial systems usually have the following technical characteristics: a common database, common data element definitions, standardized processing for transactions, and multiple applications integrated through a common database or are interfaced to meet defined requirements.

If software developers are to understand emerging business requirements in terms of functionality rather than technical architecture, they need to address them directly. The place to start is with a review of what financial and accounting systems do.

Accounting captures financial data, records and aggregates it, and prepares statements that communicate to decision-makers necessary information about business units, transactions, and events. Early accounting systems processed transactions, stored historical information, and used that information to answer questions about the past, present, and future.

Today's accounting systems are a collection of methods for capturing and transforming financial data. An important task for accounting is to report the financial position of the firm and the performance of its business units to facilitate decision-making. The accounting system is usually thought of in two types: financial and management accounting. Financial accounting collects, classifies, and reports financially based transactions subject to numerous disclosure requirements. The reports are used outside the company by shareholders, investors, creditors, financial analysts, and the IRS. Financial accounting activities include collecting, processing, maintaining, transmitting, and reporting data about financial events; supporting financial planning or budgeting activities; and supporting the preparation of financial statements.

Management accounting provides a financial analysis of management decisions and activities. The reports generated by the management accounting system are used internally. These are the report cards by which operations managers are evaluated. Compared to financial accounting, management accounting is fairly new, having evolved from simple cost accounting systems. Management accounting activities include reporting historical transactions to internal and external parties, accumulating and reporting cost information, safeguarding the assets of a company, and providing insight into the value of future transactions.

Financial Intranets

Finance and accounting software has traditionally not been trendsetting. Accounting software, for instance, provided a way to enter transactions and manage those transactions to form an audit trail. The primary concern of accounting software was transaction entry and back office management of the audit trail, critically important but not very exciting.

Today business managers need a lot more from the information locked inside accounting databases. The information is there but it is very difficult to obtain. Intranets can solve this problem because they allow the integration necessary to give managers the accounting information they need, in the specific form they need it, at the time they need it, and where they need it.

Well-managed companies watch their financial records carefully, setting clear objectives for their managers. Providing secure access to important financial information in an easy-to-use way is a top priority. By using internal Web applications, finance departments can more easily disseminate this information to key managers by securely posting corporate finance information (see Figure 4.2) or by providing simple forms-based query capabilities (see Figure 4.3). This information can take hundreds of specific forms rather than one general view or report, like the typical set of financial statements.

Figure 4.2: Sample Posting: Corporate Finance Information

WRIST I/O 2000 DEVELOPMENT   Info Add...

Experience the Web (url)	01/01/1997 Info
Focus Group Report.doc	01/01/1997 Info View
HomePage.html	01/01/1997 Info View
Part and Supplier Specification.doc	01/01/1997 Info View
Policies & Procedures (compound doc)	01/01/1997 Info View
Supplier Query	01/01/1997 Info Run
LCD Change Request Workflow	01/01/1997 Info Initiate
Images	01/01/1997 Info View

Go to:

Livelink™ Version 7.1.1. © Copyright 1997 Open Text Corporation and Open Text U.S.A. Inc.

Figure 4.3: Sample Forms-Based Query

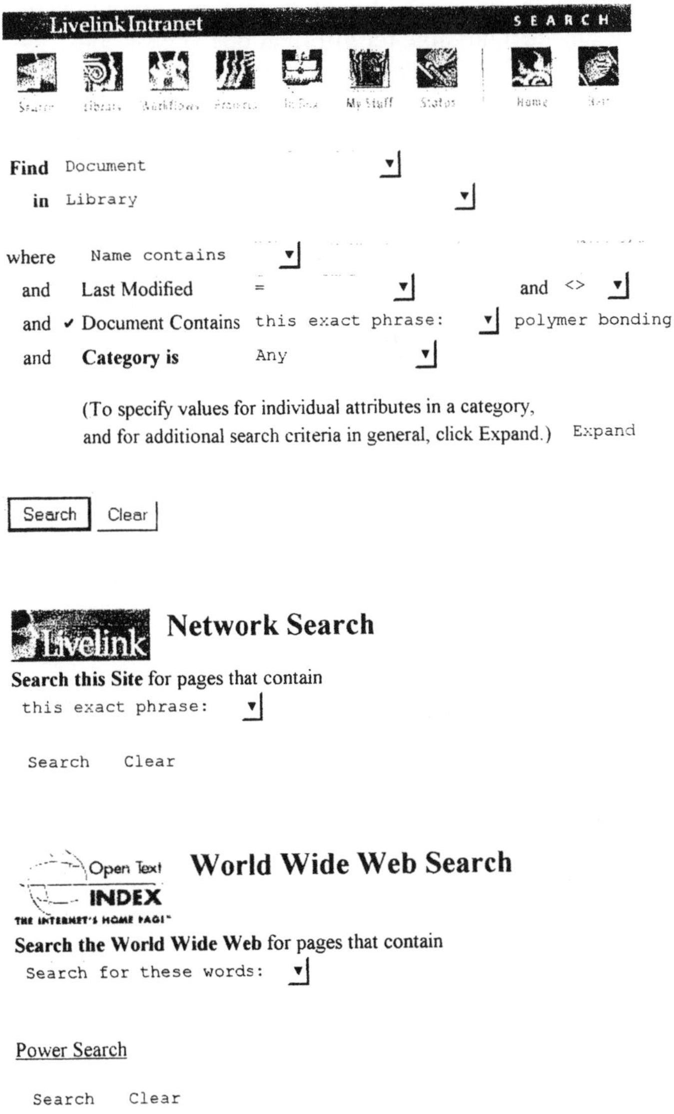

Find Document ⯆

 in Library ⯆

where Name contains ⯆

and Last Modified = ⯆ and <> ⯆

and ✔ Document Contains this exact phrase: ⯆ polymer bonding

and **Category is** Any ⯆

(To specify values for individual attributes in a category,
and for additional search criteria in general, click Expand.) Expand

Search | Clear

Network Search

Search this Site for pages that contain
this exact phrase: ⯆

Search Clear

World Wide Web Search

Search the World Wide Web for pages that contain
Search for these words: ⯆

Power Search

Search Clear

Accountants need to recognize the inevitable changes technology is bringing about and look for new ways to add value to the business. This value must be aligned with the needs of the business process. Integrated systems technologies make it possible for information to be put into a system once and moved to all the different places where it's needed. This frees accountants from having to manually move information from one place to another because there was no other way to accomplish the task.

Finally, the large financial systems developed in the era of mainframe computers have become too costly to maintain, too troublesome to document, inefficient, ineffective, or even strategically dangerous because they are difficult to change as business conditions evolve. After Deloitte & Touche surveyed senior financial and accounting executives at 200 corporations, they reported that 68% of the respondents planned to implement a new system within the next two years. Of this group, 80% intended to purchase packaged solutions and 64% preferred client/server hardware platforms.

These statistics reveal that systems based in new technology are well positioned to benefit from the major surge in demand expected over the next few years. The rapid growth of Intranet accounting applications has been considered partly a replacement cycle phenomenon. It's estimated that the average enterprise general ledger in a Fortune 100 company is 15 to 17 years old. Virtually all of these are running on (mainly IBM) mainframes. A significant majority were developed internally. Their replacement is being driven by high maintenance costs and the desire that accounting provide decision support data and facilitate business process reengineering.

The Purpose of Financial Intranets

Successful Intranet implementation should tackle four problems that the systems they replace are not equipped to handle: production control, the effect of daily operations on short-term and long-term strategy, cost control, and the lack of control of report generation.

Given increasingly global sourcing, financial flows related to production are becoming more complicated. Managers currently rely on a patchwork of systems—accounts payable, accounts receivable, fixed-asset management, purchasing, and general ledger—to support financial management activities. These systems worked well when their primary responsibility was to collect and present historical information. Not surprisingly, most of these systems are only equipped to handle routine transactions; little consideration was ever given to their connection to other business activities. For example, if the general ledger and the procurement systems are linked through an integrated information process, the financial analyst can get an accurate picture of accounts payable. By integrating financial functions into decision-making, the organization can make timely and accurate assessment of the financial consequences of its strategic and operational decisions, regardless of the type of decision or where it is made.

While many financial systems are just adequate for accounting purposes, they often fail to give line managers the requisite operating information or provide timely performance information to senior management. To be useful, strategic information must be compiled from the overabundance of operational data being stored; overnight batch reports are no longer sufficient. Managers need to see the whole business operation modeled. The ability to construct queries on the fly and to follow up quickly with questions that drill even deeper into the data is necessary if managers are to fully understand the business environment before making critical decisions. Changing market conditions and specific business situations, such as inventory levels and detailed analysis of customers' behavior, can point analysts down potentially profitable paths that they could not have anticipated. That's why systems should be developed to help managers make better strategic decisions.

To achieve better cost control new technology must be used. As businesses downsize and cut cost to survive, there is a growing need for faster, more accurate, and more useful financial information. Usually, this is easier said than done. Many companies, especially those that are large or highly decentralized, find it difficult to get at the information they need to effectively manage their businesses. These companies are restrained by inflexible legacy systems and an environment of non-standardization. This creates difficulties in simple reorganization, much less managing better in a rapidly changing world.

As for the lack of control of report generating, a major problem is bottlenecking. The report generating process often has difficulty integrating all the data required to make a comprehensive and informative assessment for managers to work with. Moreover, as companies become more widespread and powerful, the balance of data processing power has shifted away from central Information Systems staffs to individuals in functional departments. By tying together desktop computers, inexpensive Intranets allow businesses to integrate their information systems to a greater extent than was previously possible.

The need for integration is a key driver of the financial Intranet marketplace. Many organizations are planning to integrate their accounting systems into their networks over the next several years. Financial executives desire the ease of use and timeliness that this will afford. Information systems managers, faced with scarce resources, believe this will smooth out system development and management processes, saving time and money.

Financial Analysis and Management Accounting

While managing the transaction aspects of financial flows is important, so is using financial information for control purposes. The area of financial management that is essential to support the operations and strategy of the company is called management accounting. Management accounting is vital for business planning, decision-making, budgeting, and controlling, including overhead cost management, activity-based costing, product cost controlling, and sales and profit analysis.

Gathering data for management accounting is challenging. Few companies maintain a single, integrated set of records for all their divisions and the departments within them. In practice, to consolidate their data, companies tie together data from many sources, including databases and spreadsheets. The process adds to the time and cost required to perform consolidations at the end of a period, as well as to create and track budgets and forecasts. At the functional level, consolidation can set the finance organization free from the central IS structure with a set of applications that are powerful but easy to use.

Once the data is gathered, financial analysis software tools allow people with authorized access to find the data they need, drill down into it, and see the results in seconds, without waiting for MIS or even corporate accounting. This information is meant not only for executives, but also for a everyone who wants to make better decisions on a daily basis.

Online Analytical Processing (OLAP)

Analytical tools, called OLAP, transforms warehoused corporate data into strategic information. When users of warehousing applications want better access and analysis of the data, OLAP tools can help them with everything from basic navigation and browsing to multifaceted data analysis.

OLAP applications can span a variety of organizational functions. Finance departments use OLAP for budgeting, activity-based costing, financial performance analysis, and financial modeling. Managers use it for ad hoc analysis of data in multiple dimensions to get the insight they need for better decision-making. OLAP lets managers probe and access corporate data in bits and pieces rather than through traditional means of query, giving them consistently fast access to a wide variety of data organized by criteria that match the real dimensions of the modern enterprise.

OLAP uses a multidimensional view of aggregate data to provide quick access to strategic information. The key feature is the ability to transform data into so-called multidimensional form, providing views that inherent represent an actual business model. Managers typically look at financial data by scenario, organization, product line, and time; and at sales data by product, geography, channel, and time. Database design should not prejudice which operations can be performed on a dimension or how rapidly those operations are performed. Managers must be able to analyze data across any dimension, at any level of aggregation, with equal ease. OLAP software should support these views of data in natural and responsive fashion, insulating users of the information from complex query syntax. Above all, managers shouldn't have to understand complex computer languages to use OLAP.

Intranet Demonstration

This section presents the AICPA (American Institute of Certified Public Accounts) demonstration Intranet (see Figure 4.4 on page 104) at *www.kvg.com/information* to show you the kinds of information you can get in one place, with one interface:

- Daily flash reports
- Review of daily cash receipts and checks
- Customer information
- Personnel manual
- Lists
- Project tracking
- Employee communication
- E-commerce links

The demo screen covers:

1. Production (Figure 4.5, page 105)—Compare Dollars: This screen can show who is going to be the employee of the year and who is going to need help.

Figure 4.4: AICPA Demonstration Intranet (*www.kvg.com/information*)

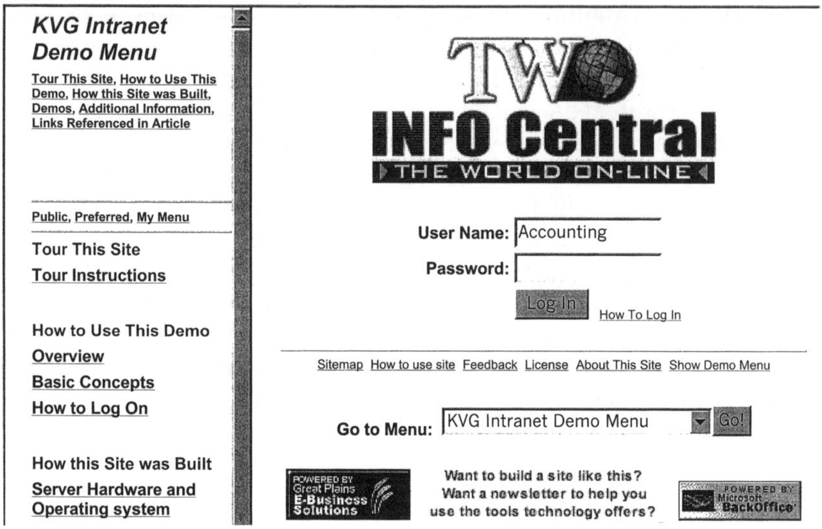

KVG Intranet Demo Menu

Tour This Site, How to Use This Demo, How this Site was Built, Demos, Additional Information, Links Referenced in Article

Public, Preferred, My Menu

Tour This Site

Tour Instructions

How to Use This Demo

Overview

Basic Concepts

How to Log On

How this Site was Built

Server Hardware and Operating system

INFO Central
THE WORLD ON-LINE

User Name: Accounting
Password:

Log In   How To Log In

Sitemap   How to use site   Feedback   License   About This Site   Show Demo Menu

Go to Menu: KVG Intranet Demo Menu   Go!

Want to build a site like this? Want a newsletter to help you use the tools technology offers?

2. Accounts Receivable (Figure 4.6)—Aging: Intranets organize accounts receivable by aging.

3. General Ledger Transactions (Figure 4.7)—Intranets give you a variety of options for handling your general ledger.

Summary

The role of Intranets is to respond to management needs for comprehensive and timely business information. A company's accumulated data constitute a valuable resource; in most organizations, those in charge are very aware of this fact. Yet the approach of simply collecting data has serious shortcomings. It neither succeeds in giving corporate decision makers data in a form they can understand and use nor permits easy access to information.

Incompatible accounting and information systems are causing management tremendous problems. In the past, companies have attempted to support financial information systems by using mainframes that are rigid in structure, expensive to maintain, and difficult to update when business requirements change. At the other end of the spectrum, firms generate business reports by assembling them manually using spreadsheets from

Figure 4.5: AICPA Demonstration Screen: Production—Compare Dollars

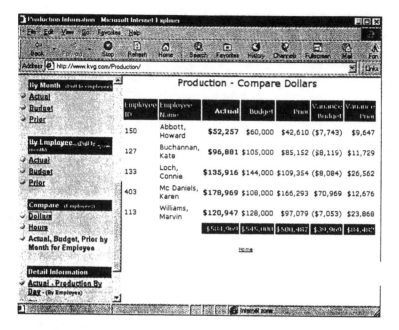

Figure 4.6: AICPA Demonstration Screen: Accounts Receivable

KVG Intranet Demo Menu

Tour This Site, How to Use This
Demo, How this Site was Built,
Demos, Additional Information,
Links Referenced in Article

Public, Preferred, My Menu

Tour This Site

Tour Instructions

How to Use This Demo

Overview

Basic Concepts

How to Log On

How this Site was Built

Server Hardware and
Operating system

Tools used to Build Site

Accounts Receivable - Aging

Sort By: Total Current 31 to 60 61 to 90 91 to 120 120 +

Customer Name	Total	Current	31 to 60	61 to 90	91 to 120	120
Aaron Fitz Electrical	17,198	14,574	0	0	2,156	4(
Adam Park Resort	17,195	13,970	689	2,536	0	
Advanced Paper Co.	4,327	1,685	1,320	1,288	0	:
Advanced Tech Satellite System	6,735	6,735	0	0	0	
Alton Manufacturing	68,955	68,955	0	0	0	
American Electrical Contractor	7,800	4,590	1,240	1,970	0	
American Science Museum	26,161	0	5,000	21,161	0	
Associated Insurance Company	398	398	0	0	0	
Astor Suites	4,339	4,339	0	0	0	
Atmore Retirement Center	13,104	1,570	6,764	1,333	868	2,5(
Baker's Emporium Inc.	0	0	0	0	0	
Beatrice Foods	289	289	0	0	0	
Berry Medical Center	51,824	51,824	0	0	0	
Boyle's Country Inn's	16,812	12,018	0	2,413	2,380	
Breakthrough	13,109	0	3,838	3,860	3,480	1,9

Figure 4.7: AICPA Demonstration Screen: General Ledger Transactions

KVG Intranet Demo Menu	General Ledger Transactions
Tour This Site, How to Use This Demo, How this Site was Built, Demos, Additional Information, Links Referenced in Article	Account: **000-1100-00** From: **1/1/98** To: **1/31/98** Sort By: **Date**
	Create Import File Instructions

Cash - Operating Account

Beginning Balance:	**338,562.25**
Transactions (net):	**40,701.99**
Ending Balance:	**379,264.24**

Public, Preferred, My Menu

Tour This Site

Tour Instructions

Account	Date	Amount	JE	Source	Reference
000-1100-00	1/1/98	(1,847.50)	13	CMTRX	
000-1100-00	1/13/98	(5,000.00)	482	PMPAY	Comnet Enterprises, Inc
000-1100-00	1/13/98	(21,918.15)	618	PMPAY	International Wire
000-1100-00	1/13/98	(36,382.83)	619	PMPAY	Green Lake Wire Company

How to Use This Demo
Overview
Basic Concepts
How to Log On

How this Site was Built
Server Hardware and
Operating system

general ledgers and other operating systems. This approach cannot handle large volumes of data primarily because it would require extensive data rekeying and manual consolidation. In addition, spreadsheets have limited capabilities for information sharing and lack the necessary control to ensure consistency across the corporation.

As business requirements have changed, there has been an increasing push for ways to analyze significant amounts of data in real time so that management can look at different scenarios and make decisions in hours rather than in weeks. Inevitably, broad access to data and to the analytic tools that ease the analysis of the data will change decision-making. Quick and easy analysis of up-to-the-minute and accurate on-the-fly data is a powerful competitive weapon.

Intranet technology can help you collect, aggregate, and consolidate business information from fragmented computer systems and transactional databases in a number of ways; usually Intranets replace existing systems with more efficient alternatives.

Intranet applications can start as small "pilots" and scale upward over time, gradually facilitating access to an increasing breadth of information, thus improving both employee productivity and satisfaction and bolstering the company's competitive position.

References

"Corporate Finance Network," at
http://www.corpfinet.com/welcome.html.

"Corporate Intranets," at
http://www.moonspinners.com/moonspinners/intranet.html.

"Enterprise Solutions," at
http://home.netscape.com/comprod/at_work/index.html.

"Finance Applications," at *http://www.itWeb.com/intranet/corp_16.htm.*

Hoffman, Charles, "Intranets," Journal of Accountancy, October 1998, pp. 31-37.

"Intranet Applications: A White Paper," at
http://www.thehost.com/intra01.htm.

"Intranets," at *http://www.mgl.co.uk/iservices/intranet.html.*

"Intranets Refine Corporate Information Systems: A White Paper," at
http://www.netscape.com/comprod/at_work/white_paper/indepth.html.

"Livelink Intranet Suite by Opentext Corporation," at
http://www.opentext.com/.

"The Web World #1 Guide to Finance," at
http://www.euro.net/innovation/Web_Word_Base/TWW1-html/FinTOC1.html.

Chapter 5
MARKETING AND ADVERTISING

Introduction

The potential of the Internet and the World Wide Web (WWW) is most exciting. Predictions of sales over the Internet are wide-ranging, from a low of $7 billion to a high of $16 billion in 2000.

The Internet allows retailers to reach both customers and suppliers and provides another medium for retailers to expand internationally at relatively low cost. Technology allows businesses to provide higher value and greater convenience to their customers.

CDNow, a music store, and other specialized online retailers like the Amazon.com bookstore, PC makers like Dell, and flower and gift stores are thriving, proving that Internet retailing can work when properly done. The "best-of-breed" stores dominate each category; these specialized companies are the ones that can out-innovate competitors to retain customers.

While many business retailers like Amazon.com are moving aggressively onto the Internet, many more are proceeding cautiously, using it as a means to advertise merchandise and providing a toll-free telephone number for customer orders. Many retailers are reluctant to devote more resources to the Internet until they feel more confident of consumer interest.

Recent surveys have found that Americans are concerned about giving out credit card information online. Emerging cryptographic techniques are likely to alleviate this concern. For example, MasterCard and Visa are jointly developing Secure Electronic Transfer (SET) technology to make credit card transactions safer by encrypting the consumers' credit card numbers. Even the merchants will not be able to see the numbers.

This will prevent unscrupulous merchants from selling a product over the Internet solely to collect credit card numbers. As technology improves and consumers become more comfortable with the Internet, it's likely that privacy/encryption issues will cease to be a serious barrier to Internet commerce.

Internet speed is holding back both consumers and retailers. Relatively slow speed means that consumers have to wait for images to download for viewing. However, given the competition in the communications industry, consumers will soon benefit from faster and more affordable access to the Internet.

Selling merchandise over the Internet makes it possible to reach international as well as domestic consumers, although outside the United States the cost to connect to the Internet is sometimes two to three times the cost in the U.S. These costs are expected to decrease in the future; the number of users of the Internet is expected to be about 35 million in 2000. The rapid expansion of the Internet in the United States and internationally means commercial Web sites will become a profitable distribution channel for businesses.

Consumers are likely to benefit greatly from retailing on the Internet. Search engines now under development will enable consumers to find merchandise on the Internet at the lowest price. This will lead to significant changes in how business is conducted. There will be tremendous pressure on retailers to cut their margins. As a result of these competitive pressures, retail prices are expected to drop by up to 30 percent over the next 10 to 15 years. It's often easier for the online customer to search and compare information on brands and prices, and emerging technology will allow them to view 3-D images of the product. Instead of just reading a description and looking at a photograph, a consumer will be able to visually inspect the product from virtually any angle.

The Internet can help a business do much more. It's a great tool for conducting marketing research, gathering both primary and secondary data. Information is the key factor in e-commerce. It's clear that the Internet is going to be a major distribution channel for businesses in the near future.

The Web and the Internet

Businesses, universities, governmental bodies and non-profit entities are content providers on the Internet. Their computers are set up to allow others to examine their data. Users connect with these sites primarily to obtain useful or entertaining content.

Many content providers are also advertisers. Their Web sites contain paid announcements to entice users to visit an advertiser's Web site. As a distribution channel, the Internet is like an electronic streetscape. The aim of advertisers is to bring customers into their electronic storefronts, their Web sites.

The birth of the World Wide Web (WWW) has revolutionized the use of the Internet. Hyperlinks allow users to connect from one computer to another by clicking on highlighted links. The IP addressing system provides a way of identifying the computers on the Internet. An IP address is defined by four 8-bit numbers. Each 8-bit number is equal to 1 byte; it can represent up to 256 sites, numbered from 0 to 255. The four 8-bit numbers are separated by periods.

Each IP address is unique. Because numeric IP addresses tend to be harder to remember by humans, domain names are typically used. Each domain name corresponds to one IP address.

Domain names are organized in a hierarchy. A domain name is typically made up of two parts: a top-level domain name and a unique name. You can determine the type of site they are linked to by looking at the top-level domain name. The most common top-level domains are:

- .com   commercial organizations
- .edu   educational institutions
- .gov   government entities
- .org   non-profit organizations
- .net   Internet service providers

Other top-level domain names belong to countries: *us* for the United States, *il* for Israel, *mx* for Mexico, *kr* for South Korea and *pk* for Pakistan. Seven new top-level domain names were added in 1997: *arts, firm, info, nom, rec, store, web*. Additional information about domain name registration may be obtained from:

- *www.yahoo.com/Computers_and_Internet/Internet/Domain_ Registration/.*

Market Analysis

Don't overlook the wealth of marketing information available on the Internet. It's a great source of both primary and secondary marketing data, though it does have to be evaluated for credibility. Information on the Internet is not generally reviewed, evaluated, or censored by anyone other than the owner of the information, so it may not necessarily be correct or reliable. On the other hand, information on the Internet can and is generally updated frequently, while printed matter tends to become obsolete. The information on the Internet can be kept current. In the end, it's up to you to evaluate the quality of information you get from the Web.

Market research is an integral part of product development and design. Products should be tested at each design stage. This is expensive and time-consuming. Budgetary constraints sometimes limit a company's ability to conduct market research properly, and companies want to reduce research time as well as save on expenses.

One solution is interactive multimedia research. Using sound and video multimedia, researchers can test the design features of a new product on a greater number of respondents in a greater number of markets, providing a more diverse and representative sample. Multimedia research eliminates the need for actual prototypes or using concept boards or storyboards to conduct tests. Multimedia research also eliminates the need to make multiple copies of items to use in several test markets.

Conventional market research techniques can lead to fatigue, boredom, and strain on the respondents. Respondents in a focus group may have to evaluate several concepts or designs in a single session. The stress caused by boredom or fatigue can then affect objectivity and may lead to biased responses.

The primary disadvantage of interactive multimedia research is that physical substance is lacking. Respondents cannot touch, feel, manipulate, or use the product. For some products, this can have significant adverse effects. The disadvantages can be mitigated, however, by providing some samples of the product along with multimedia sounds and video. Reliability and validity are not affected, and the process is much shorter.

Secondary Data

Market researchers can obtain information about consumers and competitors from the Net. Market research can help you determine the opportunities and pitfalls of a given strategy. Product mix and planning, pricing, promotion, and distribution are all affected by market research data. While primary data may be collected, for example, from online surveys, it's often cost-effective to also look at secondary data online. Much of this is free and readily available. Demographic and cultural trends can be identified. Information is available about the economic, legal, and political factors that affect marketing decisions. Information on competitors can easily be obtained online.

US Census Bureau

The US Census Bureau (*www.census.gov*) is an excellent source of demographic data. As with most government Web sites, the information is free. While the official census only takes place every ten years, other surveys provide more recent data.

You can use a variety of data access tools available to extract and display Census Information:

- Census Bureau information may be located by subject or topic using a keyword search.

- Map searches are available through *DataMap*.

- *CenStats*, a Web-based subscription service, provides interactive search and display access to various databases.

- *CenStore* contains information about the products sold by the Census Bureau and the U.S. Government Printing Office. An "economic clock" displays current economic indicators including:
  –U.S. international trade in goods and services
  –Advance monthly retail sales
  –Housing starts
  –Advance report on durable goods manufacturers' shipments and orders
  –Manufacturers' shipments, inventories, and orders
  –Manufacturing and trade inventories and sales
  –Quarterly financial report for manufacturing, mining, and trade corporations

American Demographics Marketing Tools

The Web site of American Demographics Marketing Tools (*www.demographics.com*) contains a wealth of information. *American Demographics Magazine* analyzes consumer trends for business leaders. The Web site allows users to search its databases. Users who find the material useful are expected to subscribe to the print edition. The same company's *Marketing Tools* magazine provides information on marketing tactics and techniques. Its search engine allows you to search the information on this site using keywords or phrases.

Business Marketing Association (BMA)

The needs of business-to-business marketers are different from those of consumer marketers. The Business Marketing Association (*www.marketing.org*) serves those needs. It contains surveys, reports, newsletters, articles, and several hundred data files concerning marketing and communications. The site provides information about education, training, professional certification, membership benefits, and other resources.

U.S. Postal Service (USPS)

The U.S. Postal Service (*www.usps.gov/ncsc*) Web site is an excellent source for postal information. ZIP+4 Codes can be looked up. There is also a link to find city and ZIP Code associations, and there is a frequently asked questions (FAQs) section, information about preferred address abbreviations, and rate information. It's possible to track express mail packages through this site.

Adlaw

The Adlaw (*www.adlaw.com*) Web site is an excellent source of information on the legal issues related to marketing and advertising; it contains law reports, news, and legal commentary. Adlaw even has a law library for market researchers. Information of current legislation about marketing and advertising is available.

Primary Data

When secondary data is not available, or when the marketing department decides it wants to find its own information directly, you can collect primary data to solve a specific problem. It's generally more cost-effective to use secondary data—collecting primary data tends to be expensive and time-consuming—but primary data tends to be more relevant.

Once the marketing problem is identified, you must decide:

- What data you need to solve the problem
- Who will provide the data
- How the data will be collected

Data collection is one activity you can do successfully on the Internet. Two common techniques are:

- Sending questionnaires by e-mail
- Posting questionnaires on Web sites

Collecting data on the Internet is generally much faster and more economical than traditional techniques. It's often easier to get people to participate. Net questionnaires are still somewhat novel; many people surfing may find it interesting to respond to the survey. However, others may get upset if they are sent unwanted or "junk" e-mail. The source of the e-mail is of special ethical concern. For example, it's unethical to obtain e-mail addressed from newsgroups without permission.

Participants might be more truthful in their responses because they are interacting with a nonjudgmental computer and not a human being. On the other hand, some participants may take advantage of their anonymity to answer questions untruthfully. For example, they may lie about their age or sex.

Data captured electronically can easily be statistically analyzed. It's not prone to data entry errors by researchers. *Respondents*, however, are more likely to make data entry mistakes; they make fewer mistakes writing than typing. In traditional data collection researchers have some control over data entry mistakes made by their staff. Data can, for example, be checked by another individual for errors. This option is not available in electronically captured data. One way to overcome this problem is by building redundancy checks into questionnaires.

The Internet is diverse. A large number of users from all over the world can participate in your marketing study—but this means you may have little control over who participates in the study and the resulting sample size. Still, while you need to be cautious in collecting primary data on the Internet, the new possibilities are exciting.

Developing Web Sites

Interactive Web Sites

Successful Web sites provide valuable information beyond what is available in print or from competing businesses. The content should be relevant, reliable, and accurate. It should be easy for a customer to navigate the Web site and locate information. The information should download quickly. Extensive graphics and multimedia capabilities that make downloading drag may frustrate customers. This means, in part, that you must have a good understanding of the type of equipment and communication lines used by your customers.

Creating and maintaining an *interactive* Web site is technologically complex; it requires much greater resources. Companies often forego interactive pages and place ads with only product and price information, hoping that Web surfers will automatically be motivated to buy their product.

It's dangerous to make that assumption. Users can choose between thousands and thousands of sites. Every company needs to capture roaming surfers. Success on the net requires developing customers and serving them well.

One successful technique is to offer Web visitors special deals. It's beneficial to fully integrate Internet operations with other types of marketing activities. Above all, the Web site must be designed so that it's appropriate for the target audience.

From a technical perspective it's not desirable to use too much technology. The Web site should not be testing the latest gizmos; they can detract from building rapport with customers. High-quality interactive Web sites must be carefully programmed. PERL (Practical Extraction and Report Language) is used extensively; it's available free and enough programmers know PERL to provide ongoing support. In designing Web pages, the dimensions of the graphics should always be included in the HTML code for faster displays. It's easy to add free features, such as Real Audio and Real Video (*www.real.com*).

Several search engines are available either free or at nominal cost. Some search engines, however, can cost several thousand dollars.

With limits on download speeds, it's imprudent to have too much graphics or animation at your Web site. However, as download speeds increase, Web graphics are likely to change from two-dimensional to three-dimensional (3-D). 3-D imaging technology will greatly help consumers buying over the Internet because they will be able to visually inspect the product at virtually any angle.

Your marketers should be following new developments in 3-D technology closely. Within a few years, 3-D graphics and virtual reality modeling language (VRML) applications will become the norm. These technologies require faster processors and modems, increased bandwidth, graphics accelerators, and better authoring tools. Web browsers will have to support 3-D technology.

Web designers and marketers offer you custom Web pages. They can create highly personalized Web pages that increase the likelihood of future visits. For example, your site could monitor which visitors are interested in which items on the site and process that information to personalize the Web page for each visitor. Alternatively, the visitor could answer a few questions about specific interests and receive a customized Web page.

Product development lead-time is expected to be reduced with 3-D modeling. Multimedia techniques like interactive applications with 3-D modeling, animation, video, and sound are offering companies of all types new ways to market their products. Well-designed multimedia tools make it easy to market and sell products or services; they offer speed, accuracy and easy updates. Multimedia presentations are generally more refined; they may even eliminate the need for salespeople.

Interactive multimedia brochures are becoming increasing popular; presently, they're an effective supplement to printed matter. The cost of developing interactive Web sites is higher than the cost of a typical printed color brochure. However, companies integrating interactive multimedia technology into their marketing plans are seeing positive results.

Companies often release images of the product when making new product announcements. Sometimes, the design process is not even complete when these announcements are made. The companies gain insight from customer feedback into whether the product should be developed further. This is much cheaper than developing actual prototypes, which in any case may be unfeasible. 3-D modeling is an effective way to show how the product works and to create an illusion that the product actually exists.

Your Web site should have search capabilities. Your material should be updated frequently. Let the users know the last time the material was updated.

A tremendous amount of work is required to set up and maintain the Web site. Don't underestimate the number of possible visitors. Basic rules should be established at an initial stage. For instance, you must decide how much control your firm will exercise. Will any chat rooms be carefully moderated, or will users be able to say and post anything? From a legal perspective, it's prudent to include a statement with all online messages stating that the views expressed are those of the users and not the company or its management and the company is not responsible for the content.

If you wish to moderate discussions, be prepared to read all posted messages. Alternatively, enlist some volunteers to act as moderators; you can reward them by giving them special discounts or other benefits. Moderators should be given editorial rules and policies. They should be able to change discussion topics as necessary. At the same time, don't over-moderate. Let the users talk about what they want; otherwise they're likely to lose interest.

When setting up the Web site think about a system to measure if your goals are being met. Perhaps you have a goal of bringing in a certain number of new customers. Set up a way to measure your progress. Some questions you might want answers include:

- Are more people joining your chat group than leaving it? What's the net gain per week or per month?
- Where are the new people coming from?
- Are existing customers referring new ones?
- Are existing customers satisfied?
- What are the buying habits of your customers?

Take basic precautions in building your company's Web site. Don't expect your visitors to have the latest and best equipment. Keep in mind that many users will not update to the latest version of the browser or other software. Try to make the Web page easy to view on different size monitors.

CD/Net

One problem with viewing graphic-intensive Web pages is that they take a long time to download with typical Internet connections. Blau Marketing Technologies (203-254-3700 or *www.blau.com*) has come up with a solution to this problem in CD/Net. CD/Net combines the advantages of compact discs (CD) and the Internet. The CD-ROM content is in HTML format. Hyperlinks allow users to access information from the Internet in real time. Because the multimedia capability comes directly from the user's computer, it takes significantly less time for information to appear on the screen. Though the major increase in speed expected soon in the U.S. and other developed countries may make this technology less appealing, for international marketers, especially in developing countries that lack a communications infrastructure, it may prove invaluable.

Building Customer Loyalty

Building a virtual online community is an excellent way to attract visitors to your Web site. People with different motivations are going to be attracted to it. Some users are just browsers, curious or seeking specific information. They're not likely to participate extensively in the online community. Other users may have a problem and want help from people who've had the same problem. Still others may be interested primarily in offering their expertise. Communities work because users enjoy being part of them and enjoy discussing the main topic.

The aim should be to build an online community that is self-sufficient, needing no formal supervision. Members should monitor and police themselves. Allowing users to download files makes the site significantly more attractive. Providing answers to Frequently Asked Questions (FAQs) is extremely helpful, especially if there's an automatic response system that can e-mail responses. Many communities also provide links to similar sites.

Some online communities offer special events. Setting up specific times for special discussions is an excellent way to encourage users to visit your site. Special events may host a well-known expert. Top management can also participate from time to time. You can offer special discounts to regular visitors to your site.

The increased use of e-commerce is likely to lead to lower prices. Customers will be more easily able to compare prices and play one vendor off against another. Vendor delivery costs are likely to be reduced and customers will demand concessions. Many transaction costs will be reduced with automated negotiations.

While customers want a low price, that is not the only factor that affects their decisions. With reduced profit margins, for companies to survive, they must have a strategy for growth and provide value-added services.

One option is to create a Web site that's not purely self-serving. The Web site should be a source of information to the consumer, not just another place for company "hype." The site should allow customers or potential customers to interact. Saturn has had considerable success giving its car-buying customers access to each other. Customers should be allowed to discuss the product's price, quality, etc., without censorship. For example, Amazon.com allows customers to post online book reviews.

Online customers want instant responses, so answer e-mail quickly. On-time delivery of products is another key factor in gaining customer loyalty.

It's important to put the customers' interest first. Customers will be loyal to a brand or product if the company makes them feel important. Loyalty generates repeat purchases. This is especially important because the cost of retaining customers is significantly lower than the cost of acquiring new ones. Repeat customers are also likely to spend more than new customers.

Incentives and electronic coupons are often successful in encouraging individuals to visit a specific Web site. Online customers are generally more educated consumers and demand better value for their money.

Many prospective customers are not immediately ready to buy. The aim should be to encourage them to take some action, perhaps request information such as a brochure, catalog, or price quotation. It should be easy for visitors to send you e-mail. A "hot link" to your e-mail address should appear on each Web page. All e-mail addresses from correspondents should be to a mailing list for new product announcements and news releases—but always give people the option to remove their names from the mailing list.

Sending unsolicited e-mail is not generally a good way to increase Web traffic. Mass unsolicited commercial e-mail is known as "spam." Spam is, at a minimum, a nuisance to Web users. Some may consider it an invasion of privacy. Sending junk mail thus costs money with no revenue benefits.

The rate of growth of Web users is expected to decrease in the U.S. but increase in the rest of the world. The Internet transcends national boundaries. A single Web site is unlikely to serve the needs of the entire world. Businesses must be prepared to comply with the different rules of different countries. A different strategy will generally be needed for penetrating markets in each new country. The overseas growth opportunities are simply tremendous.

Advertising on Your Web Site

Advertising is used to accomplish several objectives:

- Inform consumers
- Increase demand
- Increase or decrease demand elasticity
- Discourage entry by potential competitors
- Differentiate the firm from current competitors

Advertising on the Internet is relatively new. While most firms spend a significant amount on advertising, little of this goes to the Internet—yet. It's clear that the Internet's share of total ad expenditures will grow because it offers new opportunities to marketers and it's easier to target customers on the Internet. It's possible to give customers detailed product information and answer their questions. Internet advertising is an active not a passive activity.

There are two models of advertising, the "push" model, and the "pull" model. In the push model, the seller selects a target audience and decides on the content of the advertisement. In the pull model, buyers have greater input. Both are used extensively on the Internet.

Traditional marketing and selling techniques are not as successful on the Internet. Traditionally, the marketing strategy was to broadcast to a vast number of prospective customers. Such media as radio, television, billboards, and newspapers were used to deliver short, high-impact messages. Because media space is limited, it sells at a premium. You can fit only a little information in the limited space. Hence, the aim is to project an intangible image of quality.

Broadcast-type advertising is likely to receive a negative reaction from online users. Some network service providers have specific rules against unwanted advertising. People on the Internet want interactivity rather than the passive, one-way advertising that is the norm with traditional broadcast advertising. If you want to succeed in e-commerce provide a high level of interactivity and detailed information. Storage capacity on the Internet is virtually unlimited and very inexpensive; you can share vast amounts of information with interested customers.

Banner Ads

Though banner ads dominate the Internet, they take up considerable bandwidth and slow the downloading of Web pages. Consumers tolerate them to avoid paying fees for Web content. Some advertisers pay fees based on the number of people that see the ads. However, most advertisers insist on paying fees based on the number of "clicks" that bring potential customers to the advertiser's Web site.

Web Storefronts

Creating and maintaining a Web site, a Web "storefront", can be costly but most businesses simply can't ignore the medium. Consumers generally have more confidence in sales advice provided through a Web site; there is a general distrust of salespersons in stores. Computerized sales information is uniform; that gives it greater credibility. People believe that computers have no incentive to lie.

Most companies now have at least a basic Web site. In creating yours, ask yourself:

- Who are your customers likely to be?
- What are their characteristics?
- Where are customers of the kind you want likely to be on the Internet?
- What mailing lists or news groups do targeted customers use? Mailing lists and news groups tend to be concentrated on very specific topics.
- What will turn customers "on" or "off"?

To achieve the maximum return on investment from the Internet, marketing managers must find ways to integrate online marketing into their general marketing program. The Internet offers significant benefits to customers. Customers can check for product availability and get specifications and pricing information 24 hours a day. Implementing features like this often leads to higher sales and cost savings in providing customer service.

Advertising your company's Web site is critical. Customers must know about the Web site before they can use it. All printed matter, as well as other media, should encourage users to visit it. All ads, brochures, business cards, letterheads, and any other material should have your Web site address on it. The Web site address should have the same prominence as your address or phone number.

Search engines like Yahoo! Excite, and Lycos are an excellent source of Web visitors. The Web site should be registered on as many search engines as possible; at the very least, it should be registered on all the major ones. It's prudent to re-register after a few months to enhance the chances of your Web site appearing in a person's search. Your home page should contain invisible key words or "metatags." If any key word on your home page matches a customer's search request, your Web site will be suggested.

Reciprocal linking arrangements are another great way to make your site known. Related sites should be asked to include links to your site. An advantage of this is that as some search engines capture link data your company's site is more likely to be found by visitors.

You can also advertise in Web directories. The listings generally cost a few hundred dollars a year.

Don't abandon your company's successful marketing practices just because you're marketing on the Internet. Marketing strategies that work in basic print are likely to work on the Web as well. For example, if your company offers certain promotions to its print customers and the promotions work, offering them on the Internet should also work.

However, the benefits of the special electronic and interactive aspects of the Internet should not be ignored. The Internet is not passive like print media. It's much easier for you to learn the browsing and purchasing habits of your Internet customers than of magazine readers, for instance, and capture the data automatically. You can ask customers to fill out an interactive questionnaire with name, address, telephone number, and other information if they want to receive a free catalog of your company's products.

The Internet presents marketers with unique opportunities; only companies that successfully exploit these opportunities will succeed in the competitive world of e-commerce. It's essential to let customers buy products online. Online customers also want instant information. At a minimum, they want to know the features of a product, its price, current inventory status, how long it will take for them to get it, and the company's return policy.

E-mail is now a key channel of communication between companies and customers, so budget resources to develop e-mail content and deliver it widely. to hordes of people. There are companies that specialize in delivering customized e-mail messages. But note that sending unsolicited e-mail on the Internet often does not pay off. E-mail should generally be sent only to those who have requested information.

To get people to read your e-mail, you must build a relationship with them. Address them personally. Some jurisdictions require that the return address on the e-mail be real. Sending unsolicited bulk e-mail is generally not illegal, but many Internet users consider it a nuisance. Still, it's popular because it's considerably cheaper than traditional bulk mailing.

But sending unsolicited e-mail can cause many problems. The Internet culture has a strong bias against any type of random sales pitch. Recipients of unsolicited e-mail will often complain to your ISP, which may terminate the accounts of companies that send junk mail. People (and companies) who send spam are demonstrating that they don't care about their reputations; who wants to do business with someone like that? And many people don't want to respond to a spam mailing by asking to be removed from the list; spammers consider that an acknowledgement that the recipient is reading junk e-mail and may send even more.

It's possible to send commercial e-mail to recipients who have stated their willingness to receive it. Many companies specialize in direct e-mail marketing. While this targeted direct e-mail marketing is more expensive than unsolicited junk e-mail, it's far more effective.

An extensive list of opt-in e-mail lists is available from *The Directory of E-mail List Source* (*www.copywriter.com/lists/*). Other businesses that provide "opt-in" mailing lists include:

- *www.bonusmail.com*
- *www.bulletmail.com*
- *www.htmail.com/customer.html*
- *www.postmasterdirect.com/*
- *www.targ-it.com/*

Opt-in lists work because businesses and consumers are given incentives to receive commercial e-mail messages. Sometimes Web promotions like contests and sweepstakes are used to encourage people to visit Web sites. These campaigns often cost significantly less than long-term banner advertisements. Consumers are willing to volunteer their time and attention in return for a reward. People disclose information about themselves and you can tell them about your product.

As we said earlier, banner ads are very common and useful on the Web. To catch attention, banner ads should have a colorful background that contrasts with the background Web page. Use simple animation to draw attention, but don't become obtrusive. Don't use deceptive techniques that may frustrate or anger the consumer.

A successful Internet marketing technique is to have a sign-up form on your Web site to allow visitors to register for an e-mail newsletter. Amazon.com offers its visitors another valuable service. Visitors may register to receive e-mail about new books on specified topics. Some travel club Web sites will e-mail members about new discounts on airlines or travel packages. Users give permission to be contacted again via e-mail.

Include instructions at the beginning and end of all your advertising e-mail messages letting recipients know how they can remove their names permanently from future mailings. You may also ask members to forward your e-mail message to people they know who share similar interests.

Use signature files whenever you send e-mail. The signature file contains your Uniform Resource Locator (URL) and e-mail address so that people may contact you. It's like handing out your electronic business card and it's unobtrusive as long as you don't include too much information in it.

Electronic Assurance Services

To give consumers greater confidence in transacting online, the American Institute of Certified Public Accountants (AICPA) and the Canadian Institute of Chartered Accountants (CICA) have jointly developed the WebTrust program. It's an electronic seal that provides certain assurances. A Certified Public Accountant (CPA) or a Chartered Accountant (CA), after a careful examination, places the WebTrustseal on a Web site to indicate that the site's business practices and controls meet all WebTrust criteria. After issuing the initial seal, the CPA or CA must update the evaluation quarterly to assure that all guidelines for authenticity, security, and privacy are being followed.

Selling Online

Letting customers order online enhances the likelihood of a sale. It's much easier for a customer to click the "purchase" button on a Web site than to call the company. However, customers should not be forced to order only through the Internet. Many customers don't yet feel comfortable about giving their credit card numbers online. Giving customers a choice, such as ordering through the telephone or fax, would help increase the company's sales.

Online ordering gives a company a marketing edge. If your tracking program notices that a person has repeatedly visited your Web site without placing an order, you can make him a special offer to encourage him to buy.

Cross selling is another advantage of online ordering. Assume a customer is ordering a backpacking tent from your sporting goods Web site. This gives you a wealth of information and creates a great cross-selling opportunity: you can remind the customer to buy sealant to waterproof the tent, or a tarpaulin to protect the tent floor. He might also be interested in hiking shoes, backpacks, sleeping bags, trail maps, and insect repellents. Your sporting goods Web site could offer customers a chance to browse through your "hiking checklist" to make sure they haven't forgotten something important, like a first aid kit, for their hiking trip.

The checklist should not be self-serving; it should be of value to consumers, not just a list of items you want to sell. For example, your company may not sell portable water purification systems, but these should be on the checklist, perhaps with links to Web sites that sell them. An added advantage is that the linked site might have a reciprocal link back to yours.

Make it easy for customers to make an informed buying decision. Encourage them to upgrade their product choices. Many people might be willing to spend more for a better quality product if they were educated on its benefits. Quantity discounts might also encourage further sales.

In fact, because the information on your Web site can be updated quickly, if you see that a product is selling below expectation, you can offer everyone a special discount to encourage sales.

Customers should be able to save their order forms so they can add or delete items as they browse through the Web site. If they don't want to order or pay for products immediately, give them the option to save their order form for another day. Make it easy for customers to order the same products again, or to modify previous orders. Keep the ordering process clear and simple. If certain customers are offered special prices, make sure the adjustments occur automatically.

It's possible to buy keywords on search engines like Yahoo! or Alta Vista. Each time a user types a search phrase that matches those keywords, your company's advertising banner will appear along with the search results. This can help increase visits to your Web site significantly.

Customer Service

Respond to e-mail with speed. Online customers demand immediate feedback; lack of a prompt reply to e-mail is a sure way to lose customers. If staff requirements make it impossible to respond in less than 24 hours, at least send an immediate automated response acknowledging receipt of the message. Automated systems are useful for answering FAQs, but they have to be monitored because they can sometimes fail due to bugs or other problems. In any case customers want humans to respond to their messages, so they may be unhappy with an automated response.

When responding make sure you understand the question and that your reply clearly addresses the specific problem. Don't respond in generalities; be precise and specific. After a reasonable interval, send a follow-up e-mail to make sure that the customer is satisfied that his concerns have been addressed. Be polite, even if a customer is rude; try to understand the problem.

Legal Concerns

Be careful in setting up links to other Web sites from your Web site.
Most Webmasters want to publicize their site. They request links from directories and related sites and submit their URLs to search engines. However, recent litigation suggests that such links may not always be welcomed. Ticketmaster sued Microsoft for what has become known as "deep linking." A click at Microsoft's site took users to a page deep within Ticketmaster's site. Such linking deprived Ticketmaster of advertising dollars from banner ads that were bypassed. Meanwhile, Microsoft's advertising revenue increased through the use of Ticketmaster's trademarks.

Similarly, the *Washington Post* sued Total News: Total News had created a Web site that linked to 1,200 news sites. A click on the Total News site brought up the *Post's* news pages in a frame within the Total News site. Only the Total News URL was displayed. The *Post* argued that Total News had unfairly used its property. The case was settled out of court when Total News agreed to cease its framing practices. It's prudent to indicate on your site the source of linked materials. Also include a message that you will remove any link at the request of the owner of the linked site.

To prevent others from deep linking to your site, several options are available. For example, you can use dynamic URLs that permit access to your internal pages only from other pages within the site.

Placement on Search Engines

Most Internet search engines use a keyword density preference system in listing search results. A new pay per placement search engine (*www.goto.com*) uses a real-time competitive bidding process. It offers Web site operators preferred placement within search results. The aim of Goto.com is to function like an electronic yellow pages; consumers using the engine are completely aware that advertisers have paid for preferential placement.

Tracking Web Traffic

You need to know how many people visit your site and how many are viewing each page. Web servers can track that information. Typically, you can get:

- The name of the host
- The visitor's login name, if authentication is mandatory
- The date and time of the "hit"
- The type of request
- Who referred the user
- The visitor's "IP" address
- The number of bytes transferred
- Cookies (electronic data) sent by the visitor
- Cookies (electronic data) sent by the Web server
- The path of the file served

There is a distinction between a *hit* and a *page view*. A hit is recorded when any file (graphic, sound, etc.) is requested from the server. For instance, if a user requests a page that contains five graphics, the access log will count five hits. In contrast, the page view measure indicates when a page as a whole is viewed. It's relatively easy to determine the number of hits to a site using a hit counter. For a more accurate analysis, scrutinize the Web server logs. This will tell you about the number of failed hits as well as their status code.

Though page view information is more useful, it's harder to get. You have to differentiate between those hits that are or those that are not page views. Common ways of doing this are by looking at the type of file, whether it's HTML or graphic or sound. You might also be able to differentiate based on the name of the file requested from the server. Looking at the Web server's response code is yet another option. You may also want to differentiate between internally and externally generated page views. You want to know the page views not only for your home page, but for other pages as well. Users may have bypassed your home page and linked directly to one of your other pages.

It's useful to know where visitors are coming from. Are they coming from an advertisement banner? From a link at another Web site? Page views by referrer can help you decide whether the banner advertisement is worthwhile. It will also give you insight into the interests of your visitors. The referrer log can be useful in determining what links are most useful. How many people are coming from AOL or CompuServe or another service provider?

You can do page view analysis by time of day. Is your site being accessed during work hours or after? Most home users dial up with slower speed modems. If most visits are after working hours, use fewer graphics for faster download. It's possible to determine the hardware platform (PC versus Mac) operating system being used by the visitor as well as the type of browser and its version. The agent log records information about the browser, file transfer protocol (FTP) client, or search engine robot that accessed the Web page. If browsers with different capabilities or different versions are being used by a substantial number of visitors, it might make sense to offer pages in dual versions.

It's generally more difficult to determine the number of visitors than the number of page views. You may not know if the same person or different people are repeatedly viewing your pages. The following may be used to track visitors:

- IP address

- User names (if registration is required)

- Cookies (electronic data)

IP address is perhaps the easiest way of counting visitors. By counting the number of unique IP addresses, you can get an approximation of the number of visitors. However, the method tends to be unreliable because most people get a different IP address each time they connect. Many ISPs assign addresses dynamically in order to use the IP addresses more efficiently. When the first visitor disconnects, the same IP address is available to another customer, so the same IP address doesn't necessarily mean that the same visitor came to your site twice. Still, the method may give a reasonable approximation if the results are tabulated over a relatively short time. Over an extended period, accuracy decreases significantly.

Some sites require visitors to log in using their user name. This makes tracking visitors much easier, though there's always the possibility that two or more individuals, perhaps spouses, will share the same user id and password. Moreover, unless you can explain why logging in is necessary, many people will not stay to visit your Web site. Some sites reward people for the extra effort of logging in by providing special access to registered users.

"Cookies" can help you determine the number of visitors. It's possible to define a cookie that will have a unique value for each visitor. Some people, however, may turn off cookies in their Web browser. They may also delete cookies, so even this may not be a reliable measure of visitors.

The Web server log should be analyzed periodically; it contains vital information that can help you understand your visitors. For most businesses, weekly analysis of the logs should be sufficient. You can do it easily with a log file analysis program.

Find out how visitors found your site so you can increase traffic to your site. For example:

- What key words did visitors use on the search engine to locate your site?
- What search engines appear most often in the log files?
- Are some search engines missing from the log file?
- Did most visitors enter through your home page?
- What pages are popular or unpopular?
- From what pages do most visitors exit?
- What path through the Web site do most users take?
- Do the popular pages have something in common?
- How might the unpopular pages be improved?
- Are other sites linking to pages with greater traffic?
- What pages on your site generate the most sales leads?
- Is there a navigation problem? If so, how might it be corrected?

Traffic log analysis will help you improve your site. For example, you could include something on pages from which most visitors exit to keep their interest and guide them to other pages on your site. A profile of your visitors will help you determine if you're attracting your target audience:

- Why did they visit?
- Where did they come from?
- From what kind of organizations are they visiting your site?
- What countries are they coming from?

- What pages did they view?
- Did they request anything by e-mail?
- Did they download anything?

Web servers store different kinds of information in separate files, generally in ASCII format. Web-site analysis software packages that can transform raw data into useful information, with charts, tables, graphs and reports, can also analyze Web server log files. All errors encountered during the visit are logged, including time-outs, lost connections, not found, and other types of failures. Scanning error reports can help you determine if any of your files are missing that could make it hard for your visitors to access pages.

All log file analyzers can analyze files from several type of servers. However, they differ in their ability to analyze files. Some programs require that you transfer the log files to the vendor for analysis; this is especially helpful if the log files are very large. The internal computer doesn't have to process the data. There's also the benefit of added credibility, since the results are analyzed by a third party. However, if you want to keep the information confidential, log file analysis software packages are available. The answers to the following questions will help you choose the right software package:

- Will the package produce the reports, charts, tables, and graphs that you need?
- Can the software package process the log files typically generated by your server? (Many packages cannot handle very large log files.)
- Is the package easy to learn and use?
- Is the software available for your platform? Is it available for multiple platforms? Basic packages run on your Web server and automatically generate reports. More advanced programs offer sophisticated analysis, but are typically run on a separate system.
- Does the software have to be run locally, or can it access the log files at other sites?
- Does the package have database capabilities?
- Can the software import and export in different file formats?
- Does the package offer drill-down capabilities? How many layers of data can you view and analyze?

- Does the package allow you to analyze data based on different units of time, such as hourly, daily, weekly, monthly, quarterly, annually?

- Can the log file analyzer automatically resolve numeric IP addresses and provide information on their owners?

- How large a site can the software handle? Will you outgrow it quickly?

- How many sites can the software handle? Can it track several sites at once? If you have several Web sites, can the software do a meta-analysis of all your sites?

- Does it offer real-time report access? For example, can you analyze data for the last 10 minutes of activity on your site?

- Does the software package offer data integration and synthesis capabilities? Can it integrate sales and other business information, whether or not it's Web-based?

- How much does the software package cost? Will a shareware or freeware package do? Or do you need a comprehensive package capable of advanced analysis?

The number of page views can sometimes be misleading. People may be visiting your site, but not sticking around long enough to read your message. This may happen if your graphics take too long to download.

Before reports, tables and charts can be generated, the log analyzer packages needs to process log-file data. This is time consuming, especially for larger files. All the log analysis packages generate some predefined reports and let you build custom reports using data filters.

Traffic analysis packages have their limitations. For instance, they don't provide any information about server reliability or integrity. Furthermore, if you need independently audited statistics of Web traffic, you must enlist the services of an external firm. Typically, reports produced by the analysis packages include:

- The number of times specific pages were requested over a given period of time

- Pages downloaded most often

- Pages downloaded least often

- Trends for visitor activity at specific times of the day or the week

- The most common entry points
- The most common exit points
- Average time per visit (usually in seconds)

A list of traffic log analysis tools can be obtained from Yahoo! at:

- *www.yahoo.com/Computers_and_Internet/Software/Internet/ World_Wide_Web/ Servers/Log_Analysis_Tools/.*

Organizing Your Web Site

Each Web site contains one or more *presentations.* If the site contains only one presentation, the term Web site and presentation can be used interchangeably. Each Web presentation consists of one or more pages. The *home* page is the first page of your presentation. The key to organizing a site is to answer a few basic questions:

- What is the purpose of your Web site?
- What type of information do you want visitors to see?
- Why will people visit your site?
- Are visitors looking for specific information?
- Are the visitors going to read each page in detail, or are they just going to scan it?

Your Web site should include information about your company. Typical items in the company profile are as follows:

- What the company does or sells, its products and their prices
- New product announcements
- Company address, phone number, and other location-related information
- Customer service and support information
- Company policies
- Job openings at the company

- Company financial information, including its stock-market symbol, the exchange it trades on, and current and historical share prices
- Visitor guest-book to learn the profile of prospective customers
- Online survey to get feedback from visitors on everything from your company's products to your Web site
- Links to related sites

It should always be possible for users to determine exactly where they are in your Web site. There are several ways to organize Web presentations.

- A *linear* structure is very simple, just like a printed document. Its rigid structure is ideal for situations where you don't want Web visitors to skip around; that is, you want them to read the information in a strict order. The entire Web presentation should not be linear. It should be used only in the few situations where such rigidity is warranted.
- In a *hierarchical* or *tree* structure, you start with a main menu. Visitors select a topic from the main menu, then from a sub-menu, and so forth. It's easy for visitors to navigate and know their exact position. Each hierarchical level should have a consistent interface. Avoid having too many levels. Users can easily get frustrated if they have to hunt through several pages to find information.
- A combination of *linear* and *hierarchical* structures is popular, especially when multiple linear documents are put online. The FAQ (frequently asked questions) section of Web sites typically follows this structure. The visitor is allowed to move vertically (hierarchical) as well as horizontally (linear). This can sometimes be confusing, making it hard to navigate. Provide links on each page to move forward and backward, as well as to return to the beginning.
- A *Web* structure is free-flowing. It's useful when the content is not all closely related. It encourages users to browse. But it's almost like a maze, so it's easy for users to get lost.

Always provide a way for users to get back to the home page. A map of the overall structure is extremely helpful. The map doesn't necessarily have to be a graphic; it should just convey enough information to keep the user oriented.

Visitors won't have the patience to remain at your site if the material isn't properly organized. Most users will scan or browse and not read everything. You must catch a prospective customer's eye quickly, so keep in mind that you should:

- Use headings to summarize topics.

- Enhance menu links with navigation. Always have a link to the home page.

- Use lists to summarize related items.

- Highlight important information, but don't overemphasize. Too much visual emphasis tends to make things unreadable.

- Keep paragraphs short, with the most important information in the first sentence.

- Make sure each Web page is complete by itself. The user should be able to jump into your Web site anywhere and still have a sense of orientation.

- Make each link serve a purpose. Ensure that each is relevant to the content.

- Use graphic images, but don't overdo it. Keep the images small. Consider download times when using any graphics or animation.

- Don't split topics across pages. Keep related items together. If a topic is too large for a single page, break it into self-contained subtopics. Don't create too many or too few pages.

- Include information about the Webmaster, with an e-mail address.

- Don't forget to include a copyright or trademark or service mark.

- Include the URL of each page at the bottom. This is especially helpful if users print your pages so they can later identify where they got the information.

Storefront and Shopping Cart Software

A "shopping cart" program is essential for any business that wants to sell multiple products over the Internet. The software, which runs on the ISP's computer, makes it easy for the customers to search, browse, select, and order your products.

A customer who likes a product can put the product in a virtual shopping cart, then, after selecting all the products they want, pay for them together. These software packages work seamlessly with SSL secure servers; customers are unlikely to give their credit card numbers online without such security.

At any point, the customer can see a running total of the amount spent, including taxes, shipping, and special sales discounts. The customer can easily remove an item from the shopping cart at any time. It's also possible to "pause" your shopping and continue it later in a different session.

Recently "storefront" software packages integrated with shopping cart programs have appeared. When a company offers a large number of products, customers should easily be able to find what they need. Typically a sophisticated navigation system is needed. While it's possible to have a set of related products on a single page, each page often contains only one product.

Storefront software keeps track of customer information, including home mailing address. The address can be used to calculate sales tax, if any, as well as shipping costs. Some programs can help customers more accurately determine shipping costs by connecting with United Parcel Service's Quick Cost Calculator at *www.ups.com/tools/tools.html*. The storefront software automatically generates a receipt and order confirmation and e-mails it to customers.

Storefront software offers you as a merchant several advantages. A successful store is always innovating. Storefront software lets you quickly add or delete products, change prices, organize promotions, or give discounts to a certain set of customers. Items out of stock can be temporarily hidden. More sophisticated packages can incorporate extra information, such as size, color, or model type. Each combination of the product generally has a unique number for tracking inventory and fulfilling orders. Data from the storefront software can be integrated into a company's accounting and inventory system.

The membership feature of storefront software packages lets you keep track of the browsing and shopping habits of prospective and actual customers for general and special discount offers. Prospective customers may be offered a special discount if they provide basic information about themselves, and then e-mailed information about special sales promotions. The first time a prospective customer visits, the server can send a cookie to the browser to help you identify the visitor in subsequent visits.

Most storefront packages offer a variety of reports and statistics. They can generate reports on products that were viewed or products that were actually bought. They may also tell you the path most customers take through your site.

Internet Malls

Malls on the Internet are becoming popular. Internet malls are like real malls: Several shops feed customers to each other, which allows for economies of scale, especially in promoting and advertising the mall. Some Internet malls charge storefronts a percentage of the sale transaction, but there are many free malls that will link to your site.

Many malls running shopping cart programs will not share the e-mail of the purchaser. Many others limit the ability of merchants to advertise on their own, and require shoppers to enter the mall through the main Web entrance.

Selecting an ISP as a Host

To publish Web pages, you need a Web server. Your customers' browsers will be requesting files from your Web server. Web servers and browsers communicate using the Hyper Text Transfer Protocol (HTTP). Web servers also perform some basic file management functions and maintain a log of activities.

It's possible to set up your own server but you can also use an ISP to host your Web pages. The cost of setting up a private server as well as maintaining the technology is significant. The greatest ongoing expense typically is the communication charge for obtaining adequate bandwidth.

A commercial ISP is often the best choice. However, ISPs sometimes have restrictions. For example, you may not be able to run Common Gateway Interface (CGI) scripts, which are essential for interactivity. Disk space may be limited. Most ISPs charge a flat monthly fee. However, if your site is very popular or your Web pages consume a lot of disk space as well as bandwidth, you may be asked to pay more. However, one major advantage of using an ISP is access to its technological expertise. ISPs have professional site administrators to make sure there are no technical problems. Most ISPs offer "virtual hosting" that lets you have your own domain name rather than using the ISP's with a subdirectory designating your site. Virtual hosting is essential from a marketing perspective.

An ISP anywhere in the world can host your site. U.S businesses will probably want a domestic ISP because overseas Internet connections are typically slower. You can get local dial-up Internet access to save on toll calls and send files to the ISP host using File Transfer Protocol (FTP). Select an ISP based on service as well as price.

Before committing to any ISP, visit the Web sites of their customers. See how fast pages download and whether you can get to the Web sites easily. Some ISPs may be pursuing this as a sideline, working only on part-time on hosting sites. Their prices are usually significantly cheaper, but the drawbacks are significant. Such companies may not have full technical expertise. They may not have the hardware capability you need. They may lack good technical support and customer service—it's dangerous to set up a business Web site with someone who doesn't provide appropriate technical support. These ISPs are also not likely to be able to handle the volume of hits generated by a successful Web site.

Many local dial-up Internet access providers also host Web pages. Sometimes, these ISPs don't understand the needs of businesses. It's generally safer to use an ISP that specializes in Web hosting, not dial-up access. Their bandwidth is not compromised by their dial-up Internet customers.

Larger ISPs may charge more, but they normally provide adequate technical support. They usually have the latest hardware and offer fast connection. But if they have a large number of customers, they may not be as eager for your business as smaller ISPs.

Larger ISPs are the only choice if your site is likely to generate a lot of hits. They offer 24-hour technical support and have redundant connections to the Internet. Many provide mirror sites. Their reliability tends to be exceptional.

In choosing an ISP, ask:

- How many businesses are hosted by each of the ISP's computers?
- How much space is assigned for Web pages? Are e-mail and log files counted towards assigned space?
- Is virtual hosting possible?
- Is access provided to the CGI bin directory?
- How many e-mail addresses are allowed? Can you set up multiple "aliases?" Can different aliases be forwarded to multiple e-mail addresses?

- Is it possible to have multiple Post Office Protocol (POP) e-mail boxes?

- What type of contract will you have to sign? For how long? Can you easily leave the ISP if you're not satisfied?

- During what hours is technical support available?

- Does the ISP offer mailing list management programs?

- Does it offer autoresponders to e-mail messages?

- What statistical data about visitors to your site will the ISP provide?

- Does the ISP provide SSL security for credit card transactions?

- Who are some of the ISP's current customers?

- How slow is the site during peak hours?

- How long has the ISP in business?

- Are there many complaints against the ISP? (Check with the Better Business Bureau and your state consumer affairs office.)

Check references before choosing an ISP. Ask them about the quality of service. Is the ISP reliable? How often has the system been down, and for how long? How long has the customer been with the ISP? How accessible and knowledgeable is the technical support? "Would you recommend this ISP"?

It's essential to have your own domain name. This way you always have the option to transfer to another ISP if your ISP fails to meet your expectations. A list of ISPs can be obtained from Yahoo at:

- *www.yahoo.com/Business_and_Economy/Companies/Internet_ Services/Access_Providers/*

The List™ at http://thelist.internet.com/ is also an excellent place to search for ISPs. You can locate them by area code or country code, either in the United States or in Canada.

References

Choi, S., Stahl, D., & Whinston, A. *Economics of E-commerce.*
    Indianapolis: Macmillan Technical Publishing, 1997, p. 224.

Chapter 6
ELECTRONIC DATA
INTERCHANGE*

Introduction

The exchange of electronic messages between trading partners is a critical part of e-commerce. It allows the trading partners to exchange data faster, cheaper, and more accurately. Electronic Data Interchange (EDI) structures the messages in a pre-arranged format to facilitate automatic computer processing.

Several factors, including advances in hardware, software, and communication technologies, are increasing the role of EDI in business transactions. As trade agreements like NAFTA, Mercosur, and the Europe Economic Union lift trade barriers, EDI is a tool businesses need to remain competitive. The boundaries between manufacturers, suppliers, and customers tend to disappear with EDI. The expectation for growth in EDI applications is very high.

EDI is a fast, inexpensive, and secure way of transmitting purchase orders, invoices, shipping notices, other business documents, and payments. Sending faxes or e-mail messages or sharing files through a network, a modem, or a bulletin board do not satisfy the definition of EDI because they don't use standardized machine-processable structured data formats. Non-EDI file transfers require trading partners to generate computer files in an identical format. With EDI, when the sender sends a document, translation software automatically converts the proprietary format into an agreed standard. When the receiver gets the document, the receiver's EDI translation software automatically changes it into the receiver's proprietary format.

---

*Juliana Cheong contributed to this chapter. The authors greatly appreciate her research assistance.

Integrated EDI saves rekeying data. Data from documents like purchase orders is automatically integrated into a company's computer system. EDI increases the productivity of trading partners. It reduces the cycle time of data interchange, eliminates paper work, reduces postage costs, and improves accuracy. It makes it easy to implement just-in-time inventory management. It improves capital management by reducing investment in inventories and receivables and by providing better control over payables. The amount of lead-time to respond to customers' requests is greatly reduced.

For e-commerce to succeed, trading partners must have trust in the data. Special controls are essential in an EDI environment. Paper-based audit techniques are ineffective. Computerized audits are necessary to ensure that the electronic records are correct. For example, tests can check whether the number sequence of sales invoices is being maintained. If not, the computer can trace the gaps and generate a variance report for the auditor.

The auditor, however, cannot rely only on the computer. Electronic Data Processing (EDP) auditors need to ensure that computer programs are properly written and unauthorized alterations are not made.

EDI has been progressing in the U.S. in one form or another since the mid-1960s. Still, in most companies, it's in the very early stages.

Companies have been using value added networks (VANs) to store and forward data. Using VANs, the trading partners do not need direct connections in order to send or receive the data. The sender's computer can transmit the data to a VAN and the VAN will transmit the data to the trading partner's computer system. VANs, however, are proprietary and relatively expensive. In contrast, the Internet provides a relatively low-cost method for retailers to communicate, without diminishing the major benefits of VANs.

The use of the Internet for EDI will reduce the cost of transmitting data considerably. However, because the Internet is open, special security precautions must be taken. As Internet traffic flows over circuits operated by government, academic, and private organizations, encryption is required for security.

Implementing EDI

Before EDI is implemented, ask which departments and functions will benefit from the change. Implementation generally means:

- Redesigning and simplifying information flows

- Converting the manual paper—based system to an electronic system

- Using the information flows in creative ways

EDI is a strategic business tool. The paper system should not simply be replaced without rethinking it. The benefits of properly implemented EDI can include:

- Reduced paper transactions and paper handling
- Reduced clerical costs, including fewer personnel
- Lower investments in inventory and receivables
- Fewer processing errors
- A faster trading cycle
- Reduced filing and storage costs
- Reduced postage expenses
- Greater confidence in data
- Improved relations with customers and suppliers
- Ability to use just-in-time and similar techniques
- Improved sales productivity
- Greater competitive position
- Less reliance on human interpretation of data
- Better record-keeping
- Faster and more accurate filling of orders
- Faster billing
- Better information for decision making
- Enhanced image

Most businesses can't afford to ignore EDI; larger organizations already use it. With the increased use of the Internet for EDI, financial considerations are no longer likely to be a significant barrier. EDI will be needed to attract and retain customers.

Senior Management

Senior management support is essential in implementing EDI. Developing an EDI system, especially a large and complex one, is costly and time-consuming. Hardware and software must be bought. There are charges for third party networks. There are ongoing costs for maintaining and supporting the system. Senior management must be concerned not only with financial resources but also with the availability of technical personnel and the effect of EDI on relations with trading partners. Therefore, no action should be taken unless top management has made a formal commitment. The management should be educated in the benefits of EDI. Sufficient resources, both human and financial, are needed for a successful implementation and it's not possible to get these resources without senior management's commitment.

Implementation Costs

The upfront costs of implementing an EDI system can range from a few thousand to several million dollars. In planning your system, estimate both variable and fixed costs for several years. The accounting department has a critical role in preparing accurate financial projections for a cost/benefit analysis that considers the time value of money.

For smaller EDI systems where the costs and benefits do not extend beyond a few years, the time value of money may be ignored. However, for larger systems you need discounted cash flow analysis, taking into account the tax effects of investing in EDI. There may be an investment tax credit or it may be possible to use accelerated depreciation. Since the computations may be complicated, many companies find it helpful to hire an external consultant to assist with cost-benefit analysis.

The Project Team

An EDI project team representing both line and staff functions should take charge of implementation, planning the schedule, and allocating necessary resources. The responsibility of each team member should be clearly defined. Schedules should be realistic and prepared with input from end users. While the team provides overall guidance, a project leader should manage daily activities.

Purchasing and sales managers should actively participate in EDI decision making. Support from their departments, as well as accounting, finance, and information technology, is essential. The project team should:

- Study the current information-gathering system
- Determine which areas, departments, or functions are likely to benefit from EDI
- Prepare a rank-ordered list of functions most likely to benefit
- Identify key trading partners
- Prepare a cost-of-implementation report
- Make a pilot implementation plan
- Select a potential pilot trading partner
- Obtain agreement from that trading partner
- Obtain agreement with other trading partners on standards
- Evaluate communication systems
- Evaluate EDI translation software
- Appraise the results of pilot testing

The EDI project team might need several months to complete its analysis. Multi-divisional companies must decide if the EDI functions should be centralized or distributed to each division and whether EDI should first be implemented on the purchases or the sales side. The overall corporate strategy must be considered.

The EDI team should be responsible for creating a strategic plan, including the goals and objectives of implementing EDI. Goals should be realistic and modifiable in response to changing market and financial needs. Periodically, progress in implementing EDI should be reviewed to ensure consistency with the long-term goals of the company. The project team should consider how personnel will be trained in the new system, giving special attention to security and to the ability to audit the system. Because legal issues in EDI tend to be complex, the legal department should have an integral role.

The EDI project team will need a comprehensive operational and financial analysis of the costs and benefits of EDI. Operational analysis studies existing business practices to determine where improvements may be warranted. For instance, the project team should consider how the data from free-standing business applications might be integrated to reduce processing time. Operational analysis should help identify the strengths and weaknesses of existing business procedures and areas suitable for EDI development. EDI should enhance information flow, not merely convert it from paper to electronic format. Operational analysis should help the team prioritize the areas likely to benefit the most from EDI conversion.

Financial analysis is cost/benefit analysis: How will qualitative factors affect the company's revenues and expenses? The analysis tends to be difficult because it may not be possible to quantify some of the costs and benefits, but it's important. Qualitative factors like the following should be considered:

- How will the reliability of daily operations be affected by EDI?
- What productivity gains can be expected?
- How will data integrity and quality be affected?
- Will decision-making be facilitated, within the company and with its trading partners?
- Will EDI give the company a competitive edge?

Feasibility

The company's current computer system should be evaluated to determine if it can handle EDI directly. (Exhibit 6.1 lists some questions to consider before acquiring EDI hardware and Exhibit 6.2 lists some factors to consider before installing EDI software.) If major modifications are necessary, it's generally better to get a new system. Ask:

- Are there enough paper-based transactions to justify a conversion to EDI?
- Are there enough suppliers or customers willing to participate in EDI?
- Are key suppliers or customers insisting that you implement EDI?
- Is there a desire to reduce the number of personnel?
- What effect will EDI have on IS management?

Pilot Testing

In the survey to identify potential trading partners, customers and suppliers can be asked if they are already placing orders using EDI. If they are, what percentage of orders are placed using EDI? How long have they been using EDI? If they are not already using EDI, do they plan to start?

Exhibit 6.1: Acquiring EDI Hardware

Questions to ask before acquiring hardware:

- Will the hardware satisfy the EDI requirements of all the trading partners?
- Will it be compatible with your translation software?
- Will it be compatible with your communication software?
- Can the hardware handle the projected transaction volume?
- Will the storage space be sufficient?
- How many concurrent users can the hardware accommodate?
- How much will the hardware cost?
- How much technical support does the vendor provide?

Exhibit 6.2: Installing EDI Software

EDI software must perform three essential functions:

- Encode outgoing data into a standardized format.
- Decode incoming data into the internal format.
- Dial the trading partner or communications network to send or receive formatted data.

The software is critical role to EDI effectiveness. You can buy it, create your own, or use the VAN's translation software. Whatever you choose to do, the software should:

- Be easy to use and install.
- Allow you to create or modify data input screens.
- Allow you to customize output reports.
- Provide reporting of inbound and outbound transaction sets.
- Allow you to create or modify routines for customized operations.
- Provide error reports.
- Allow connection to multiple VANs.

Exhibit 6.2: Installing EDI Software, *Con't*

- Guide users processing electronic data.
- Be able to convert data into several different formats.
- Offer security features.
- Offer selective accessibility using passwords.
- Maintain an audit trail.
- Ensure that all transactions are properly accounted for.
- Run on the company's hardware.
- Permit batch transmissions.
- Offer scheduling flexibility.
- Support multiple versions of ASC X12 standards.
- Offer automated archiving and purging.
- Provide for automatic recover and restart.
- Be expandable to accommodate future needs.
- Contain clear documentation.
- Offer context-sensitive help.
- Be competitively priced.
- Have adequate vendor support, including training or consulting services.
- Provide for a number of installations. (How many companies have previously implemented the software?).

Rank order potential trading partners by suitability. Initially, you may wish to work with only a few or even a single partner as part of a pilot implementation to assess the ability of the system to process daily transactions. The aim of the pilot program is to identify potential problems. It should be run concurrently with existing procedures. The feedback from the pilot program is used to assess system performance, capacity, and security. As use of the EDI system is expanded, the existing system may be slowly phased out.

Ideally, the trading partners used for pilot testing should already have experience with EDI. They should also have significant paper-based transactions with your firm. Since errors are likely in the initial stages, management of the trading partners understand the risks and be willing to support your company's implementation of EDI.

The responsibilities of the trading partners should be clearly defined and a plan formulated defining the types of transactions to be automated. The plan should address data integrity and training in EDI for appropriate personnel.

Because businesses operate in an ever-changing environment, the EDI implementation process must be dynamic. It should be modified whenever company needs change. Data accuracy and reliability are critical in earning and retaining user confidence in the EDI system. Further modifications will generally be necessary whenever customers and suppliers are added to the system.

Designing the EDI System

Three factors affect data flow in EDI systems:

- *EDI standards (conventions)*: Standards are used to structure the data according to product description, code, price, and merchant information, such as merchant name and address.

- *Translation software*: The EDI translation software converts data into different formats seamlessly. It can convert internal data to a standardized format for external use and vice versa.

- *Communication*: The communication structure enables the exchange of messages between trading partners. It's possible to exchange data using magnetic media, such as tapes and discs, but most data is exchanged on networks, including private networks, third party networks (VANs), and now the Internet.

The exchange takes place in five basic steps. The data is

1. Extracted from the sender's computer applications.
2. Converted to a standardized format using translation software
3. Transmitted in that format via a communication media
4. Converted from the standardized format by the receiver's translating software
5. Imported into the receiver's computer applications

The EDI system should be kept as simple as possible. Many companies either lack the resources or simply do not need all the features of a complex system.

Information technology personnel with expertise in EDI may need to be recruited to implement and support the EDI system. Several software vendors offer EDI packages that can be customized. Larger organizations can write their own EDI programs.

There are two basic EDI design methods:

- *Point to point* EDI design is used where data is transferred electronically between trading partners, but is not processed automatically; the electronic message from the trading partners is printed for manual processing. This requires rekeying data. There are no significant advantages to this system; in fact, a company is likely to incur extra costs. The point to point system is generally used only when a company is forced into EDI by one or a few customers or suppliers. This design may also be used during the initial stages of converting to EDI, until a relationship is established with a significant number of trading partners.

- *System-to-system* design is used when the trading partners can be completely trusted. Their data is automatically processed directly into the company's applications. System security and data integrity is especially important; unauthorized users should not be able to edit files or make changes. Take precautions in setting up this system to prevent contamination of data files.

EDI Standards

EDI standards are needed to format electronic messages. They provide the rules or syntax that must be followed in creating an electronic message or documents like purchase orders, invoices, and promotional information. The group of rules for formatting a specific electronic document is a *transaction set*, which is the electronic equivalent of paper commercial documents. (*Directories* refer to the message itself and its related components: segments, data elements, and codes.) A transaction set typically consists of several data segments, which in turn consist of several data elements, such as unit price or quantity.

Standards are needed for accurate transmission of data between the trading partners. Several EDI standards are available:

- The ASC X12 standards developed by the ANSI (American National Standards Institute), also called ANSI X 12, is used predominantly in North America, Australia, and New Zealand.
- The UNTDI is used primarily in Western Europe.
- EDIFACT is the standard for international use.
- NACHA (National Automated Clearing House Association) standards are used for banking transactions.

The first three standards are used extensively by a variety of businesses. Their format is defined broadly because it has to meet the requirements of many diverse industries. Records are typically of variable length and allow for optional fields. In contrast, proprietary EDI standards tend to be highly structured with fixed record lengths and little room for variation; they use specific communication equipment and protocols. Many firms using proprietary formats they adopted earlier are now converting to generic standards.

The NACHA standards are a financial subset used to transfer payments to trading partners using financial institutions. Electronic Funds Transfer (EFT) or Fedwire allows for real-time transfer of financial information.

The aerospace, automotive, chemical, and electrical industries, among others, have adapted the ASC X12 standards for their own needs. Industry-specific conventions should be used whenever possible. Changes in informational needs as well as changes in technology affect EDI standards, which are continuously evolving; revisions are frequent. To keep track of changes, the ASC X12 standards have version and release numbers. New standards are approved to meet changing needs.

Your company's standards policy should support the most current version as well as a few prior versions. This gives trading partners a chance to upgrade without forcing anyone to comply too quickly. Otherwise, all trading partners would have to upgrade simultaneously, which would be a logistical nightmare, considering that each company may have hundreds or even thousands of trading partners.

The EDIFACT (Electronic Data Interchange for Administration, Commerce and Transport) standards sponsored by the United Nations are used extensively in Europe and Asia. EDIFACT was created by combining the best features of UNTDI and ANSI X.12. It was deemed essential that there be a common set of standards for the world without national or regional syntax standards. Many industries use only EDIFACT.

XML is new technology to facilitate Internet-based EDI. It uses tags to indicate data values in a document. The tags can be defined on the basis of a document, an application, or an industry. They may also be defined on a global basis. Its great flexibility allows XML to mimic proprietary or standard data formats, making transfers easier. The data element in XML is similar to other markup languages such as HTML with start tag, data, and end tag.

The Federal Government and EDI

The federal government is using EDI to reduce paperwork and related costs, as well as enhance the efficiency of the procurement process. The executive branch agencies have been using EDI since 1993. The Federal Acquisition Streamlining Act (FASA) of 1994 requires that all governmental agencies use EDI. This means that only EDI-capable merchants will be able to sell to the Department of Defense (DOD) and other federal agencies.

The Federal Acquisition Computer Network (FACNET) is intended to provide a "single face" to industry. The FACNET architecture has two network entry points (NEPs), with a third coming soon to provide redundancy in case of failure. All EDI traffic must flow through these NEPs. A DOD-certified VAN provider must be used to access FACNET.

FACNET is used to inform the public of contracting opportunities. The government can also receive solicitations as well as post contract award notices on it. Businesses should be registered as trading partners with the government to remain competitive. For example, *Request for Quotation* documents are transmitted by the government to all registered trading partners.

Registration using EDI informs the government of your desire to do business with it. Each federal trading partner is assigned a distinctive identification number. In registering you are required to provide:

- Company name
- Address
- Contact number (phone or fax)
- Taxpayer identification number (TIN)
- EDI point of contact
- Contractor identification numbers
- Commercial and government entity (CAGE) code

- Data universal numbering system (DUNS)
- Standard industrial classifications (SIC)
- Version of ASC X12 standard

Value Added Networks (VANs)

While magnetic tapes or disks may be used to exchange data, most organizations use a network. As the volume of transactions increases, data exchange using magnetic media become difficult. Magnetic media is not as timely. Exchanges between a large number of trading partners become hard to manage.

Networks solve most of these problems: They can handle large transaction volume with many trading partners; they work fast; they can transmit business documents almost instantly. However, security concerns are greater with a network.

Private networks between trading partners tend to be expensive, especially if there are a large number of partners. Most businesses use VANs to communicate. VANs are like a combination of a telephone company and an electronic post office. They receive electronic documents, read the addressing information, and forward the documents to the recipient's mailbox, providing a single channel to facilitate communication. The VAN supports links to your networks. You have no responsibility for the connections of your customers or suppliers, just your own.

Most VANs route, store, and forward electronic messages 24 hours a day. Most provide reliable connectivity and support various communication speeds and protocols. They have good security, technical support, and audit trails. Most VANs offer translation services.

While VANs are typically reliable, there is always a possibility of delayed or lost transmissions. Any VAN you choose should have a back-up service to retrieve data.

Your company may have to join more than one VAN because your customers and suppliers may not all be using the same VAN. In the past, VANs were not connected to each other. Now most are. Joining one network gives you access not only to the VAN, but also to all interconnected networks.

Exchanging data on an interconnected network may mean a loss of audit trail. The audit trail is needed to ensure that a transaction can be traced from its source to its destination; it's used to verify that transactions are transmitted and processed correctly. Most networks monitor the integrity of their transmissions to ensure that the necessary EDI standards are being used. This allows retransmission of lost data.

VANs have to maintain a high level of security. DOD-certified VANs must be used if you wish to do business with the government. The information transmitted is highly sensitive.

Most VANs require you to specify in advance the type of documents that you may be transmitting electronically. Similarly, the receiver may have to specify the type of documents it will accept. The transmission will fail without the consent of both trading partners.

Most VANs offer some implementation assistance, training, and consulting services. Add-on services vary considerably. The primary business of VANs is to process and transmit a large number of electronic business transactions, however; they may not be able to provide specific guidance on implementing EDI.

A key factor in selecting a VAN should be the number of trading partners connected with it. Some of the factors to consider in selecting a VAN are given in Exhibit 6.3.

Using the Internet for EDI

At present, the scope for EDI on the Internet is somewhat limited. However, over the next few years, the Internet may overtake traditional VANs. Using the Internet for EDI can greatly reduce communication costs. A flat fee is charged for virtually unlimited Internet connection time. In contrast, the connection costs for VANs are typically much higher and additional fees may also be charged.

There are several differences between the Internet and VANs. The Internet's only function is to provide a communications pipeline. VANs, however, provide not only the communications pipeline, but also other services essential to EDI, including but not limited to EDI security. ISPs do not offer many VAN features such as:

- Translation software
- User reports
- Screening for type of message
- Screening for authorized trading partners
- Checking to ensure that transmissions comply with standards
- Warning of non-delivery
- Backup system

Exhibit 6.3: Factors to Consider in Choosing a VAN

- What are the basic fees? The startup costs? The ongoing costs?
- What are the additional costs beyond basic fees?
- Are there discounts for volume?
- What billing data is provided?
- What communication speeds and protocols are supported?
- What are the security features?
- What compliance testing is done to ensure data integrity?
- What data backup and recovery services are offered?
- What transmission status reports are provided? What other types of reports are provided?
- What transaction filtering services are offered so that only desired solicitations are received?
- Is the VAN certified by the Department of Defense for trading with the US government?
- Does the VAN provide consulting services?
- Does the VAN furnish training services?
- Does the VAN limit the number or type of transactions?
- How reliable is the service?
- When is customer support available? 24 hours a day? If not, when?
- Can the VAN profile business transactions?
- What translation software does the VAN use? Will you have a choice?
- How often is transaction data forwarded by the VAN?
- How long can transaction data be retrieved?
- Will you need to join multiple VANs to reach all trading partners?
- Who is liable for lost transmission data?
- What current VAN clients are like your organization? What has been their experience?
- What additional special services does the Van offer?

ISPs do not provide customer support for EDI-specific questions. This means that the ISP will not generally give you implementation assistance, train your employees, or provide technical support for EDI, as is routine with VANs.

There are two basic ways the Internet can currently be used for EDI:

- *File Transfer Protocol (FTP)*: FTP is used to download files from the Internet. Using FTP application software, EDI files may be sent or retrieved. It's possible to automate the process so that the sender can automatically convert application data into a standardized format and FTP the file to another computer. The recipient computer automatically translates the FTP file for use in its application software. Though FTP is easy to use, file transfers using FTP are not secure.

- *E-mail*: The sender can simply attach EDI files to an e-mail message. The receiver retrieves the file from the e-mail, translates it, and imports the data into its application software. This approach, like FTP, is not secure. E-mail messages can get lost. That's why it's essential for the parties to acknowledge receiving the e-mail.

The Web offers opportunities for partial EDI. Web technology allows global access to all types of data, text, sound, and video. The Internet has become popular because its open and standard protocols are simple and adaptable. It represents a major shift away from closed proprietary systems.

Many businesses have opened virtual storefronts on the Internet. Customers can visit their electronic store, browse through their catalog, and place orders. The data the customers input is captured for use by internal application software. This, however, is not a true EDI because customers have to physically key in the data; the input process on site is not currently automated.

Intranets and Extranets offer additional opportunities for EDI. Intranet users at a business can access the Internet but firewalls keep outsiders from accessing the confidential data of the business. On an Intranet one protocol connects all users to the Web server. Intranets run on standard protocols supported by any computer.

An Extranet is a bridge between the public Internet and a private Intranet. The Extranet makes it possible to connect several organizations behind virtual firewalls. For example, suppliers, distributors, contractors, customers, and trusted others outside the organization can benefit from establishing an Extranet. The Internet is used to provide access to the public; the Intranet serves the internal business; Extranets provide a critical link between these two extremes. Extranets are where the majority of business activity occurs. They enable commerce through the Web at a very low cost and allow companies to maintain one-to-one relationships with their customers, members, staff and others.

Intranets and Extranets:

- Can be navigated easily (the internal home page provides links to information)
- Can integrate distributed computing strategy (localized web servers reside near the content author)
- Allow for rapid prototyping (can be measured in days or even hours)
- Are accessible by most computing platforms
- Are scaleable (start small, build as requirements permit)
- Can incorporate a variety of media types (video, audio, interactive applications)
- Can be tied into "legacy" information sources (databases, existing word processing documents, groupware databases)
- Are inexpensive to start, with minimal investment in infrastructure
- Have open platform architecture that accommodates a large (and increasing) number of add-on applications
- Offer a distributed computing strategy that uses computing resources more effectively
- Are more timely than traditional information (paper) delivery

The information on an Extranet may be restricted to the collaborating organizations or may be available publicly. To enhance security, privately owned or leased transmission lines may be used.

Extranets are extremely powerful. Efficiencies for collaborating companies are achieved through economies of scale and other returns on investment. Extranets may be used to integrate across distributed, cross-platform, and heterogeneous system environments.

While Extranets rely on simple Internet based technology, the process is not effortless. Consensus by the organizations on a common goal is important. Information should be maintained, but not duplicated, by all the collaborating organizations. The interface should be simple. An

Extranet Web committee can make system maintenance more cohesive and facilitate the use of the Extranet.

The more accessible a computer is, the more susceptible it's to attacks. When setting up an Intranet or Extranet, you want the advantages of an accessible computer but you also want to limit exposure to security attacks. One solution is to install a *firewall.*

A firewall limits access to selected gateways. A *gateway* is a computer or a router that selectively passes information between the inside and outside networks. It rejects all incoming traffic not specifically directed to itself. A *proxy server* is a program that mediates application-specific traffic through the firewall. It makes secure access less difficult and generally has additional logging, user authentication, and protocol-specific security capabilities. You may build your own firewall or use an ISP that provides firewall and gateway service between your network and the Internet. Add-on security tools can restrict usage by preventing users from performing certain acts or seeing restricted data.

Electronic Contracting

EDI allows for electronic contracting, though not all electronic messages set up contract. Messages with purely informational content do not create an electronic contract; nor do interfirm messages.

Electronic contracting is routine in business. Examples of electronic documents with offer and acceptance implications are:

- Purchase orders

- Invoices

- Payments

- Solicitation and submission of bids

- Filing documents electronically with a government

- Advertising of goods or services

Trading partner or EDI agreements are essential in electronic contracting. Trading partner agreements do not cover third parties, such as VANs. Several model trading partners' agreements have been published by the legal and EDI community (e.g., the American Bar Association, the EDI Council of Canada). Agreements have also been developed for specific industries and countries. Most entities will want to modify model trading agreements to suit their own needs. An agreement allows the parties to legally enforce electronic contracts.

A trading partner agreement should specify:

- The intent of parties to transact electronically
- Whether all trade or only a specific portion of the trade between the two parties is covered
- What constitutes offer and acceptance are essential (which transaction sets will constitute a legally enforceable acceptance)
- The understanding of the parties with respect to electronic payments for trade.
- That the parties will not repudiate the validity, integrity or reliability of an EDI transaction and will consider it equivalent to a paper-based transaction
- The time and place of receipt of EDI communications. There are several possibilities; receipt can take place when:
  −A message leaves the sender's computer system.
  −A message arrives at the receiver's computer system.
  −A message arrives at the receiver's mailbox on a third party's computer system (e.g., VAN).
  −The recipient sends an acknowledgement of the message.
  −The original sender receives the acknowledgement.

Acknowledgments provide proof of transaction's integrity and authority. Cryptographic methods should be used whenever possible, especially when the authenticity of the transaction is critical. Sometimes electronic signatures are used to verify a message's integrity; typically, these signatures are created cryptographically. A signature does not have to be cryptographically enhanced. As long as the EDI system is trustworthy, a non-cryptographic signature is deemed sufficient signature for purposes of offer and acceptance. The location of the signature in messages should be agreed on in advance.

Give special attention to security in drafting a trading partners agreement. Security supports confidence that transactions are authentic, and ensures that the transactions remain confidential. Security and trustworthiness are in fact essential to the enforceability of an electronic contract.

To be enforceable, trading agreements generally need *commercially reasonable security*. However, the definition of commercially reasonable differs from industry to industry; for example, the banking industry demands a much higher level of security than the average. Among the responsibilities of each party should be the extent to which one party is responsible for ensuring the security of its trading partner, and what actions will be if security is breached. Basic security risks in EDI include:

- Access violations
- Message modifications
- Interruptions or delays
- Message rerouting
- Message repudiation

Without access controls, an unauthorized individual could initiate a transaction by pretending to be authorized, sending fictitious purchase orders or making fictitious payments. The reliability and integrity of an EDI system breaks down without access controls. Security is greater when different access control techniques are combined. The most common security techniques are based on:

- Something a person knows, such as a password
- Something a person possesses, such as magnetic cards or electronic keys
- Some unique attribute of a person, such as fingerprints, voice prints, or retinal patterns

Unauthorized individuals may intentionally modify electronic messages, but they may also be modified unintentionally through hardware, software, or transmission error. Authenticating messages is a major concern, especially when a transaction is being repudiated. To minimize the risk of accidental repudiation, specify irrevocable proof, such as a digital signature.

Managing Electronic Record

You need written policies for electronic records management. All trading partners should keep records of each transaction for auditing and governmental regulation purposes. Maintaining audit trails is essential. The Foreign Corrupt Practices Act (FCPA), which applies to all publicly held companies, specifies certain controls for ensuring that transactions are executed with management authorization and records that must be kept. Similarly, the financial and tax records needed to comply with Internal Revenue Service (IRS) requirements must be retained as long as they are "material"—for tax purposes, at least three years.

Maintaining audit trails is more difficult in an electronic environment where there is no a visible trail as there is in a paper based-environment. Program your computers to provide an audit trail; most commercial software packages have at least some audit trail capability.

Maintaining an audit trail is especially important with EDI. EDI transactions go through several systems. Any data used for EDI needs to be translated into a standardized format; the translation software can maintain the audit trail. Any communication sent over the network can be accounted for by communication software. Data translated into an internal format by the recipient can be trailed, as can data used by the recipient's application software.

In an EDI environment, a weakness in any system can create problems for all the trading partners. Therefore, each function at each stage should be reviewed to make sure appropriate controls are in place.

Resources

Baum, M., & Perritt, H. *Electronic Contracting, Publishing, and EDI Law*. New York: John Wiley & Sons, 1991.

Bort, R., & Bielfeldt, G. *Handbook of EDI*. New York: Warren, Gorham & Lamont, 1997.

Thierauf, R., *Electronic Data Interchange in Finance and Accounting*. Connecticut: Quorum Books, 1990.

Sources of EDI Information

* CommerceNet: *http://www.commerce.net/*
* Data Interchange Standards Association (DISA): *http://www.disa.org*
* Defense Acquisition Revolution Reform Net: *http://www.far.npr.gov/*
* Defense Technical Information Center (DTIC):
  http://www.dtic.dla.mil

- Department of Defense E-commerce Office: *http://www.acq.osd.mil/ec/*

- EDI World Institute: *http://www.ediwi.ca/ediwi/*

- E-commerce Strategies, Inc.: *http://www.ecom.com/buyersguide*

- Federal EDI Secretariat: *http://snad.ncsl.nist.gov/dartg/edi/fededi.html*

- FedWorld: *http://www.fedworld.gov*

- FinanceNet: *http://www.financenet.gov/*

- General Services Administration: *http://www.gsa.gov/*

- Government Printing Office: *http://www.access.gpo.gov/su_docs/*

- ISO Online: *http://www.iso.ch/*

- Jim's EDI Emporium: *http://www.ibmpcug.co.uk./~jws/index.html*

- National Performance Review: *http://www.npr.gov*

- Premenos Corporation: *http://www.premenos.com*

- Rawlins EDI Consulting: *http://www.metronet.com/homepages/rawlins/*

- SBA Online: *http://www.sbaonline.sba.gov*

- Sterling Commerce: *http://www.sterling.com*

- Unidex: *http://www.wwa.com/unidex/edi/*

- USENIX: *http://www.usenix.org/*

Chapter 7
ELECTRONIC BANKING
AND PAYMENTS

The most fundamental view of e-commerce for business is effective interaction with customers and business partners (see Figure 7.1). That's why electronic banking and payments are an integral part of e-commerce.

Figure 7.1: E-Commerce—Effective Interaction

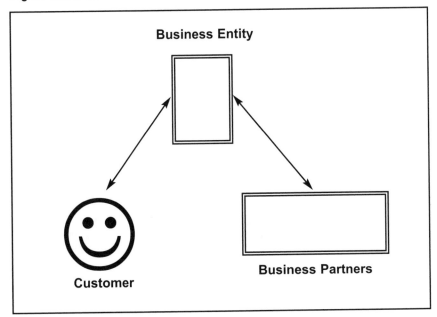

New systems are constantly being proposed and tried with varying levels of success. Microsoft (*www.microsoft.com*), IBM (*www.ibm.com*), Hewlett Packard (*www.hp.com*), Sun Microsystems (*www.sun.com*), Netscape (*www.netscape.com*), Cybercash (*www.cybercash.com*), and Verifone (*www.verifone.com*) are all developing software that allows use of a Web browser for e-commerce applications. Intuit (*www.intuit.com*) in the area of personal finance and Charles Schwab (*www.eschwab.com*), Datek Online (*www.datek.com*), and E Trade (*www.etrade.com*) in the area of online stock trading are also contributing to the advancement of e-commerce.

At the same time the Secured Electronic Transaction (SET) protocol is evolving. Companies like Visa (*www.visa.com*) and MasterCard (*www.mastercard.com*), in collaboration with software vendors, are developing encrypted electronic transactions that protect the identity of the customer and prevent fraudulent usage.

Electronic data interchange (EDI), a protocol for business-to-business transactions over private networks, has been in use for quite some time now. EDI is secure and the transactions are in real time. However, the Internet is far less expensive and reaches more people; a simple form of the Internet payment system is illustrated in Figure 7.2.

Figure 7.2: Simple Form of Internet Payment System

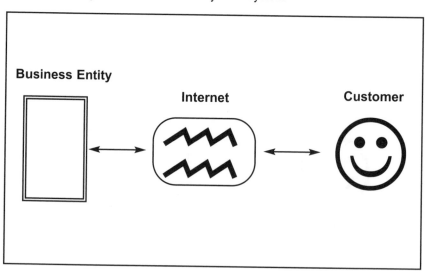

Electronic Banking

Electronic banking encompasses the gamut of financial transactions among financial institutions, individuals, corporations, proprietorships, and government. In order to improve profitability, banking organizations, like others, are trying to control costs and reduce operating expenses. Technology and innovation are the tools. Computer networking, Internet, and business analysis solutions lower service costs while still providing good customer service. Other factors are increased computer literacy among consumers, greater consumer awareness, and an explosion in installed PCs.

Large businesses have traditionally used computers for financial operations both within and outside their organizations. However, today even medium and small businesses are demanding from banking institutions the electronic service previously enjoyed only by large business.

The proliferation of PCs in households is spawning another revolution, this one in the personal banking area. Home banking systems offer access to the customer's account and the ability to transfer funds, pay bills, and download personal account information. Proprietary services let customers connect to their banks over a dial-up private connection. Web-based banking lets them connect to their banks over the Internet. Use of off-the-shelf software to manage personal finances is increasing. Almost all major banks—for example, Bank of America (*www.bofa.com*), Figure 7.3 on page 166, and Wells Fargo (*www.wellsfargo.com*)—allow their customers to conduct transactions online.

Electronic Payment

An electronic payment is in many ways like a conventional physical payment. The exchange is usually a digital financial instrument backed by a bank or an intermediary. Electronic financial transactions are expected to grow to 118 billion by the end of 2000—an average annual growth rate of 12%. In comparison, paper transactions show an average annual growth of 2.5% for the same period. The growth in electronic banking and commerce is fueled by

- Increasing numbers of Internet users
- Reduced operational and processing costs due to improvements in technology
- The affordability of high performance technology.

Figure 7.3: Bank of American Web Page

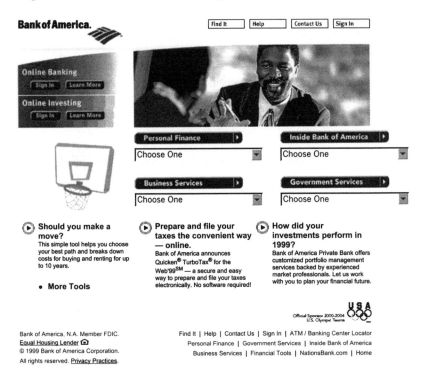

Traditionally, large businesses have made electronic payments with EDI or electronic fund transfer (EFT), but high administrative and technology costs forced smaller operators to contend with conventional physical payment methods. A further limiting factor was the inability of EFT systems and protocols to handle small amounts of money. These issues have been resolved; it's now possible to make small, immediate (real-time) payments for goods and services using a Web browser.

Many different techniques are being used to ensure that transactions and customers are secure, among them public-key cryptography, cipher text, symmetric encryption, digital signature, digital certificates, and spoofing. Firewalls, secure web servers, and virtual private networks reduce the risks of outside attack on our systems.

Other areas of technology, such as *transactional commerce* and Web portals, enhance e-commerce. Transactional commerce is the application of customer-specific information to guide transactions in real time. It's the integration of real-time interactions of customers with their profile databases. Companies like Amazon.com (*www.amazon.com*) integrate customer-specific information to track shipments dispatched through United Parcel Service and post information in real time to customers.

Financial Intermediaries

Financial intermediaries, economic agents, stand between the parties to a contract, performing functions necessary to fulfillment of the contract. These agents include the merchant server, payment acquiring bank, issuing bank, credit card processor, third party processors, brokers, agents, traders, and mediators. A second category of intermediaries that are not economic agents but participate in e-commerce activities are equipment providers, network access providers, information access providers, and web portals. In the absence of an intermediary, a seller will be forced to identify and serve individual buyers, resulting in decreased efficiency. Intermediaries:

- Provide information to buyers on the availability of products and services.
- Help buyers identify sellers.
- Provide an efficient means of exchanging information between buyers and sellers.
- Conduct or assist in the execution of electronic transactions.
- Provide after sale-support.

The need for an intermediary becomes pronounced when business is conducted over the Internet because of the spread and disparity of buyers and sellers. Buyers need to identify possible suppliers or service providers within our budget, satisfying our quality requirement, and at our preferred location. We need to ensure that the financial transactions are secure and accurate. We want value for our money. On the other hand, sellers need to identify possible customers, offer quality service at reasonable cost, and ensure that transactions are secure and accurate. It's these critical functions of e-commerce that intermediaries provide best.

Identifying Buyers and Sellers

Web portals are search sites that contain databases of generic information. They include Netscape (*www.netscape.com*), Yahoo (*www.yahoo.com*),

Infoseek (*www.infoseek.com*), Microsoft (*www.msn.com*), Excite (*www.excite.com*), Alta Vista (*www.digital.altavista.com*), and Lycos (*www.lycos.com*). These sites help identify products, services, articles, and other Web sites. By using these portal sites a customer can identify product and service providers and get information on the quality and cost of what they want. Some offer information on specific products and services. At Car-Point (*www.carpoint.msn.com*) you can find all kinds of information on cars, vans and SUVs (sports utility vehicles); At Expedia (*www.expedia.msn.com*) you can plan and make reservations for your next vacation.

Customers truly benefit when they quote the price they want to pay and the sellers decide if they want to accept that price. Price Line (*www.priceline.com*) offers such a service for buying air travel tickets and cars,. Customers quote the price they want to pay and depending on the availability they can get cheaper air travel.

Execution of Transactions

Financial intermediaries are responsible for transaction management, chargeback and return, capture and settlement, inventory, accounting, fulfillment and authorization, and settlement. Intermediaries use systems from First Virtual (*www.firstvirtual.com*), CyberCash *(www.cybercash.com)*, and Verifone *(www.verifone.com)*, to protect against merchant fraud. Some intermediaries issue digital certificates for firms to use in identifying themselves.

Conventional Payments

Payment is a financial exchange between a customer and a business entity. The instruments of these financial exchanges in a conventional payment system are cash, cashier's check, check, and credit card payment, over the counter, over the telephone, or through the mail. Offline payment systems that demand physical presence are by far the safest.

Cash, cashier's check, and regular check are particularly safe; credit card payments are less secure. Because the payments are not in real time, there is an inherent delay in processing the payment that introduces a financial risk for the business.

Nevertheless, the sense of security that all conventional payment systems have generated over time is very high. However, the traditional payment system has many problems. Some of the issues are:

- *Lack of Convenience*: The need for the physical presence—either in person or on the telephone—for both parties limits transactional freedom. For customers this translates into a delay in acquiring the product or service and results in higher cost; for the seller it introduces a loss of revenue due to reduced or lost sales.

- *Non-Real-Time Payments*: Conventional payments are not real time. The delay in actual realization depends on the type of payment—check payments may take up to a week, credit card payments a couple of weeks.

- *Lack of Security*: Signatures can be forged, credit card numbers can be stolen, or merchants can commit fraud.

- *Higher Cost of Payments*: Each transaction costs a fixed amount of money. For smaller payments these costs barely cover expenses.

Yet these payments are here to stay. The convenience offered by traditional payment systems for physical transactions will always be unmatched, though we have seen some shifts in the use of check cards (debit cards) and electronic payment by traditional methods, like use of credit cards over the telephone.

Many modern payments are electronic. Automated teller machines, online transactions (secure and non-secure), electronic fund transfer, credit card authorizations and payments, check card authorizations and payments, and electronic check verification all use some form of electronic communication.

Electronic payments emerged with the simple concept of wire transfer. Human operators conducted these transfers with minimal verification over private voice networks. Over time EFT graduated to using private digital networks, enabling banks and other organizations to reduce the fund transfer time. Refinements in electronic payment mechanisms have concentrated on:

- Minimizing banking cost,

- Speeding up payment,

- Minimizing fraud, and

- Improving customer satisfaction.

The most notable feature of today's electronic payment systems is user interaction. Earlier electronic payment systems could not allow end-user interaction, thereby increasing the cost and the time for payment completion. With increasing user interaction the cost of making payments is coming down. This makes possible electronic payment of smaller amounts, called micropayments, possible. Consumers can use credit cards, digital cash, microcash, and electronic checks for making payments electronically.

Credit Cards

Electronic payments with a credit card follow the same procedure as conventional credit card payments. Customers give their credit card number to the merchant. The merchant verifies the ability of the customer to make payment with the bank or credit card issuer and creates a purchase slip for endorsement. Eventually, the merchant uses this purchase slip to collect the payment.

However, now the process to a large extent is automated. In an online scenario, the customer uses the Web browser to fill in the online order form. This form is processed by the Web server, which forwards the authorization request to the bank. The bank then pays the merchant.

In a non-secure transaction, all the data communication is plain text; anyone snooping on the line can read it. In a secure environment all or parts of the information are encrypted—most importantly, the credit card information. In order to protect customers from possible credit card fraud by everyone including merchants, we use a trusted third party to decrypt the credit card numbers. These third party systems are available from First Virtual, CyberCash, or Verifone.

CyberCash and Verifone both use helper applications called *Wallet* for the Web browser. A Wallet essentially encrypts the credit card number and passes the encrypted number to the third party server for verification. The merchant does not see the number at all (see Figure 7.4 on page 171).

First Virtual issues a VirtualPIN to the customer, who then uses the PIN instead of the credit card number. When FirstVirtual receives the PIN, it converts it to a credit card number to clear the purchase.

Electronic Checking

Two firms—Financial Services Technology Corporation (FSTC) and CyberCash—have systems for letting customers use electronic checks to pay merchants. FSTC uses a format like a paper check. Electronically initiated, these checks are signed with a digital signature. FSTC allows different instruction mechanisms like certified check and electronic charge slip that the customer specifies at the time of making the purchase. CyberCash uses an extension of its Wallet application. CyberCash does not handle the check payment itself; instead the check is passed on to an electronic payments handler.

Figure 7.4: Third Party Verification of Information

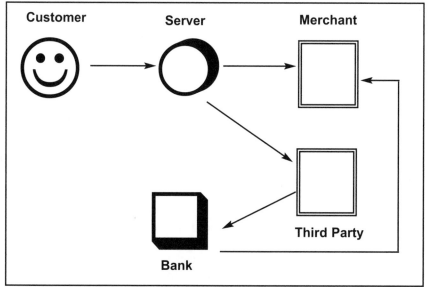

In both cases, electronic checks are handled by an electronic payments handler, which could be a bank, a clearinghouse, or any other financial agency authorized to process the payments.

Digital Cash

Digital cash, also called e-cash, is best suited for making real-time payments over the Internet, though setting up and using digital cash is more complicated than using conventional cash. First, banks issue *tokens* to their customers. A token is an electronic object with a unique serial number. Customers then use these tokens to make purchases. The merchants present these tokens to the customer's bank for processing and payment. The bank handles the tokens as it would a physical check. It prevents reuse of the tokens by comparing the unique serial numbers.

The addition of *blind signature*, developed by DigiCash, to e-cash makes it look more like actual cash. The person holding the cash is not identified with the cash. E-cash with a blind signature has to be honored by the issuing bank, which has no knowledge of who tendered the payment.

A major advantage of digital cash, also called *microcash*, is the removal of financial intermediaries from smaller transactions. Merchants can accept digital cash for purchases or services. Once they have collected enough digital cash from customers, they can use it themselves to pay for purchases or services over the Internet, or they can convert it to regular cash by presenting it to the bank. Microcash can be used to buy small items online, such as an image, a sound clip, a document, and a game session.

Legal and Business Issues

Banking is a mature industry, closely monitored by the government. However, electronic payment is in the hands of consumers. Some of the issues the difference raises are record-keeping, proofs of purchase, and privacy.

Record keeping and proofs of purchase are the easiest to manage in an electronic environment. All transactions move in stages through a number of computers. It's possible to keep permanent records at each significant processing computer. If a record is lost, it should be fairly simple to reconstruct the entire transaction and fill in the missing link.

In electronic transactions it can be easy to invade the privacy of consumers. Since we can reconstruct transactions, purchases, spending and receipts, privacy must be given a great deal of thought. Privacy must also be secured against eavesdropping.

As technology evolves and consumers become more confident in the system, we should see an increase in e-commerce. For e-commerce to be successful, consumers must feel comfortable about privacy and be confident of their control over their finances. Ultimately, the success of e-commerce depends on consumer satisfaction.

Resources

IBM E-Business (*www.ibm.com/e-business*), a generally helpful e-commerce resource.

KalaKota, R., & Whinston, A.B., *E-commerce—A Manager's Guide.* Addison Wesley, 1997.

Kosiur, David, *Understanding E-commerce.* Microsoft Press, 1997.

Net Business (*www.techweb.com/netbiz*), a collection of case studies in e-commerce.

ZDNet E-Business (*www.zdnet.com/icom/e-business*), a guide to e-commerce emphasizing tax issues.

Chapter 8
NETWORK SECURITY

Networks may be broadly classified as either *wide area networks* (WANs) or *local area networks* (LANs). Both need network security. The computers in a WAN may be anywhere from several to thousands of miles apart; the computers in a LAN are usually closer together, all in one building or plant. Data switching equipment is common in LANs, rare in WANs.

On the Internet, you need security to prevent unauthorized changes to your Web site. For businesses selling information-related products over the Internet, such as software vendors that allow paying customers to download upgrades, there has to be a way to discriminate between paying customers and non-paying users.

Security administrators confront the risk that an attacker will be able to break into a network. The attacker may be anyone; the attacks may range from direct attacks by both hackers and insiders to automated attacks like those using network worms-a virus that seeks out all the data in memory or on a disk in order to alter it. Such an attacker might obtain:

- *Read Access:* The attacker can read or copy confidential information.

- *Write Access:* The attacker can write to your network, perhaps infecting the system with a virus or planting Trojan horses or back doors. The attacker may also destroy confidential information.

- *Denial of Service:* The purpose of some attacks is simply to deny normal network services to authorized services. An attack may consume CPU time or network bandwidth or fill up memory.

Security risks in using a server on the Internet include inappropriate configuration of FTP (file transfer protocol) settings. If your server allows FTP access, it must be so configured as to prevent unauthorized modifications to files.

You need a secure communication link for data transmission between interconnected host computer systems of a network. A major security technique on the network is cryptography. Cryptographic algorithms may be either *symmetric* (private key) or *asymmetric* (public key). The two popular encryption methods are *link-level* security and *end-to-end* security. Link-level safeguards traffic independently on every communication link; end-to-end safeguards messages from source to destination. Link-level enciphers the communications line at the bit level; data is deciphered when it enters the nodes. End-to-end enciphers information at the entry point and deciphers information at the exit point; unlike in link-level, information inside the nodes remains secure.

There should be a list of authorized users, created after you ask yourself:

- Who is allowed into the facilities?
- When may they enter?
- For what purposes?

A variety of tools can help the security manager implement the security plan, among them encryption tools, route and packet filtering, and firewalls.

Your company should have both a network security policy and an internal corporate security policy. You must decide how critical it is to protect the integrity of your computing system and the security of your Web site.

Distribute the internal security plan to everyone who uses the system. Give employees written guidance on the proper use of passwords, reminding them about what should not be used as passwords and scheduling how often passwords must be changed.

There must be positive authentication before a user can access online applications in a network environment, or certain other applications. Make sure information is available only on a need-to-know basis.

Set controls for accessing a specific terminal or application, enumerating date and time constraints along with file usage. Unauthorized use can deactivate or lock a terminal. Diskless workstations may make the network environment safer.

Passwords

Most LAN or communication software packages contain encryption and security features, including passwords. However, passwords often are not enough protection. People generally don't pick good passwords or change them often enough. From a security perspective it's not too difficult for hackers to breach security by guessing passwords.

People tend to make certain mistakes with their passwords. Passwords should never be shared with others; nor should they be written down. Passwords should be easy to remember. If you need to write the password down to remember it, you've defeated its purpose. Advise system users that:

- They not select a password that is a word in English or any language. Hackers often use dictionaries to guess passwords.

- They should avoid obvious patterns like *123456, 12468, asdf* or *qwerty*, from the keyboard.

- Geographical names like Vegas or Florida should not be used.

- Many computer systems require that the password contain numerals as well as letters. Many people just add 1 to a word (e.g., CAT1 or 1CAT). Hackers know this, so they can overcome it easily.

- Using a combination of upper and lower case and non-alphabetic characters can make it more difficult for hackers to guess passwords.

- An excellent technique to create a password is to use the first letters of each word of a phrase. For example, "I was born in New York" would yield the password IWBINY. This is not a word that can be guessed easily, but it's easy for the user to remember.

- Users should change their passwords periodically. You can force this by programming the computer system to require new passwords at certain intervals. The system should check that users don't use the same password again, or pick one they've used recently.

All users should be given security guidelines, and give new users a short course in security precautions and how to select a good password. The following Web site provides information about selecting a good password. It also helps users evaluate the strength of their existing password(s):

http://www.symantec.com/avcenter/security/passwords/password analysis.html

Though passwords give good protection from casual or amateur hackers, professional or experienced hackers can usually bypass the password system. In the UNIX environment, which is quite common, there are software programs that can help even hackers with limited knowledge to find or guess passwords.

The aim of most hackers is to obtain unlimited access to a computer system. To do this, they:

- Find bugs or errors in the system software
- Take advantage of an incorrect installation
- Look for human errors

Many hackers are authorized users whose access to the system is limited. These hackers will have a valid user id and password, and will look for weaknesses in the system.

In most UNIX systems, passwords are stored in an encrypted file. Some systems use a shadow password file where the original data is stored. Passwords are generally encrypted using the data encryption standard (DES) algorithm. A key is used to encrypt and decrypt passwords.

The type of encryption method used is essentially irreversible: While it's easy to encrypt a password, it's extremely difficult, almost impossible, to decrypt it. Nonetheless hackers can discover passwords through brute force. A hacker can find a password consisting of only six lowercase characters rather quickly. It's therefore critical that passwords for accounts that are likely to attract hackers not consist of simply lowercase characters.

A serious design flaw can sometimes result in the creation of a "universal" password, one that satisfies the requirements of the login program without the hacker actually knowing the correct password. For example, a hacker could enter an overly long password that would end up overwriting the actual password, thus allowing the hacker unauthorized access.

Modem Connections

Any time a user connects to the network using a modem, there are additional risks, but these can be minimized.

Simply keeping the telephone number secret is not sufficient. Many hackers dial through the entire prefix of telephone numbers until they randomly discover your telephone number.

In the past, many companies used dial-back techniques to reduce the dial-in modem risk. Nowadays, caller-id can accomplish the same objective. Essentially, the network allows users access only from pre-identified telephone numbers. The obvious disadvantage is that the telephone numbers of authorized users must be arranged in advance. This is difficult for users who travel.

Another way to minimize risk from dial-in modems is to use hardware encryption devices on both ends of the connection. These devices, however, tend to be expensive.

A good telecommunications software program will have numerous protocol options, enabling communications with different types of equipment. Some programs error-check information or software programs received. Desirable features in telecommunications programs include menus providing help, telephone directory storage, and automatic log-on and redial.

Saboteurs' Tools

While in recent years ingenious procedures have been developed to preserve computer security, many computer systems are still astonishingly insecure. Saboteurs may use a wide variety of tools and techniques to overcome security, among them:

Trojan Horse: The saboteur places a hidden program within the normal programs of a business. The computer continues to function normally while the hidden program collects data, makes secret modifications to programs and files, erases or destroys data, or even causes a complete shutdown. Trojan horses can be programmed to destroy all traces of their existence after execution.

Salami Techniques: The perpetrator makes secret notations to a computer program, causing very small changes that are unlikely to be discovered, but whose cumulative effect can be substantial. For example, the perpetrator may steal 10 cents from the paycheck of each employee and transfer it to his own account.

Back Door or Trap Door: In developing a program, programmers sometimes insert a code to allow them to bypass the standard security procedures. Once the programming is complete, the code may remain in the program either accidentally or intentionally. Attackers rely on this extra code to bypass security.

Time Bomb/Logic Bomb: A code can be inserted into a computer program that causes damage when a predefined condition occurs.

Masquerade: A computer program is written that simulates the real program. For example, a program may be written to simulate the log-in screen and related dialogue. When a user attempts to log in, the program captures the user's ID and password and displays an error message, prompting the user to log in again. The second time, the user does log in and the user may never know that the first log-in was a ruse to get the ID.

Scavenging: A computer normally doesn't erase data that is no longer needed. When the user "deletes" data, the information is not actually destroyed but the space is made available for the computer to write on later. A scavenger may thus be able to steal sensitive data that the user thought had been deleted but that was still on the computer.

Viruses: Viruses are like Trojan horses except that the illegal code can replicate itself. A virus can rapidly spread throughout the system; eradicating it can be expensive and cumbersome. To guard against viruses, be careful in using documents or programs from diskettes or in copying software from outside the company. Only use disks from verified sources. The best precaution is to use a commercial virus scanner like McAfee's or Norton's on all downloaded files before using them. Virus protection and detection is crucial.

Data Manipulation: The most common and easiest way to commit fraud is to add or alter the data before or during input. The best way to detect this is to use audit software to scrutinize transactions and review audit trails that indicate additions, changes, and deletions made to data files. The use of batch totals, hash totals, check digits can also help prevent this type of crime.

A *batch total* is a reconciliation between the total daily transactions processed and total determined manually by someone other than the computer operator. Material deviations must be investigated.

A *hash total* is adding values that would not typically be added together so the total has no meaning other than for control purposes. Examples are employee and product numbers.

A *check digit* is used to ascertain whether an identification number (e.g., account number, employee number) has been correctly entered by adding a calculation to the identification number and comparing the outcome to the check digit.

Piggybacking: Piggybacking is often used to gain access to controlled areas. Physical piggybacking occurs when an authorized employee goes through a door using a magnetic ID card, and an unauthorized employee enters the premises behind him. The unauthorized employee is then in a position to commit a crime. In electronic piggybacking, an authorized employee leaves his terminal or desktop and an unauthorized individual uses it to gain access.

Designing Networks

The architecture of a network includes hardware, software, information link controls, standards, topologies, and protocols. A protocol is how computers communicate and transfer information. Each component within the architecture must be secured to assure reliable data exchanges. Otherwise, the integrity of the system may be compromised.

In designing the network, consider three factors:

1. You need get the best possible response time and throughput. Minimizing response time entails shortening delays between transmission and receipt of data; this is especially important for interactive sessions. Throughput means transmitting the maximum amount of data per unit of time.

2. The data should be transmitted along the least-cost path within the network, as long as other factors, like reliability, are not compromised. The least-cost path is generally the shortest channel between devices using the fewest intermediate components. Low priority data can be transmitted over relatively inexpensive telephone lines; high priority data can be transmitted over expensive high-speed satellite channels.

3. Reliability should be maximized to assure proper receipt of all data traffic. Network reliability encompasses the ability not only to deliver error-free data but also to recover from errors or lost data. The network's diagnostic system should be able to locate problems with components and perhaps even isolate the malfunctioning component from the network.

Network Topologies

The network configuration or topology is the physical shape of the network, the layout of linking stations. A *node* is a workstation. A *bridge* is a connection between two similar networks. *Protocols* are software implementations providing support for network data transmission. A *server* is a micro or a peripheral performing tasks like data storage within a LAN.

Exhibit 8.1. Network Media
The considerations in selecting a network medium are:

- Technical reliability
- Type of business
- Number of users who will need to access data simultaneously
- Frequency of updating
- Physical layout of existing equipment
- Number of micros
- Compatibility
- Cost
- Geographic dispersion
- Type of network operating software and support available
- Availability of application software
- Ability to add additional workstations
- Restriction to PCs (can cheaper terminals be used?)
- Ease of access in sharing equipment and data
- Need to access disparate equipment, like other networks and main-frames
- Processing needs
- Speed
- Data storage ability
- Maintenance
- Noise
- Connectivity mechanism
- Ability of network to conduct tasks without corrupting data

Network servers are of several types. A *dedicated* server is a central computer used only to manage network traffic. A computer that is used as a local workstation is called a *nondedicated* server. In general, dedicated servers provide faster network performance because they don't take requests from both local users and network stations. Nor are these machines susceptible to crashes caused by a local user's error.

Dedicated servers are expensive and cannot be disconnected from the network and used as stand-alone computers. *Nondedicated* servers have a higher price-performance ratio for companies that need occasional use of the server as a local workstation.

The most common types of network topologies are:

- The *hierarchical topology* (also called vertical or tree structure) is attractive for several reasons. The software to control the network is simple and the topology provides a concentration point for control and error resolution. However, it also presents potential bottleneck and reliability problems. Network capabilities may be completely lost if there is a failure at a higher level.

- The *horizontal topology* (or *bus topology*) is popular in LANs. Its advantages include simple traffic flow between devices. This topology permits all devices to receive every transmission; in other words, a single station broadcasts to multiple stations. The biggest disadvantage is that because all computers share a single channel, a failure in the communication channel brings down the whole network. Redundant channels get around this problem. Another disadvantage with this topology is that the absence of concentration points makes it hard to resolve problems; it's more difficult to isolate faults to any particular component. A bus network usually needs a minimum distance between taps to reduce noise. A bus topology, which suggested for shared databases, is not good for single-message switching. It does employ minimum topology to fill a geographic area, while at the same time having complete connectivity.

- The *star topology* is a very popular configuration. The software for star topology is not complex and controlling traffic is simple. All traffic emanates from the hub or the center of the star. In a way, the star configuration is like the hierarchical network, but its distributed processing capabilities are more limited. The hub routes data traffic to other components. It also isolates faults, which is relatively simple in the star configuration. Like the hierarchical network the star is subject to bottleneck at the hub and may have serious reliability problems; the problem can be minimized by establishing a redundant backup of the hub node. A star network is best when there is a need to process data at many locations with day-end distribution to different remote users. Here, information for general use is sent to the host computer for processing. It's easy to identify errors in the system, since each communication must go through the central controller. Maintenance is easy if the central computer fails the network. There's a high initial cost in setting up the system because in addition to the cost of the host each node requires hookup to the host computer. But expansion is easy; all that's needed is to run a wire from the terminal to the host.

- Data in a *ring* network flows in a circle, usually in one direction only. Bottlenecks like those found in the hierarchical or star networks, are relatively uncommon. The primary disadvantage is that a single channel ties all the components in a network; the entire network can be lost if the channel between two nodes fails. Establishing a backup channel can usually alleviate this problem. Other ways to overcome it are by using switches to automatically route the traffic around a failed node or installing redundant cables. A ring network is more reliable and less expensive when there is minimal communication between micros. This type of network is best when there are several users at different locations who have to continually access updated data. Here, more than one transmission can occur simultaneously. The system is always current. The ring network permits accountants within the firm to create and update shared databases. With a ring, there is greater likelihood of error compared to a star because numerous parties handle data. In light of this, the accountant should recommend that data in a ring system make an entire circle before being removed from the network.

- The *mesh topology* is very reliable, though complex. Its structure makes it relatively immune to bottlenecks and other failures. The multiplicity of paths makes it relatively easy to route traffic around failed components or busy nodes.

LANs and WANs

The major differences between WANs and LANs are that their topologies usually take different shapes. A WAN structure tends to be more irregular. Since an organization generally leases lines at a considerable cost, it tries to keep the lines fully utilized. To do this, data for a geographical area is often routed through one channel; hence the irregular shape of the WAN network.

Since channels in a LAN network are relatively inexpensive, the owners of a LAN are generally not concerned with utilization of channels. Furthermore, since LANs usually reside in a single building or a plant, they tend to be inherently more structured.

LANs are flexible, fast, and compatible. They maximize equipment utilization, reduce processing cost, reduce errors, and ease information flow. LANs use ordinary telephone lines, coaxial cables, fiber optics, and other devices like interfaces. Fiber optics support good performance and reliability but their cost is high. LAN performance depends on physical design, protocols supported, and transmission bandwidth. Bandwidth is the frequency range of a channel and reflects transmission speed along the network. As more devices become part of the LAN, transmission speed decreases.

Two or more LANs may be connected. Each node becomes a cluster of stations (subnetworks). Among the advantages of interfacing networks:

- Total network costs are lower.
- There is flexibility in having individual subnetworks meet particular needs.
- More reliable and higher cost subnetworks can be used for critical activities.
- If one LAN fails, the other still functions.

The disadvantages of interfacing networks are that:

- Complexity is greater.
- Some network functions may not be able to cross network boundaries.

Communications Security

Communication systems are used to link data between two or more sites. The communication system should be reliable, private and secure. Communication systems are often affected by environmental factors, hardware malfunction, and software problems.

Attacks on computers that don't require physical access fall under the domain of communications security. The increased use of computer technology has also increased dependence on telecommunications. All types of data, including sound, video, and traditional data, are transferred between computers over networks. Communications security means ensuring that the physical links between the computer networks function at all times. This also means that data is being transmitted, breakdowns, delays, and disturbances are prevented. It's important to prevent unauthorized individuals from tapping, modifying, or otherwise intercepting data transmission. Considerations in communications security are:

Line security—restricting unauthorized access to the communication lines connecting the various parts of the computer systems.

Transmission security—preventing unauthorized interception of communication.

Digital signature—used to authenticate the sender or message. A secure digital signature process is comprised of (1) a method of signing a document that makes forgery infeasible and (2) validating that the signature is the one whose it purports to be.

Cryptographic security—rendering information unintelligible if transmission is intercepted by unauthorized individuals. When the information is to be used, it can be decoded. Security coding (encryption) of sensitive data is necessary; one common method is the data encryption standard (DES). For even greater security, there is double encryption in which data is encrypted twice using two different keys. (You can may also encrypt files on a hard disk to prevent an intruder from reading them.)

Emission security—preventing the emission of electromagnetic radiation, which can be intercepted by unauthorized individuals.

Technical security—preventing the use of devices like a microphone, transmitters, or wiretaps to intercept data in transmission. Security modems allow only authorized users to access confidential data. A modem may have graduated levels of security. Different users may be assigned different security codes. There can be password and call-back features or built-in audit trails allowing you to monitor who is accessing files.

Many companies use value-added networks (VANs), which offer both communication services and specialized data processing. Generally, a client company has no direct control over a VAN's security. However, VAN security has a direct effect on the client's overall security.

Communication security may be in the form of:

- *Access control:* Guards against improper use of the network. For example, KERBEROS is commercial authentication software that is added to a security system to assure that a user is not an impostor. It does this by encrypting passwords transmitted around networks. Password control and user authentication devices may be used, like Security Dynamics' SecurID (800-SECURID) and Vasco Data Security's Access Key II (800-238-2726). Do not accept a collect call if it's not from a network user: Hackers don't typically spend their own funds. Review data communications billings and verify each host-to-host connection. Review all dial-up terminal users. Are the telephone numbers unlisted and changed periodically? Control specialists should try to make unauthorized access to the network to test whether the security is working properly.

- *Identification:* Identifies the origin of a communication within the network through digital signals or notarization.

- *Data confidentiality:* Prevents unauthorized disclosure of information within the communication process.

- *Data integrity:* Guards against unauthorized changes (e.g., adding, deleting) of data at both the receiving and sending points, perhaps through cryptographic methods. Anti-virus software should be installed at both the network server and workstations. Detection programs alert users when viruses enter the system.

- *Authentication:* Substantiates the fact that an originating or user entity within the network is actually who it claims to be and that the information being transmitted is appropriate. Examples of authentication controls are passwords, time stamping, synchronized checks, nonrepudiation, and multiple-way handshakes. Biometric methods measure body characteristics with equipment attached to the workstation. Retinal laser beams may also be used. Keystroke dynamics are another possibility.

- *Digital signature:* Signs messages with a private key.

- *Routing control:* Inhibits data flow to network elements such as relays, links, or subnetworks identified as not secure.

- *Traffic padding:* A traffic analysis of data for reasonableness.

- *Interference minimization:* Eliminates or controls radar/radio transmission interference. There are various ways to backup data in networks. For a small network, one workstation may be used as the backup and restore for other nodes. In a large network where the failure of one node could have disastrous effects on the entire system, several servers may do backups. Access to backup files must be strictly controlled.

Token-Ring and Ethernet Networks

Token-Ring and Ethernet networks work on the broadcast principle: They send information in units called frames. Each frame contains information about a variety of items, including the sender's and the receiver's address. The sender broadcasts a frame that every receiver can see. At any given moment only one computer in the network is broadcasting and all other computers act as receivers. Another computer may broadcast after the first computer finishes. While all machines on a network can see the broadcasting computer's frame, under ideal conditions only the computer whose address matches the receiver's address in the frame should be able to access the frame's contents.

Sniffers

Sniffers are programs designed to capture certain information. Network managers often use sniffers to analyze network traffic and network statistics. Hackers, however, may use sniffers to steal information like passwords.

Certain actions can minimize sniffing risk. The most obvious is to limit access. If the hacker is unable to access the LAN, sniffers cannot be used. However, it's often possible to restrict access to networks too tightly; hence, other alternatives need to be considered. Switched versions of token-ring and Ethernet networks may minimize sniffing. With a switched LAN, each user has his own port on the switch. A virtual connection is established with the destination port for each frame sent. If destination address in the frame does not match, the risk associated with sniffing is significantly reduced. Switched networks tend to be more expensive. Moreover, it's rare to find completely switched networks.

Probably the best way to minimize sniffing risk is to encrypt data. In such a system, it's important that the key is never sent over the network. Traditional information, such as the time, is used to enhance the encryption scheme.

Data Flow

Data switching equipment routes data through the network to its destinations; for instance, it routes data around failed or busy devices or channels.

Routers at each site communicate with routers at other sites. Routers provide information about the individuals and the resources available in the LAN. They direct the flow of information. It's possible to configure the routers so that certain types of routers, such as FTP or Telenet, do not allow either incoming or outgoing access. It's also possible to enable certain routers to receive information from only certain network addresses.

Route and packet filtering requires significant technical knowledge as well as time. Most routers do not provide a security or audit trail. You need to know:

- Who tried to break in to the computer system.

- How often they tried.

- What methods were used to attempt the break-in.

Data Transmission

Data transmission between computers in a network uses one of three methods.

- *Simplex transmission* is in one direction only. An example is radio or television transmission. Simplex transmission is rare in computer networks.

- *Half-duplex transmission* is found in many systems. Here, information can flow in both directions—but not flow in both directions simultaneously. In other words, once a query is transmitted from one device, it must wait for a response.

- A *full-duplex system* can transmit information in both directions simultaneously; it doesn't have the stop-and-wait aspect of half-duplex systems. For high throughput and fast response time, full-duplex transmission is common.

Security Layers

Security should be provided in different layers for networking facilities, telecommunication elements, host computers, and subnetworks.

Network traffic may be over many subnetworks, each with its own security depending on confidentiality and importance. Therefore, different security and controls may be required. Security aspects of each subnetwork have to be distributed to the gateways so as to incorporate security and controls in routing decisions.

Backup capability is especially important for networks. If one computer fails, another computer in the network must be able to take over the load. This might be critical in certain industries such as the financial.

Secure Sockets Layer

When the *Secure Sockets Layer* (SSL) is enabled, a Web browser will display a lock or another symbol to indicate that the data transfer is secure. Another way to tell that the Web site is secure is by looking at its address: The Web site address should start with "https://" rather than simply "http://."

Most Web-based monetary transactions are secured using SSL. Many Web server/client products support SSL connections. To transact on the Web, you need access to such a server as well as a digital certificate. While using SSL for encryption greatly enhances security and confidentiality, it does slow the interchange. All the data has to be encrypted and then decrypted.

SSL, a protocol developed by Netscape,[1] operates by layering a security protocol on top of an underlying connection transport protocol like HTTP, Telnet, NNTP, FTP, or TCP/IP. SSL is built in to Netscape's client and server products. In building a Web site, you can enable SSL by configuring a security-enabled http (https) process on the server. Web pages that require SSL access can be specified. Common Gateway Interface (CGI) routines can be written on the server side to integrate SSL into existing applications.

SSL provides data encryption and checks for data integrity. It provides server authentication and, if required, client authentication for a TCP/IP connection. SSL is open and nonproprietary. Encryption, decryption, and authentication are transparent for applications using SSL.

SSL is used extensively to encrypt and authenticate communications between clients and servers on the Web. The *Transport Layer Security* (TLS) standard by the Internet Engineering Task Force (IETF) is based on SSL.

A user can confirm and authenticate an SSL server's identity when sending sensitive information, such as a credit card number, to the server. The digital certificate is used to prove authenticity. Certificate Authorities (CA) such as VeriSign Inc. issue digital certificates. Anyone with the correct software can become a certificate authority, but there are

---

[1]For the latest information about SSL connections, visit Netscape's Web-site at:
http://developer1.netscape.com/docs/manuals/security/sslin/contents.htm

only certain trusted CAs that a Web browser will accept. It's possible to tell the Web browser which CA to accept.

Public-key cryptography techniques may be used to check if a server's certificate and public ID are valid and were issued by a trusted CA. Similarly, a server can confirm a user's identity by checking that the client's certificate and public ID are valid and were issued by a trusted CA.

Public key cryptography greatly facilitates key management. Without public key cryptography, encrypted communication could take place only if all the users shared the keys. The users would need a secure connection to share the secret key, and each user would have to maintain different keys for different partners.

Public key cryptography allows parties to communicate securely without sharing secret keys. Each party establishes a key pair, one private and one public key. The public key, available to all nodes on a network, is used to encrypt messages to the node. The private key is used to decrypt the messages. It never leaves its node.

Public key cryptography is used to create digital signatures and sign documents. A document is signed using the private key, but other users can verify the signature with the public key. The digital certificate consists of the name and other information about the user along with the user's public key. A trusted certificate authority signs the information on the digital certificate and verifies the identity of a user. The following steps are typical:

- A user creates a public/private key pair.
- The private key is stored with the user.
- The public key is given to a trusted authority.
- The trusted authority creates a digital signature for the user and provides a digital certificate.
- The digital certificate may be published or attached to messages the user digitally signs.
- Other users may verify the signature and authenticate the user's identity using the digital certificate.

The *Transmission Control Protocol/Internet Protocol* (TCP/IP) gives the rules for transporting and routing data over the Internet. Protocols like the HyperText Transport Protocol (HTTP) use the TCP/IP to carry out tasks like displaying Web pages. The SSL protocol runs in the middle between TCP/IP and higher-level protocols like HTTP. SSL utilizes TCP/IP on behalf of the higher-level protocols. This allows SSL-enabled clients and servers to authenticate themselves and makes an encrypted connection possible.

The confidentiality of an SSL connection is ensured through encryption. An SSL connection also provides assurance that the data has not been tampered with or altered in transit.

The "strength" of an SSL connection depends on the bit level. For example, 40-bit SSL connections tend to be rather weak; a 128-bit SSL connection is extremely strong: 128 bits is approximately 240 septillion times (340,000,000,000,000,000,000,000,000) larger than 40 bits.

128-bit encryption is available only for American and Canadian residents; it's presently illegal for US companies to export internationally anything above a 56-bit encryption. Software security companies are trying to overcome these export restrictions by developing encryption technology outside the United States.

The SSL protocol includes two subprotocols. The *SSL Record Protocol* defines the format that will be used for data transmission. The *SSL Handshake Protocol* determines how the record protocol will exchange data between an SSL server and an SSL client when the SSL connection is first established. It can either authenticate the server to the client or the client to the server. It also allows client and server to select from various cryptographic algorithms or ciphers supported by both.

Both public-key and symmetric key encryptions are used by the SSL protocol. While symmetric key encryption tends to be faster, public-key encryption provides better authentication. Among the common ciphers:

- The *Data Encryption Standard* (DES) is a popular encryption algorithm; triple DES applies DES three times and supports 168-bit encryption. Its key size makes it one of the strongest ciphers supported by SSL.

- The *Digital Signature Algorithm* (DSA) is used to authenticate digital signatures.

- The *Key Exchange Algorithm* (KEA) is used for key exchange.

- The *Message Digest* (MD5) algorithm.

- *RSA* is a popular public-key algorithm used for both authentication and encryption.

- The *Secure Hash Algorithm* (SHA-1).

• *SKIPJACK* is a classified symmetric-key algorithm used in FORTEZZA-compliant hardware. The FORTEZZA encryption system is used by U.S. government agencies for sensitive but not classified data. FORTEZZA ciphers use the KEA for SSL instead of the RSA key-exchange algorithm. FORTEZZA cards and DSA are used for client authentication.

Performance can suffer when using public key cryptography. Therefore, it's typically applied only to digital signatures or small amounts of data. Performance can suffer when using public key cryptography. Therefore, public key encryption is typically limited to digital signatures or encrypting a small amount of data. RSA public-key cryptography is most common in commercial applications, for encryption, decryption, digital signatures, and authentication. Symmetric key encryption, such as DES, is typically used for encrypting bulk data.

Ciphers for both client and server can easily be enabled or disabled. During the handshake Performance can suffer when using public key cryptography. Therefore, public key encryption is typically limited to digital signatures or encrypting a small amount of data (see Exhibit 8.2), client and server determine the strongest common cipher suite, which is used for the SSL connection.

Security administrators should decide which cipher suites to enable or disable. Consider the nature of the data, the need for confidentiality and security, the speed of the cipher—and the national origin of the parties, because certain ciphers may only be used within the USA and Canada. If an organization disables the weaker ciphers, it automatically restricts access to American and Canadian clients; a client elsewhere may access the server only if it has a special Global Server ID.

Authentication

For server authentication, the client encrypts the pre-master secret with the server's public key. The server's private key alone can decrypt the pre-master secret. This gives the client reasonable assurance about the server's identity.

For client authentication, the client encrypts random pieces of data using the client's private key. In other words, it creates a digital signature that can be validated using the public key in the client's certificate only if the corresponding private key had been used. If the server cannot validate the digital signature, authentication fails and the session will be terminated.

Exhibit 8.2: The SSL "Handshake"

The following sequence typically takes place in an SSL connection (handshake):

- The client provides the server with its SSL version number, cipher settings, and other communications-related data.
- The server gives the client the same information for itself.
- The server sends its certificate and may ask for the client's certificate.
- The client authenticates the server. If the server cannot be authenticated, the client is warned that an encrypted and authenticated connection cannot be established.
- The client creates a "pre-master" secret for the SSL connection, encrypts it with the server's public key, and sends it to the server. At the server's request, the client may also sign and send data to authenticate itself.
- The session will be terminated if the server cannot authenticate the client.
- The server uses its private key to decrypt the pre-master secret and to generate the "master" secret. The client generates the master secret using the same pre-master secret.
- Using the master secret, session keys are generated by both the client and the server. These symmetric session keys are used to encrypt and decrypt data. The keys ensure that the data is not tampered with between sending and receiving, and that data integrity has not been compromised.
- The SSL session begins once the SSL handshake is completed. Both client and server use the session keys to encrypt and decrypt data and to verify data integrity.

SSLRef

SSLRef is an advanced tool-kit designed to help developers provide security features in TCP/IP applications using the SSL protocol. ANSI C source code is provided for incorporation into TCP/IP applications. SSLRef may be downloaded for free for noncommercial use. While there are no license restrictions on SSLRef, there are export restrictions.

Kerberos

Kerberos is a network authentication protocol that uses secret-key cryptography. After authenticating client/server identity, Kerberos may be used to encrypt data. Kerberos does not send across any data that may allow an attacker to learn secret information and impersonate the user.

Kerberos is available free in the form of source code from Massachusetts Institute of Technology. It's also available in commercial software products from several vendors.

In the traditional environment, a user's identity is verified or authenticated by checking the user's password during the login process. Without Kerberos authentication, the user would need to enter a password to access each network service. This is, at a minimum, inconvenient. Moreover, it still does not provide security when accessing services on a remote machine. Without encryption, it would be easy for anyone to intercept the password during transit. Instead of passwords Kerberos uses a series of encrypted messages to prove that a client is running on behalf of a particular user. The client, to prove its identity, presents a ticket issued by the Kerberos Authentication Server. Secret information (such as a password) that only an authorized user would know, is contained in the ticket.

Kerberos is not effective against password-guessing attacks. It's therefore essential for the user to select a good password. Otherwise, a hacker who intercepts a few encrypted messages may launch an attack by randomly trying passwords to see if the messages decrypt correctly. A hacker who can guess the password will be able to impersonate the user.

Kerberos assumes that workstations are reasonably secure and only the network connections are vulnerable. A trusted path for passwords is required. For example, if the password is entered into a program containing a Trojan horse (i.e., the program has been modified to capture certain information), Kerberos will not provide any protection. Moreover, if transmissions between user and authentication program can be intercepted, Kerberos will be ineffective.

Both user and network service must have keys registered with the Kerberos Authentication Server. The user's key is derived from a user-selected password. The network service key is selected randomly.

Many types of software used by the international community require Kerberos. An international version, Bones, was created because the United States restricts export of cryptography. All the DES routines have been stripped from Bones, which is used as a substitute to "trick" other software into believing that Kerberos is installed. International users can get Encrypted Bones, E-Bones, which does provide encryption.

To use Kerberos, you need a Kerberos principal, which is like a regular account on a machine. Certain information, such as the user name and password, is associated with each principal. The information is encrypted and stored in the Kerberos database. Kerberos is essentially transparent from the user's perspective. To be effective, Kerberos has to be integrated into the computer system. Kerberos protects only data from software that is configured to use Kerberos.

Because the Kerberos Authentication Server maintains a database of passwords or encryption keys, it's critical to protect the server system. The server, if possible, should be physically secure. Ideally, the machine should be dedicated to running the authentication server. Access to the machine should be strictly restricted.

While Kerberos is free from MIT, it's not officially supported. Several companies have taken reference implementations from MIT and provide commercially supported products.

Each user's initial password has to be registered with the authentication server; the procedure depends upon the number of users. Inperson registration is the best control if the number of users is small. Other procedures, like a login program on a trusted system, may be used when the number of users is large.

Several tools can enhance the security provided by Kerberos. Kerberos cannot protect against a hacker guessing or stealing user passwords; one-time passwords generated by special devices eliminate that problem. Commercial products are available that combine one-time passwords with Kerberos.

Additional information about Kerberos is available from http://nii.isi.edu/info/kerberos/ or http://nii.isi.edu/publications/kerberos-neuman-tso.html.

The Web sites for some vendors that sell or support Kerberos are:

- *http://www.cybersafe.com*
- *http://www.latticesoft.com>*
- *http://www.stonecast.net*
- *http://www.wrq.com*

Firewalls

Firewalls overcome some of the problems associated with route and packet filtering. The firewall is a buffer between an internal network and the external world. The purpose of a firewall is to allow authorized traffic and restrict unauthorized traffic.

It's possible to configure the network so that outgoing data may travel freely across the firewall but incoming data is restricted. It's also possible to configure it so that only e-mail may go in and out of the computer; no other communication is allowed. Senior management determines the kind of access to permit or deny.

Firewalls may also block certain types of services that are known to cause problems. Most firewalls are configured to protect against unauthenticated interactive logins from external networks.

Unlike dial-in modem connections, firewalls perform logging and auditing functions. For example, data may be obtained about the number of login attempts and password failures.

Many organizations are overly concerned about threats from sources external to the organization. However, firewalls can't protect against internal threats. It's easy for internal users to steal proprietary data because they don't have to go through the firewall. Other routes to the corporate network as well as threats from internal users should be considered; firewalls should be only one part of your security plan.

While several firewall vendors offer virus protection tools, firewalls are not very effective against viruses. A virus can come from many sources, not only via transfers from the Internet. Virus protection should also be part of your overall security plan. Protect against viruses from all sources, especially internal sources where floppy disks are exchanged. Install virus-scanning software on each machine to run automatically whenever the machine is booted.

Firewall policies should consider the nature of the data to be protected. If the data requires a very high level of security, perhaps it should not be accessible via the Internet. It may be wise to isolate top secret data even from the main corporate network.

Setting up a Firewall

The cost of setting up a firewall can range from virtually free to several thousands, even hundreds of thousands, of dollars. In choosing a firewall system, consider not only the setup cost but also the cost of ongoing maintenance and support.

At one end, the firewall may be set up to block all services except those that are absolutely essential to establish connection. At the other end, the firewall may simply be used for monitoring and audit. Most organizations wouldn't want to be at either extreme. The sensitivity of your data will determine your organization's stance, but you must decide explicitly what services should be permitted, denied, or simply monitored.

There are two basic types of firewalls:

Network-level firewalls rely on the source/destination addresses and ports in individual IP packets. These firewalls generally route traffic directly and require an assigned IP address. Network-level firewalls are typically fast and transparent to users.

Application-level firewalls typically act as hosts running proxy servers. A *proxy server* or application gateway mediates traffic between a protected network and the Internet. Proxy servers are used to prevent traffic from passing directly through networks. Greater logging or support for user authentication is provided.

Application-level firewalls do not allow any traffic directly between networks. While improvements have been made, the performance of application-level firewalls may not be as good and they may not be as transparent to the user as network-level firewalls.

Future firewalls will integrate network-level and application-level characteristics. Network-level firewalls will keep better track of information that goes through them, and application-level firewalls will become more transparent. The overall effect will be better performance with elaborate logging and auditing functions.

Encryption of data passing through the firewall is increasingly common. With encryption you can have multiple points of connectivity with the Internet without being concerned about password or data sniffing programs.

Resources required to protect a site using a firewall are likely to vary considerably due to variations in traffic type and system load. System scalability is important. A faster CPU won't necessarily enhance performance. Sufficient RAM is critical for busy systems to perform adequately. A denial-of-service attack can be easily launched against a system with insufficient RAM. At the very least, the system should have a backlog.

Security of the DMZ

The DMZ or *demilitarized zone* of a firewall is that part of the network that does not belong to either the internal network or the Internet. This is generally the area between the Internet access router and the *bastion host.* The bastion host is a system that has been fortified against attacks. Bastion hosts may be part of the firewall.

Putting access *control lists* on the access router creates a DMZ. An access control list contains the rules that define which packets are permitted or denied passage. The access router connects your internal network with the Internet. An access router is your company's first line of defense against attacks from the Internet. Creating a DMZ allows only authorized services to be accessible by hosts on the Internet.

If a system has several services that mandate different security levels, one option is to divide the DMZ into separate zones. The effects of a security breach can be minimized by putting together hosts with similar levels of risks so that even an attacker gaining access by exploiting some bug or coming through the Web server will not be able to attack your private network if the bastion hosts are on a separate LAN.

Most organizations don't secure their Web servers strictly and allow services for Internet users that entail certain risks. Unauthenticated users might be able to run executable programs on the Web server. While this might be reasonable, it's unacceptable to run such programs on a bastion host, where the entire security mechanism can be compromised.

Services should be split up not only by host but also by network. Trust between hosts on the networks should also be limited.

Use redundant components to achieve maximum security. A single failure, such as a software bug, should not compromise the entire security mechanism. Risk from software bugs can easily be reduced by:

- Keeping up-to-date on software fix patches
- Using well-known products that have been around a while
- Running only necessary services

Organizational Policy

Which services you decide to permit and which to deny will depend to a great extent on the function of the firewall. Much depends on whether your organization's primary concern is with allowing access or with maintaining security.

When deciding which services to permit, ask:

- What effect will allowing this service have on firewall security?
- How does permitting the service affect firewall architecture?
- Will an attacker be able to exploit an inherent weakness?
- How well-known is the service?
- Is the protocol for this service published?

You may want to restrict Web access to prevent users from viewing sites not related to their work. While firewalls may be used to block access, it's relatively easy for individuals to find an alternate route to a blocked site. Site-blocking products are typically not effective. For example, inappropriate Web pages may be fetched through e-mail. It's virtually impossible to block everything.

Attackers sometime decide to launch denial of service attacks by crashing, flooding, or disrupting the network or firewall. Due to the distributed nature of networks, it's virtually impossible to prevent such attacks. For time-critical jobs on the Internet, you must have a contingency plan in case the network is attacked or its capability degraded.

FTP (File Transfer Protocol) is usually supported in firewalls by either using a proxy server or allowing connections to networks at a restricted port range. Sometimes FTP can be achieved by allowing users to download files via the Web. Telnet is generally supported by an application proxy. Configuring a router to permit outbound connections using screening rules can also support Telnet. Both Gopher and Archie can be supported through Web proxies.

The following are additional Internet sources for firewalls:

- *http://sunsite.unc.edu/LDP/HOWTO/Firewall-HOWTO.html*
- *FTP://FTP.tis.com/pub/firewalls/*
- *http://www.clark.net/pub/mjr/pubs/index.shtml*
- *FTP://FTP.research.att.com/dist/internet_security/*
- *http://www.net.tamu.edu/FTP/security/TAMU/*
- *http://www.cs.purdue.edu/coast/firewalls/*

Pretty Good Privacy (PGP)

Pretty Good Privacy (PGP) can be used to encrypt e-mail messages or sign messages digitally, thus ensuring privacy. Encrypted e-mail that is intercepted will appear to be garbage to the unauthorized recipient. Digital signatures can be used when the content of the message is not secret but the sender wants to authenticate his identity and confirm that he wrote the message. PGP has proven very effective.

PGP relies on a public key encryption scheme. With public key encryption, there is no need for a secure channel over which to share the key. The public key used to encrypt the data is readily available to the public. The decryption key is private. No one has access to it except the intended recipient.

PGP is available free for non-commercial use. ViaCrypt PGP, available for commercial use in the U.S. and Canada, costs less than $100. For the international community, commercial versions of PGP are available from Ascom Systec AG (*IDEA@ascom.ch*).

To use PGP you need two key rings, one public and one private. The public key ring holds your public key and the public keys of people known to you. The private key ring holds the secret or private key or keys.

Public key is much slower than conventional encryption. PGP combines two algorithms, RSA and IDEA, to encrypt plain text. It's essentially impossible to break the encryption algorithm using brute force. PGP's IDEA encryption scheme currently calls for a 128-bit key. This means that 2^{128} possible key combinations would be available. The fastest current technology would still take several trillion years to break the encryption scheme.

To launch a successful attack against PGP, an attacker would have to understand the mathematical transformation that takes place between plain text and cipher text. The complexity of the transformation makes it extremely difficult to solve the mathematical problem.

At present, PGP gives you three choices for key size: 512, 768, or 1024 bits. It's also possible to specify the number of bits for your key. As key size increases, encryption becomes more secure. The key size affects the program's running time during generation. A 1024-bit key takes approximately 8 times longer to generate than a 384-bit key. This is a one-time process that doesn't need to be repeated unless another key pair is generated. Only the RSA portion is affected by the key size during encryption; the main body of the message is not affected. Therefore, it's best to use the 1024-bit key size. Some versions of PGP allow key sizes up to 2048-bits. Generating such a key takes a considerable amount of time, but it, too, is a one-time process. Users running certain versions of PGP may be unable to handle very large keys.

Each time PGP is run, for enhanced security a different session key is generated. This session key is used for IDEA.

Using PGP, it's possible to apply a digital signature to a message. A trusted copy of the sender's public encryption key can be used to check the signature on the message. It's impossible for anyone else to create the signature without the secret key. This will also detect if someone has tampered with the message. Digital signature protects the entire message.

If the contents of a message are not secret, but it's essential to allow others to verify the authenticity of the sender, clear-signing digital signatures may be used. Clear signing works only on text files, not on binary files.

Key signatures authenticate that the signature really belongs to the sender and not an impostor. If the sender's key is not available but a trusted source has added his signature to the sender's key, you may infer that you have a valid copy of the sender's key. A chain of trust may be established: A trusts B, who trusts C; therefore A may trust C. PGP can be configured to specify the number of levels in the chain of trust. Be cautious in dealing with keys several levels removed from your immediate trusted source.

You may sign someone's key if you wish to inform others that you believe the key belongs to that person. Other people may rely on your signature to decide whether or not that person's key is valid.

A key-signing party is used to get together various users of PGP. The purpose is to extend the degree of trust on the Web.

If the secret key ring is stolen or lost, the key should be revoked, though if a strong pass phrase was used to encrypt the secret key ring, there is little chance of damage. Both the pass phase and the secret key ring are needed to decrypt a message. Using a backup copy of the secret key ring, a key revocation certificate may be generated and uploaded to one of the public key servers. Before uploading the revocation certificate, it's useful to add a new ID to the old key to inform others what your new key ID will be. But without a backup copy of the secret key ring, it's impossible to create a revocation certificate.

Public key servers are used to make available one's public key. Everyone can use the public database to encrypt messages for you. Although there are several public key servers, it's only necessary to send your key to one of them. It will then send your key to other public key servers. Keys may be submitted or extracted using the following site: http://pgp5.ai.mit.edu/.

Further information about PGP may be obtained from the following Internet sites:

- *http://dir.yahoo.com/Computers_and_Internet/Security_and_ Encryption/ PGP___Pretty_Good_Privacy/*

- *http://www.pgpi.com/links/*

- *http://home.epix.net/~alf/Security/*

- *http://Web.mit.edu/network/pgp.html*

- *http://thegate.gamers.org/~tony/pgp.html*

- *http://www.nai.com/default_pgp.asp*

SATAN: Security Analysis Tool for Auditing Networks

The Security Analysis Tool for Auditing Networks (SATAN) helps security administrators identify network security problems. Dan Farmer and Wietse Venema, who wrote SATAN, explain in their December 1993 paper, *Improving the Security of Your Site by Breaking Into It* (*http://www.fish.com/~zen/satan/satan-demo/admin-guide-to-cracking.html*), that they wrote SATAN because as computer systems are becoming more dependent on networks, they are thus more vulnerable to attacks via networks.

SATAN gathers information by remotely probing various services such as *finger* or *FTP* provided by a remote host or set of hosts. Potential security flaws and bugs, such as incorrectly setup or configured network services or known system bugs, are identified. SATAN's expert system may be used to further investigate potential security problems. A SATAN demo is available at *http://www.fish.com/satan/*.

SATAN consists of several programs. Each tests for a specific weakness. Additional programs may be added by putting their executable files into SATAN's main directory; these programs must have the .sat extension. The entire SATAN package, including source code and documentation, is freely available via FTP from various sites, including the following:

North America:

- *FTP://FTP.mcs.anl.gov/pub/security*
- *FTP://coast.cs.purdue.edu/pub/tools/unix/satan*
- *FTP://vixen.cso.uiuc.edu/security/satan-1.1.1.tar.Z*
- *FTP://FTP.acsu.buffalo.edu/pub/security/satan-1.1.1.tar.Z*
- *FTP://FTP.acsu.buffalo.edu/pub/security/satan-1.1.1.tar.gz*
- *FTP://FTP.net.ohio-state.edu/pub/security/satan/satan-1.1.1.tar.Z*
- *FTP://FTP.cerf.net/pub/software/unix/security/*
- *FTP://FTP.tisl.ukans.edu/pub/security/satan-1.1.1.tar.Z*
- *FTP://FTP.tcst.com/pub/security/satan-1.1.1.tar.Z*
- *FTP://FTP.orst.edu/pub/packages/satan/satan-1.1.1.tar.Z*

- *FTP://ciac.llnl.gov/pub/ciac/sectools/unix/satan/satan.tar.Z*

Australia:

- *FTP://FTP.dstc.edu.au:/pub/security/satan/satan-1.1.1.tar.Z*
- *FTP://coombs.anu.edu.au/pub/security/satan/*
- *FTP://FTP.auscert.org.au/pub/mirrors/FTP.win.tue.nl/satan-1.1.1.tar.Z*

Europe:

- *FTP://FTP.denet.dk/pub/security/tools/satan/satan-1.1.1.tar.Z*
- *http://FTP.luth.se/pub/unix/security/satan-1.1.1.tar.Z*
- *FTP://FTP.luth.se/pub/unix/security/satan-1.1.1.tar.Z*
- *FTP://FTP.wi.leidenuniv.nl/pub/security*
- *FTP://FTP.cs.ruu.nl/pub/SECURITY/satan-1.1.1.tar.Z*
- *FTP://FTP.cert.dfn.de/pub/tools/net/satan/satan-1.1.1.tar.Z*
- *FTP://FTP.csi.forth.gr/pub/security/satan-1.1.1.tar.Z*
- *FTP://FTP.informatik.uni-kiel.de/pub/sources/security/MIRROR.FTP.win.tue.nl*
- *FTP://FTP.kulnet.kuleuven.ac.be/pub/mirror/FTP.win.tue.nl/security/*
- *FTP://FTP.ox.ac.uk/pub/comp/security/software/satan/satan-1.1.1.tar.Z*
- *FTP://FTP.nvg.unit.no/pub/security/satan-1.1.1.tar.Z*
- *FTP://cnit.nsk.su/pub/unix/security/satan*

Courtney software, available free on the Internet, may be thought of as the anti-SATAN. Courtney monitors attacks from SATAN. If SATAN probes your system, Courtney notifies you and gives you a chance to trace the probe. Courtney can be downloaded from *http://ciac.llnl.gov/ciac/ToolsUnixNetMon.html#Courtney*.

Automated Vulnerability Testing

Security is compromised when controls are improperly used. Generally, it's not that controls are lacking or weak but that they aren't appropriately configured. Most computer software, for example, comes with default settings. If these settings are left unchanged, security may be compromised.

The existence of controls gives management and users the false impression that their data is secure. Assuming that the controls are properly configured, they rely on them. Many hackers exploit well-known security weaknesses. They rely on common errors made by system administrators, such as not configuring the system properly or protecting the system with the latest security patches.

While incompetence or lack of time or other resources certainly contribute to this problem, many administrators may make mistakes for other reasons. Because most systems support a wide variety of services, and the security mechanism must be flexible enough to meet the needs of a variety of users. Many users are given the power to enhance or degrade security on their own. This flexibility can often lead to security weaknesses.

Many automated tools are available to audit the computer system for security weaknesses. They can quickly examine thousands of files on a multi-user computer system and identify vulnerabilities resulting from improper use of controls or mismanagement, such as poor passwords, failure to update software with security patches, inadequate virus protection, or the ability to plant Trojan horses or worms. Such automated tools, whether bought or developed in-house, typically analyze both file content and file attributes.

Tools for testing security vulnerability are different from tools that monitor activity or detect intrusion. The latter analyze activity as it occurs. Vulnerability testing tools, on the other hand, search for potential weaknesses in order to prevent unauthorized activity.

Standalone Systems

To identify vulnerabilities in a standalone system, automated testing tools analyze shared executable files, examining among others access controls and controls used to configure the system. For example, if the access controls are compromised, a hacker may be able to masquerade as an authorized user. The configuration files and shared executable files may be used to plant a Trojan horse.

Vulnerability testing tools may be used to examine the password and access system to check, for instance, whether the passwords are long enough. Short passwords can be guessed easily using brute force. These tools can also check to see if passwords are changed periodically. Passwords should be stored in an encrypted file.

To prevent the planting of a Trojan horse program, you need to take certain precautions. Start-up files are often used to plant Trojan horses because start-up files are always executed, so they should be protected from modification and write access in a user's personal file space should be limited.

System configuration files and shared binaries must be protected. Vulnerability testing tools can check to see if modification privileges for system binaries are restricted to systems staff. Only system staff should be able to modify system start-up scripts. Secure defaults should be specified.

In a networked environment, computer systems generally share data and other resources. Security controls for access paths in networks can be reviewed with vulnerability testing tools. A network host will have the vulnerabilities not only of a stand-alone system but also of the networked system. Many systems use remote authentication, where the local host relies upon the remote system to authenticate users.

Vulnerability Testing Techniques

Vulnerability tests may audit the system or launch a mock attack. They may be passive or active, broad or narrow.

Active tests are intrusive; they identify vulnerabilities by exploiting them. In contrast, passive tests examine the system to infer the existence of vulnerabilities. An authentication system may be tested using either way. An active test may launch a dictionary attack or randomly try common or short passwords. If successful, it would log the results for review by security personnel. A *passive* test might check the protection of a password file. It may copy the password file, encrypt it, and compare encrypted strings.

Though both types of tests provide useful information, active tests are riskier than passive tests. Individual circumstances supplemented by professional judgment will guide your choice of test.

Narrow vulnerability testing programs may examine only a single vulnerability, *broad* ones the entire system. It's possible to use a series of single vulnerability tests to identify risks and vulnerabilities. While single vulnerability tests tend to be simple, they don't generally consider the complete security ramifications; they may not reveal the total effect of lack of controls. Weaknesses in multiple controls may compound the effect of the vulnerabilities.

System vulnerability tests provide better information than a series of single vulnerability tests; they make it easier to determine total risk.

Conclusion

A network is simply a set of computers (or terminals) interconnected by transmission paths. These paths are usually telephone lines; however, they may use other media, such as wireless and infrared transmission, radio waves, and satellites. The network serves one purpose: exchange of data between computers (company and individual).

Encryption must be used whenever sensitive or confidential information is transmitted. The Internet is so open that anything can be read or snatched at many locations between the originating site and the destination site. Encryption should be used not only when transmitting data but also when putting any secret or sensitive information on an Internet server.

Hackers often take advantage of common security holes to break in, as when they take advantage of a bug in a software package. It's essential to have the most current version of any software package; the most current version is likely to have the fewest bugs. Most software developers provide patches that can be downloaded to fix known security bugs.

Businesses need security for a variety of reasons. The most basic reason is that you don't want modification of data, either accidental or intentional. The more connections in your network, the more complex the system, and the greater the likelihood that security will be compromised.

Appendix 8A: Commercial Firewalls*

Product Vendor	E-mail	OS/ Hardware Platforms	Contact Information
Actane Controller Actane	info@actane.com	SNMP PC	Le California Bat D2 2, Rue Jean Andreani 13084 Aix-En-Provence CEDEX 2 FRANCE
AFS 2000 Internet Device Internet Devices	sales@internetdevices.com	-	(408) 541-1400
Alta Vista Firewall Alta Vista	-	WNT PC	-
Ascend Secure Access Firewall Ascend	info@ascend.com	PC	One Ascend Plaza 1701 Harbor Bay Parkway Alameda, CA 94502 USA (510) 769-6001
aVirt Gateway aVirt Gateway Solutions	sales@aVirt.com	PC	51 West Center, Suite 604 Orem, UT 84043 USA (800) 41-AVIRT or (801) 802-7450
BIGfire Biodata and AB Systems	sales@biodata.com.sg	-	Burg Lichtenfels D-35104 Lichtenfels, Germany Tel: ++49-6454-912070
BorderWare BorderWare Technologies	info@borderware.com	POS, PC	6695 Millcreek Drive, Unit 1 Mississauga, Ontario L5N 5R8 Europe: +44 181 893 6066 North America: 1 905 814 7900
Brimstone SOS Corporation	sales@soscorp.com	any PC	40 Broad Street, Suite 2175 New York, NY 10004 USA (800) SOS-UNIX or (212) 809-5900
Bull S.A.:Firewall and Netwall	-	UNIX/WS	-
Centri Cisco	info@cisco.com	WNT PC	170 W. Tasman Dr. San Jose, CA 95134 USA (408) 526-4000

Product Vendor	E-mail	OS/ Hardware Platforms	Contact Information
Cisco IOS Firewall Cisco	info@cisco.com	Router	170 W. Tasman Dr. San Jose, CA 95134 USA (408) 526-4000
Cisco PIX Cisco	info@cisco.com	POS	170 W. Tasman Dr. San Jose, CA 95134 USA (408) 526-4000
Citadel Citadel Data Security	info@cdsec.com	UNIX PC	Unit 3, 46 Orange Street Cape Town, 8001 South Africa Tel: +27 21 23-6065
Conclave Internet Dynamics	sales@interdyn.com	NT PC	3717 E. Thousand Oaks Blvd. Westlake, CA 91362 USA (630) 953-7706
CONNECT:Firewall Sterling Commerce	connect@sterling.com	SUN WS	4600 Lakehurst Court Dublin, OH 43016-2000 USA (800) 700-5579 or (33) 1 4417-6400
ConSeal PC Signal 9 Solutions	firewall@signal9.com	W95 PC	(613) 599-9010
COOL-FIRE Symbolic	mt@symbolic.it	-	Viale Mentana 29 I-43100 Parma, Italy Tel: +39 521 776180
CryptoSystem PyroWall RADGUARD	info@radguard.com	-	24 Raoul Wallenberg Street Tel Aviv 69719 Israel Tel: 972 3 645 5444
CSM Proxy Plus CSM-USA	Var_sales@csm-usa.com	Many PC WS	360 So. Ft. Lane Suite # 1B Layton, UT 84041 USA (801) 547-0914
CyberGuard CyberGuard Corporation	info@cybg.com	UNIX WS PC	2000 W. Commercial Blvd. Ft. Lauderdale, FL 33309 USA (954) 958-3900
Cybershield Data General	-	UNIX WS	(508) 898-5000

Product Vendor	E-mail	OS/ Hardware Platforms	Contact Information
CYCON Labyrinth CYCON Technologies	labyrinth@cycon.com	UNIX PC	11240 Waples Mill Rd., Ste. 403 Fairfax, VA 22030 USA (703) 383-0247
Digital Firewall Service Digital Equipment Corp.	email directory	UNIX WNT	United States Contact: Dick Calandrella (508) 496-8626
DEC SecurityGate for OpenVMS[*] Digital Equipment Corp.	email directory	VMS -	contacts or (508) 568-6868
Elron Firewall Elron Software	info@elronsoftware.com	POS	One Cambridge Center Cambridge, MA 02142 USA (617) 692-3000
enterWorks NetSeer Light enterWorks.com	Michael Lazar	-	19886 Ashburn Road Ashburn, VA 20147 USA (800) 505-5144 or (703) 724-3800
ExFilter V1.1.2	exfilter@exnet.com or exfiler@exnet.co.uk	SUN WS	-
FLUX EF Enhanced Firewall INS Inter Networking Systems	flux-info@ins.de	FluxOS	INS GmbH P.O. Box 101312 D-44543 Castrop-Rauxel, Germany Tel: +49 2305 101 0
Firewall-1 Check Point Software Technologies	sales@CheckPoint.com	UNIX WNT many	400 Seaport Court, Suite 105 Redwood City, CA 94063 USA (800) 429-4391
Firewall/Plus™ Network-1	sales@network-1.com Alyssa Earnhart	WNT DOS PC	(972) 606-8200 for Texas (800) 638-9751 World Headquarters
Fort Knox Firewall Device Internet Devices	sales@internetdevices.com	- PC	(408) 541-1400 x314
Freegate FreeGate Corporation	info@freegate.com	-	1208 E. Arques Sunnyvale, CA 94086 USA (408) 617-1000

Product Vendor	E-mail	OS/ Hardware Platforms	Contact Information
Gauntlet Trusted Information Systems Network Associates	tis@tis.com (us) info@eu.tis.com (non-us)	-	
GEMINI Trusted Security Firewall Gemini Computers	tft@geminisecure.com	-	(408) 373-8500
GFX Internet Firewall System GNAT Box Global Technology Associates	gfx-sales@gta.com gb-sales@gta.com	UNIX/POS PC	3504 Lake Lynda Dr., Ste. 160 Orlando, FL 32817 USA (800) 775-4GTA or (407) 380-0220
GlobeServer Data Quest Information Systems	info@dqisystems.com	LINUX PC	7509 Kingston Pike Suite 313 Knoxville, TN 37919 USA (423) 588-4757
HSC GateKeeper Herve Schauer Consultants	info@hsc.fr	-	142, rue de Rivoli 75039 Paris Cedex 01 Tel: +33 (1) 46.38.89.90
IBM Firewall for AIX IBM	peter_crotty@vnet.ibm.com	AIX WS	IBM Internet Firewall P.O. Box 12195 Mail Drop B44A/B501 RTP, NC 27709 US Tel: +1 919-254-5074
ICE.Block J. River, Inc.	info@jriver.com	UNIX PC	124 North First Street Minneapolis, MN 55401 USA (612) 339-2521
Instant Internet Deerfield Communications	info@deerfield.com	WNT, W95 PC	(517) 732-8856
Interceptor Technologic	info@tlogic.com	- PC	4170 Ashford Dunwoody Rd., Ste. 465 Atlanta, GA 30319 USA (404) 843-9111
InterLock MCI Worldcom Advanced Networks	info@ans.net	SUN WS	1875 Campus Commons Dr. Reston, VA 22091 USA (800) 456-8267 or (703) 758-7700
Inter-Ceptor Network Security International	-	-	John Shepard at (516) 674-0238

Product Vendor	E-mail	OS/ Hardware Platforms	Contact Information
IPAD 1200 Netmatrix Internet Co.	sales@ipad-canada.com	POS	Netmatrix Corporation #36001, 6449 Crowchild Tr. Calgary, Alberta Canada T3E 7C6 (403) 686-1169
IRX Firewall Livingston Enterprises	info@livingston.com sales@livingston.com	Router	4464 Willow Road Pleasanton, CA 94588 USA (510) 737-2100
Iware Internetware	Paul Singh	Novell	505 W. Olive Ave., Suite 420 Sunnyvale, CA 94086 USA (408) 244-6141
iWay-One BateTech Software	www.workgroup.co.za sales@batetech.com	WNT -	7550 W. Yale Ave., B130 Denver, CO 80227 USA (303) 763-8333
Juniper Obtuse Systems	info@obtuse.com	-	Alberta, Canada
KarlBridge/KarlBrouter KarlNet Inc	sales@KarlNet.com	Bridge/ Router	Columbus, OH USA (614) 263-KARL
Lucent Managed Firewall Lucent Technologies	firewall@lucent.com	WNT UNIX POS	480 Red Hill Road Middletown, NJ 07748 USA (800) 288-9785
MIMEsweeper Intergralis	info@us.integralis.com	WNT PC	U.K.: +44 (0) 1734 306060 US: (206) 889-5841
M>Wall MATRAnet	delplanque@matranet.com	UNIX WNT WS PC	18 rue Grange Dame Rose BP 262 - 78147 Velizy Cedex France Tel: +33 (0) 1 34 58 44 58
NetCS NetCS Informationstechnik GmbH	Oliver Korfmacher	Router	Katharinenstrasse 18 D-10711 Berlin, Germany Tel: +49.30/89660-0
NetGate™ SmallWorks	info@smallworks.com	SUN WS	(512) 338-0619
NetGuard Control Center (was Guardian) LanOptics	sales@lanoptics.com	WNT W95 PC	2445 Midway Rd. Carrollton, TX 75006 USA Tel: (972) 738-6900

Product Vendor	E-mail	OS/ Hardware Platforms	Contact Information
NetRoad/FireWARE/FireWALL Ukiah Software	-	WNT NWR PC	-
NetSafe Siemens Nixdorf	info@swn.sni.be	UNIX WS	SNS RD21 Rue de Niverlie 11 B-5020 Namur Belgium Tel: +32 (0) 81/55.47.00
Netscreen-100 Netscreen Technologies	info@netscreen.com	POS	4699 Old Ironside Drive Ste. 300 Santa Clara, CA 95054 USA Tel: (408) 970-8889
Net SecurityMaster SOLsoft SA	info@solsoft.com	UNIX WNT WS PC	4 bis, rue de la Gare 92300 Levallois-Perret France Tel: +33 147155 500
Netra Server Sun MicroSystems	-	SUN WS	SunSoft, Inc. 2550 Garcia Ave. Mountain View, CA 94043 USA (800) SUN-SOFT outside US: 1-415-960-3200
Network Systems ATM Firewall BorderGuard Network Control Facility The Security Router StorageTek Network Systems Group	webmaster@network.com	-	Tel: (800) NET INFO
Nokia IP & VPN Series Nokia Telecommunications	info@iprg.nokia.com	Router	232 Java Drive Sunnyvale, CA 94089 USA Tel: (408) 990-2000
Norman Firewall Norman Data Defense Systems	norman@norman.com	UNIX WS PS	3040 Williams Dr. 6th Floor Fairfax, VA 22031 USA (703) 573-8802
Novix FireFox	-	Novell	(800) 230-6090
Orion Zebu Systems	info@zebu.com	-	Samantha Agee (206) 781-9566

Product Vendor	E-mail	OS/ Hardware Platforms	Contact Information
Phoenix Adaptive Firewall Progressive Systems	info@progressivesystems.com	-	2000 W. Henderson Rd. Ste. 400 Columbus, OH 43220 USA (614) 326-4600
PORTUS & PORTUS-ES Livermore Software Laboratories	portusinfo@lsli.com	ALL ALL	1830 S. Kirkwood, Suite 205 Houston, TX 77077 USA (281) 759-3274
PrivateNet NEC Technologies	info@privatenet.nec.com	BSD UNIX	(800) 668-4869 Department Code: YCB
Pyramid Firewall DataTec	antoniob@datatec.co.uk	UNIX POS	650 Wharfedale Rd. Winnersh Wokingham Berkshire RG41 5TP UK Tel: 0118 925 6213
Quiotix	jbs@Quiotix.com	-	-
Raptor Axent Technologies	info@axent.com	UNIX, WNT WS, PC	2400 Research Blvd. Rockville, MD 20850 (888) 44-AXENT
SecureLan SecureAccess SecureFrame Cylink	-	-	8229 Boone Blvd., Suite 650 Vienna, VA 22182 USA (800) 449-1162
SecurIT Firewall Milkyway Networks	Info@milkyway.com	UNIX WNT WS PC	150-2650 Queensview Drive Ottawa, ON, Canada K2B 8H6 (800) 206-0922
Sidewinder, SecureZone, and Secure Computing Firewall for NT Secure Computing	sales@securecomputing.com	PC	Contact Info Worldwide Tel: +1 (408) 487-1900
Site Patrol BBN Planet Corp.	Gregg Lebovitz	-	-
SmartWall V-ONE	sales@v-one.com	-	20250 Century Blvd. Germantown, MD 20874 USA (301) 515-5200
SonicWall Sonic Systems	info@sonicsys.com	Any POS	575 N. Pastoria Ave. Sunnyvale, CA 94086 USA (408) 736-1900

Product Vendor	E-mail	OS/ Hardware Platforms	Contact Information
SPF-100/SPF-200 Sun MicroSystems	sunscreen@incog.com	POS WS, PC	Mountain View, CA 94043 USA (415) 960-3200
Sygate SyberGen	-	W95, WNT PC	-
Turnstyle Firewall System (TFS) Turnstyle Internet Module (TIM) Atlanta Systems Group	US Sales and Marketing Canada	UNIX -	USA: (516) 737-6435 CAN: (506) 453-3505
VCS Firewall The Knowledge Group	sales@ktgroup.co.uk	UNIX PC	Concorde Road Patchway, Bristol UK Tel: ++44 (0) 117 900 7500
VPCom Ashley Laurent	Jeffrey Goodwin	UNIX NT	707 West Avenue, Suite 201 Austin, TX 78701 USA (512) 322-0676
Watchguard Watchguard Technologies	sales@watchguard.com	All PC	Contacts: (888) 682-1855 or (206) 521-8340
WebSENSE NetPartners Internet Solutions	sales@netpart.com	-	9210 Sky Park Court San Diego, CA 92123 USA (800) 723-1166 or (619) 505-3020
WinGate Deerfield Communications	info@deerfield.com	WNT, W95 PC	(517) 732-8856
ZapNet! IPRoute/Secure	info@iproute.com	WNT PC	Suite 400-120, 10945 State Bridge Rd. Alpharetta, GA 30202 USA (770) 772-4567

UNIX, LINUX, WIN = Windows, W95 = Windows95, WNT= WindowsNT
POS = Proprietary or embedded operating system
WS = RISC-based workstation
PC = Intel-based person computer

Appendix 8B: Firewall Resellers

Company	Products/ Services	Email	Contact Information
ANR	NetGuard Control Center and Security consulting	info@anr.co.il	20 Admonit St. Netanya 42204 Israel Tel: 972-9-885-0480
Astra Network 0P7	Security and network consulting, Firewall installation & admin.	infosec@man.net	2633 Portage Ave. Winnipeg, MB Canada R3J (204) 987-7050
Atlantic Computing Technology USA	BorderWare	info@atlantic.com	84 Round Hill Road Wethersfield, CT 06109 (203) 257-7163
ARTICON Information Systems GmbH	BorderWare	-	-
Bell Atlantic Network Integration	Network and firewall design	sales.lead@bani.com	52 East Swedesford Road Frazer, PA 19355 USA (800) 742-2264
BRAK Systems	Firewall-1, WebSENSE and others	tony@brak.com	1 City Centre Drive, Suite 801 Mississauga, Ontario Canada L6S 4T2 (905) 272-3076
Cadre Computer Resources USA	Firewall-1, Secured ISP, Internet development	info@ccr.com	3000 Chemed Center 255 East Fifth Street Cincinnati, OH 45202 (513) 762-7350
C-CURE Belgium	Information Security Architects	luc.dooms@c-cure.be	K. Rogierstraat 27 B-2000 Antwerpen Tel: +32 (0)3 216.50.50
Centaur Commucication GmbH	Firewall-1 and others, Security cosulting	info@centaur.de	Urbanstrasse 68 74074 Heilbronn Germany Tel: +49 7131 799 0
Citadel Security Management Systems	Gauntlet, many others, and Internet consulting	infocit@citadel. com.au	726 High Street Armadale, VIC AU Tel: 03 9500 2990

Company	Products/ Services	Email	Contact Information
CleverMinds	Gauntlet, others, and security consulting	Jack Boyle	Bedford, Mass USA Tel: (781) 275-2749
Cohesive Systems	Centri Firewall Information services	info@gi.net	755 Page Mill Road Ste. A-101 Palo Alto, CA 94304 USA (800) 682-5550
Comark	Firewall-1, and others, Security consulting	webteam@comark. net	444 Scott Drive Bloomingdale, IL 60108 USA Tel: (630) 924-6700
Comnet Solutions	Shareware firewall: Midiator One	firewall@comnet. com.au	ComNet Solutions Pty Ltd Unit 4/12 Old Castle Hill Road Castle Hill, NSW 2154 Australia Tel: +61 2 899 5700
Computer Software Manufaktur (CSM)	CSM Proxy & Proxy Plus Internet Gateway with fw features	sales@csm-usa.com	P.O. Box 1105 Layton, UT 84041 USA (801) 547-0914
Com Tech Communications	Firewall-1 and others Online Security Services	rof@comtech.com.au	Australia Tel: 0412 163374
Connect GmbH	SmartWall BorderGuard NetStalker and Virus Wall	Armin Bolenius	Pichlmayrstr. 26a D-83024 Rosenheim Germany Tel: +49-8031-219820
Collage Communications	Many firewalls and network services	cyberguard@Coll Com.COM	12 Tulip Lane Palo Alto, CA 94303 USA
Comcad GmbH	Firewall-1 others, and security and network services	frank.recktenwald@ comcad.de	Industriestr. 23 51399 Burscheid Germany Tel: +49-2174-6770
Conjungi	Gauntlet	simon@conjungi.com	Seattle, Washington USA
CREDO NET	Raptor and security consulting	info@credo.net	22941 Triton Way Suite 241 Laguna Hills, CA USA (888) 88-CREDO

Company	Products/ Services	Email	Contact Information
CyberCorp	NetGuard Control Center	amuse@ cyberservices.com	2934 West Royal Lane Ste. 3136 Irving, TX 75063 USA (972) 738-6916
Cypress Systems	Raptor	rmck	P.O. Box 9070 McLean, VA 22101 USA (703) 273-2150
Data General	Cybershield and Raptor	sense@dg.com	4400 Computer Drive Westboro, MA 01580 USA (800) 4DG-OPEN
Decision-Science Applications Applications	BorderWare FireWall-1 Sidewinder and more	infosec@dsava.com	1110 N. Glebe Rd., Suite 400 Arlington, VA 22201 USA (703) 875-9600 or 243-2500
Deerfield Communications	WinGate Instant Internet	info@deerfield.com	(517) 732-8856
DFC International Ltd.	IBM Firewall	sales@dfc.com	52 Mowatt Court Thornhill, Ontario L3T 6V5 Tel: (905) 731-6449
Digital Pathways UK	Sidewinder	-	-
Dimension Data Security	Firewall-1 and security products	mouritz@ddsecurity. co.za	158 Jan Smuts Ave. Rosebank P.O. Box 3234 Parklands 2121 South Africa Tel: +27 (0)11-283-5116
DNS Telecom	SecureNet and SecurSite, Watchguard and others	preynes@dnstele com.fr	Immeuble La Fayette 2 place des vosges 92051 Paris la Difense 5 France Tel: +33 (0)1 43 34 10 17
Dynavar Networking	Ascend, Cisco PIX and many others	sales@dynavar.com	#300, 1550 - 5th Street SW Calgary, Alberta, Canada T2R 1K3 Tel: (403) 571-5000

Company	Products/ Services	Email	Contact Information
East Coast Software	NetGuard Control Center and security consulting	infotec@eastcoastsw. com.au	PO Box 6494 St Kilda Road Central, Melbourne, Victoria 3004 AUS. Tel: 61-3-9821-4848
Electric Mail	Firewall-1 and Internet products	info@elmail.co.uk	Merlin Place, Milton Road Cambridge United Kingdom Tel: +44 (0) 1223 501 333
EMJ America	AFS 2000, BorderWare and others	mrkusa@emji.net	1434 Farrington Road Apex, NC 27502 USA (800) 548-2319
Enstar Networking	Firewall-1 and security consulting	baustin@enstar.com	8304 Esters Blvd. Suite 840 Dallas, TX 75063 USA (800) 367-4254
Enterprise System Solutions	BorderWare	-	-
FishNet Consulting Services	Firewall-1, others, and security consulting	info@kcfishnet.com	7007 College Blvd. Suite 450 Overland Park, KS 66211 USA (913) 498-0711
Garrison Technologies	Security consulting, firewalls, audits, etc.	sales@garrison.com	100 Congress Ave. Suite 2100 Austin, TX 78701 USA (512) 302-0882
GearSource	NetGuard Control Center PIX	sales@GearSource.com	5015 Victor Street Dallas, TX 75214 USA (214) 821-7909
Global Data Systems	Firewalls and security	glasane@gdsconnect. com	(781) 740-8818
Global Technology Associates	GTA firewalls and security services	david@globaltech. co.uk	71 Portland Road Worthing West Sussex BN11 1QG England Tel: 44 (0) 1903 20 51 51

Company	Products/ Services	Email	Contact Information
Graphics Computer Systems	Firewall-1 and security services	sales@gcs.com.au	97 Highbury Road Burwood, Victoria Australia 3125 Tel: +61 3 9888 8522
Haystack Labs now owned by Network Associates	Stalker Intrusion detection system	info@haystack.com	10713 RR620N, Suite 521 Austin, TX 78726 USA (512) 918-3555
Herve Schauer Consultants	HSC GateKeeper	info@hsc.fr	142, rue de Rivoli 75039 Paris Cedex 01 Tel: +33 (1) 46.38.89.90
HomeCom Internet Security Services	Firewall and security sales and consulting	security@homecom. com	1900 Gallows Road Vienna, VA 22182 USA (703) 847-1702
IConNet	Internet in a Rack (IR) Network hardware and software	info@iconnet.net	-
Inflo Communications Limited	Raptor firewall and others	sales@inflo.co.uk	Mountcharles Road Donegal Town Co. Donegal Ireland Tel: +353 73 23111
Ingress Consulting Group	BorderWare and others	sales@nohackers.com	60 Guild Street Norwood, MA 02062 USA (888) INGRESS
Integralis UK Integralis USA	MIMEsweeper	msw.support@ integralis.co.uk info@us.integralis. com	U.K. +44 (0) 1734 306060 US (206) 889-5841
Intercede Ltd.	MilkyWay SecureIT	sales@intercede.co.uk	1 Castle Street, Hinckley, Leicestershire LE10 1DA UK Tel: +44 (0) 1455 250 266
INTERNET GmbH	BorderWare consulting	Ingmar Schraub	Am Burgacker 23 D-69488 Birkenau Germany Tel: +49-6201-3999-59
Jerboa	Independent security and firewall consulting	info@jerboa.com	Box 382648 Cambridge, MA 02238 USA (617) 492-8084

Company	Products/ Services	Email	Contact Information
Kerna Commuications Ltd.	Security consultants, firewall installation and support	sales@kerna.ie	3 Arbourfield Terrace, Dundrum, Dublin 14 Ireland Tel: +353-1-2964396
The Knowledge Group	VCS Firewall and Security products	sales@ktgroup.co.uk	Concorde Road Patchway, Bristol UK Tel: +44 (0) 117 900 7500
LANhouse Communications	Ascend, Centri Firewall, Gauntlet and security consulting	sales@lanhouse.com	510 King Street East Ste. 202 Toronto, Ontario, Canada M5A 1M1 Tel: (416) 367-2300
LURHQ Corporation	Security consulting, firewalls, Web server security	info@lurhq.com	P.O. Box 2861 Conway, SC 29526 USA (843) 347-1075
Madison Technology Group	Security/FW design & implementation	Steveng@microlan. com	331 Madison Ave. 6th Floor NYC, NY 10017 USA (212) 883-1000
Master Software Technology	AltaVista and CS consulting	sales@masteredge. com	92 Montvale Ave. Stoneham, MA 02180 USA (617) 438-8330
media communications eur ab	Gauntlet security consulting	neil@medcom.se	box 1144 111 81 stockholm, Sweden Tel: +46.708.432224 (GSM)
Mergent International	Gauntlet security consulting	info@mergent.com	(800) 688.1199
Midwest Systems	Gauntlet Sidewinder VAR	lschwanke@midwest-sys.com	2800 Southcross Dr. West Burnsville, MN 55306 USA (612) 894-4020
MPS Ltd.	M>Wall and security consulting	johnt@mpsuk.com	The Manor Stables Great Somerford Nr Chippenham Wiltshire SN15 5EH England Tel: +44 (0) 1249 721414

Company	Products/ Services	Email	Contact Information
NetGuard	NetGuard Control Center	solutions@ntguard. com	11350 Random Hill Road Ste. 750 Fairfax, VA 22030 USA (703) 359-8150
NetPartners Internet Solutions	WebSENSE, Firewall-1, Raptor, and others	sales@netpart.com	9665 Chesapeake Dr. Suite 350 San Diego, CA 92123 USA (800) 723-1166 or (619) 505-3020
Netrex	Secure Internet Solutions Firewall-1	info@netrex.com	3000 Town Center Suite 1100 Southfield, MI 48075 USA (800) 3.NETREX
Network Associates	Gauntlet and many security products	contacts	3965 Freedom Circle Santa Clara, CA 95054 USA (408) 988-3832
Network Security	Firewall-1, NetScreen and others	info@nsec.net	369 River Road North Tonawanda, NY 14120 USA (716) 692-8183
Obtuse Systems	Juniper	info@obtuse.com	Alberta, Canada
Breakwater Security Associates	Many firewalls and security consulting	info@breakwater.net	(206) 770-0700
Orbis Internet	Sidewinder and security consulting	dan@orbis.net	475 Cleveland Ave. North Ste. 222 St. Paul, MN 55104 USA (612) 603-9030
Qualix	Firewall-1 and security products	qdirect@qualix.com	177 Bovet Road, 2nd Floor San Mateo, CA 94402 USA (650) 572-0200
Racal Airtech Ltd	Raptor Security services	Sohbat Ali	Meadow View House Long Crendon, Aylesbury Buckinghamshire, UK HP18 9EQ Tel: 01844 201800

Company	Products/ Services	Email	Contact Information
Racal Gaurdata	Raptor Security services	Sohbat Ali	480 Spring Park Place Suite 900 Herndon, VA 22070 USA (703) 471-0892
Reese Web	Raptor	pp001261@ interramp.com	Rocky Point Harbour 3309 Diamond Knot Circle Tampa, FL 33607 USA (813) 286-7065
Sandman Security of Smoke N' Mirrors Inc	Firewall-1 Raptor and others	Ben Taylor	1165 Herndon Pkwy. Suite 200 Herndon, VA 20170 USA (703) 318-1440
Sea Change Pacific Region	BorderWare	jalsop@seachange. com michael@seawest	5159 Beckton Road Victoria, British Columbia V8Y 2C2 (604) 658-5448
Sea Change Europe Ltd UK	BorderWare	jalsop@seachange.com peter@sea-europe.co.uk	470 London Road Slough, Berks SL3 8QY, Tel: 44-1753-581800
Secure Network Systems	Many firewalls and security and network consulting	info@blanket.com	Lawrence, Kansas USA
SecureXpert Labs FSC Internet Corp	Security consulting and information FireWall-1 and others	security@securexpert.com	--
Serverware Group plc	iWay-One	sale@serverwr.de.mon. co.uk	Tel: (44) 1732-464624
Sherwood Data Systems Ltd	Karl Bridge/Karl Brouter	sales@gbnet.com	High Wycombe, UK Tel: +44 (0) 1494 464264
Silicon Graphics	Gauntlet and Security	Sales	39001 West 12 Mile Rd. Farmington, MI 48331 USA (800) 800-7441
Siemens Nixdorf	TrustedWeb	info@trustedweb.com	Fitzwilliam Court Leeson Close Dublin 2, Ireland

Company	Products/ Services	Email	Contact Information
SkyNet Czech Republic	Gauntlet	Roman.Paklik@ SkyNet.CZ	Kabatnikova 5 602 00 Brno Czech Republic Tel: +420 5 41 24 59 79
SMC Electronic Commerce Ltd	Gauntlet, many other FWs, and security consulting	info@smcgroup.co.za	52 Wierda Rd West Wierda Vally, Sandton South Africa Tel: +27 11 2694005
Softway Pty Ltd	Gauntlet and security consulting	enquiries@softway. com.au	P.O. Box 305 Strawberry Hills, NSW 2012 Australia Tel: +61 2 9698-2322
Stallion Ltd.	Firewall-1 and security services	stallion@stallion.ee	Mustamae tee 55, Tallinn 10621, Estonia Tel: +372 6 567720
Stonesoft Corporation	Stonebeat and Firewall-1	info@stone.fi	Taivalm=E4ki 9 FIN-02200 Espoo, Finland Tel: +358 9 476711 Tel: +358 9 4767 1282
StorageTek Network	ATM, NCF, BorderGuard	webmaster@network.com	Tel: (800) NET INFO
Sun Tzu Security	Firewalls and security consulting	info@suntzu.net	Tel: (414) 289-0966
Symbolic	COOL-FIRE and security services	mt@symbolic.it	Viale Mentana 29 I-43100 Parma, Italy Tel: +39 521 776180
Technology Management Systems	BlackHole	tmsinc@erols.com	Vienna, VA 22181 USA Tel: (703) 768-3139
Technology Transition Services	Fort Knox Firewall and security consulting	sales@techtranserv.com	100 Blue Run Rd. Indianola, PA 15051 USA
Trident Data Systems	SunScreen Firewall-1 and security consulting	Anthony Dinga (east) Bob Hermann (west) Charlie Johnson (midwest)	5933 W. Century Blvd. Suite 700 Los Angeles, CA 90045 USA Tel: (310) 645-6483

Company	Products/ Services	Email	Contact Information
Tripcom Systems	Firewall-1 and Internet consulting	Adam Horwitz	Naperville, IL USA Tel: (708) 778-9531
Trusted Information Systems	Gauntlet	tis@tis.com (US) info@eu.tis.com (non-US)	Tel: (301 854-6889 or (410) 442-1673
Trusted Network Solutions	Gauntlet and security consulting	-	Johannesburg, South Africa
UNIXPAC Australia	Raptor and network consulting	info@unixpac.com.au	Cremorne, Australia Tel: (02) 9953 8366 or 1 800 022 137
Uunet	Raptor and others security consulting	info@uu,net	3060 Willliams Drive Fairfax, VA 22031 USA (800) 488-6383 or (703) 206-5600
Vanstar	All major security products and consulting	Jrecor@vanstar.com	30800 Telegraph Rd. Suite 1850 Bingham Farms, MI 48312 USA (810) 540-6493
We Connect People Inc.	Security FWs, Internet consulting and more	sales@wcpinc.com	California, USA (408) 421-0857
WheelGroup	NetRanger/NetSonar, intrusion detection and other security products	sales@wheelgroup.com	13750 San Pedro Suite 670 San Antonio, TX 78232 USA (210) 494-3383
X + Open Systems Pty Ltd	Security FWs and network services	info@xplus.com.au	P.O. Box 6456 Shoppingworld North Sydney, NSW 2059 AU Tel: +61 2 9957 6152
Zeuros Limited	Raptor and network services	les@zeuros.co.uk	Tudor Barn, Frog Lane Rotherwick, Hampshire, RG27 9BE, UK Tel: 44 (0) 1256 760081
ZONEOFTRUST.COM	Security products, FWs and services	info@zoneoftrust.com	22941 Triton Way 2nd Flr. Laguna Hills, CA 92653 USA (714) 859-0196

Appendix 8C: Public Domain, Shareware, etc.

* **Drawbridge**
  Available at *net.tamu.edu*

* **Freestone by SOS Corporation**
  Freestone is an application gateway firewall package, a genetic derivative of Brimstone produced by SOS Corporation. Freestone can be retrieved from the Columbia, SOS, and COAST FTP sites

* **fwtk - firewall toolkit**
  Available from ftp.tis.com Look in /pub/firewalls and /pub/firewalls/toolkit for documentation and toolkit.

* **ISS**
  Internet Security Scanner is an auditing package that checks domains and nodes searching for well-known vulnerabilities and generating a log for the administrator to take corrective measures. For information, history, and the commercial versions by the originator, visit: *www.iss.net*. For the publicly available version, I have no current ftp site, but you might try various search engines.

* **Mediator One**
  Non commercial shareware firewall.

* **router-config tool**
  A set of KornShell scripts (known to run cleanly on UnixWare and Solaris, and with very minor tweeking on SGI's but doesn't run with pd-ksh) to build the very complex router configurations needed for high-quality packet-filtering firewalls (only generates configs for Cisco, though there are facilities for adding other router types). Software is available from the Freebird Archive.

* **SOCKS**
  The SOCKS package, developed by David Koplas and Ying Da Lee. Available by ftp from ftp.nec.com. Also see: *www.socks.nec.com*

*The source of this appendix is *www.waterw.com/~manowar/vendor.html*. Please check this web site for the latest information.

Chapter 9*
LEGAL ASPECTS OF
E-COMMERCE

Introduction

As new technologies proliferate, the laws of e-commerce are in a state of flux. Entrepreneurs and technicians who work with e-commerce must therefore operate with a degree of uncertainty.

This chapter does not purport to give legal advice. Only an attorney specifically familiar with your situation can do that. But as a participant in a commercial transaction, you must generally know the legal environment in which you operate. The purpose of this chapter is to review the legal issues that should concern entrepreneurs, technicians, and consumers who participate in e-commerce.

Jurisdiction

The business owner on Main Street, whose commercial dealings are usually with local residents, can bring matters like nonpayment of bills to local courts, which often have Small Claims divisions for the expeditious resolution of low-value disputes. Which tribunal has jurisdiction over customers or suppliers in other states or countries is not always so simple or inexpensive to decide.

When a court can exercise jurisdiction over persons and transactions has been the subject of complex analysis. Internet-based transactions

---

* This chapter was written with Kenneth H. Ryesky, adjunct assistant professor, accounting and information systems, Queens College, CUNY; member of the bar, New York, New Jersey, and Pennsylvania; B.B.A., Temple University: M.B.A., La Salle University; J.D., Temple University; M.L.S., Queens Collge CUNY; Attorney at Law, East Northport, NY.

have resulted in novel applications of traditional theories of jurisdiction, as well as a reassessment of the traditional bases for finding jurisdiction.

The entrepreneur is similarly affected by jurisdictional issues when an Internet transaction goes amiss. The mere posting of information on a Web site, without more, would generally provide little if any basis to invoke a particular court's jurisdiction. At the other extreme, the formation of a contract with a party in a given state would generally give the courts of that state jurisdiction over the contractual relationship. Transactions that cross international boundaries invoke even more complex jurisdictional issues, and are often subject to treaties and other international agreements.

This chapter is concerned only with contracts; jurisdiction in Internet-related torts or crimes is far too complex a topic to be treated adequately in this work.

Contracts

A contract is one or more mutual promises that the law will enforce. Manifestation of mutual assent by the contracting parties to an exchange and consideration has long provided the legal basis for virtually every business transaction, large or small. Though the laws of contract have remained essentially the same for many centuries, the legal system has been able to apply them successfully to new communications technologies.

The Internet is remarkable for the almost instantaneous speed at which it transmits information. The time lags inherent in older methods of communication gave rise to rules of contract law that are no longer necessary in the age of the Internet. Accordingly, rules like the old "mailbox rule," which made an acceptance effective upon its deposit into a mailbox, is all but obsolete.

Though some of the old contract rules are clearly obsolete, a consensus has yet to be formed as to just which rules do apply. Accordingly, any Internet offer you make would do well to specify definite terms and conditions for its acceptance. For example, an e-mail offer might specify that the recipient (the "offeree") can accept the terms of the offer via e-mail, and the e-mail acceptance is effective as soon as it is transmitted.

One basic feature of the Internet that has gained nearly universal familiarity is the use of the mouse-click of a "button" at a Web site. Accordingly, a Web site can provide for acceptance of contract terms by clicking a button clearly marked as an acceptance. By giving the Web site visitor the option of clicking "I Accept" or "I Do Not Accept," there is less room for a claim of ambiguity by the person considering the offer. Make your Web site offers and acceptance options as unambiguous as possible.

Many federal agencies (especially the Department of Defense) actually require vendors to submit offers and quotations via the Internet. Thus, e-commerce has become the sole means of access to much of the government contracting that has long sustained many entrepreneurs.

Intellectual Property

While tangible property like jewelry, automobiles, buildings, or furniture is the product of human physical labor, intellectual property is the intangible product of the human mind. Though intangible, intellectual property can be quite valuable. The drafters of the U.S. Constitution recognized the great value of intellectual property, especially in the Useful Arts clause in that great document, so that federal government would be empowered to issue patents and copyrights to protect intellectual property. Advances in technology since the Colonial period have given rise to varieties of intellectual property that were unknown to the Founding Fathers, but these are nonetheless given protection (and therefore, value) by virtue of the Useful Arts clause.

Intellectual property is arguably the one area of the law that has been most profoundly affected by the Internet. The great paradox of the Internet is that its most salient feature - the ease, speed, and accuracy of information transfer—poses the greatest possible threat to the integrity of intellectual property and requires owners of intellectual property to take greater pains to protect their interests.

The Internet and its underlying digital technology have further expanded the forms intellectual property might assume. With this, more potential pitfalls for the Internet entrepreneur have arisen. As an example, a single Web site might feature text or music in which an author or composer has a copyright; a logo or name that's registered as a trademark; and the photo or likeness of a well known individual that might be subject to personality rights. If the same site contains information improperly obtained from another Web site, there may also be infringement of a trade secret. Unauthorized use of these intellectual properties can entangle the site operator in costly and protracted litigation. Even the domain name can raise infringement concerns if it's similar to an established trademark or trade name; mere registration of a Uniform Resource Locator (URL) is no guarantee against infringement.

On the other hand, intellectual property rights owned or licensed to a Web site operator and rightfully used on the Web must be protected. Adequately protecting these rights can go well beyond the familiar notices of copyright or trademark; it might entail Web site access controls such as passwords, verification of the identity of the Web site accessor, and contractual clauses specifically delineating the permitted and prohibited uses of the intellectual property. Copyright, trademark, and trade name owners who know that their intellectual property is being infringed are often compelled to take legal action against the infringer, lest their intellectual property lose its value.

Privacy and Security

The Internet is not an inherently secure medium for communication. Electronic communications can be copied and recorded in computer storage at any of the numerous relay points through which an electronic message typically passes between sender and recipient. Anything that would cause embarrassment if printed on the front page of a newspaper should not be said in cyberspace!

Moreover, it's axiomatic that wherever money passes from one hand to another, information is also passed. The technologies that make e-commerce possible can extract, process, analyze, and transmit information in ways never before envisioned. All this raises personal privacy concerns.

Several federal laws address privacy issues in e-commerce, among them the Electronic Communications Privacy Act (ECPA). Violations of the ECPA can bring both criminal and civil penalties. Under the ECPA, it generally is illegal to intercept an electronic communication without the consent of the sender. Many states also have laws related to privacy in electronic communications.

A significant amount of so-called "adult material" is being sold in e-commerce. Under any circumstances, the sale of such material raises complex constitutional issues, such as the conflict between free speech concerns on one hand and the need to protect children on the other. These issues are surely complicated by e-commerce. Those who traffic in "adult material" would do well to be especially mindful of the ages and identities of those to whom they sell their wares, as parents, legislators, and community leaders strive to regain rightful control over children's exposure to undesired influences.

Even common, seemingly non-controversial, business transactions carry privacy concerns when transacted through electronic channels. Customers are rightly concerned about how merchants will use information like their names and identities. Accordingly, entrepreneurs who market their goods and services through e-commerce channels should enforce policies to safeguard customer information.

Other privacy concerns arise with regard to the employer-employee relationship. The same Internet connections that facilitate e-commerce also enable an employee to send and receive personal communications. E-commerce entrepreneurs who employ others should have clear policies about personal communications.

Such policies are not always simple and straightforward. As a practical matter, totally banning personal communications by employees often harms the interests of both employer and employee. An employee required by workplace rules to make personal communications over the pay telephone in the lobby will often extend that excursion to include a stop at the rest room, the cafeteria, a designated smoking area, or friend's desk. Permitting the same employee to use a desk computer to e-mail messages to a spouse can certainly help the employer's productivity picture.

On the other hand, employees should have no privacy expectations for personal communications conducted over company facilities. It's generally not unreasonable for the employer to declare that all communications via company facilities to or from an employee are subject to the employer's scrutiny. A sound and consistent policy about personal e-mails would be given great deference by the courts, while failure to promulgate any policy can leave the employer vulnerable to lawsuits by disgruntled employees and former employees.

Advertising on the Internet

The commercialization of the Internet has brought numerous advertising opportunities. The operators of many Web sites, especially those that provide free services such as Web search engines or electronic mail, depend largely if not solely upon advertising revenues to defray their expenses.

Requirements such as truth in advertising apply to the Internet as they would to any other advertising medium. Moreover, governmental regulation that applies to advertising in connection with specific products or services also applies to the Internet. Thus, those who use the Internet to market regulated goods or services such as financial securities, controlled medications, tobacco, insurance, automobiles, or loans must make sure their advertising complies with the law.

Unsolicited commercial electronic mail, popularly known as "spam," is one of the most controversial issues associated with e-commerce. The

Federal government and increasing numbers of states now seek to regulate spam. Though it's not clear what the regulations will eventually be, you can safely presume that there will be significant regulation that will subject the careless or unscrupulous spammer to at least civil and possibly criminal sanctions. If you use unsolicited e-mail as an advertising medium, tread with extreme caution. More and more angry spam recipients are asserting their legal remedies against spammers, with growing success.

The basic problem with spam is that while the cost to the sender is negligible, the cost to the unsolicited and involuntary recipient can be substantial. The recipient's expenses go far beyond paying for the time it takes to download the mail. A spam message, if overly verbose, can crash the recipient's computer. If a recipient's electronic mailbox at the ISP has capacity limits, unwanted spams can easily overload it, displacing more valuable correspondence.

The problem is aggravated when the unsolicited e-mail message contains a virus, or when a child receives unsolicited electronic e-mail that contains "adult" material or links to "adult" Web sites. Contrary to the self-serving assertions they commonly carry, "chain letter" and other pyramid-type electronic mail schemes are in fact illegal and also exacerbate the spam problem.

In view of the spam legislation now in process, if you want to use unsolicited e-mail, take some precautions:

1. The message must not contain any false or misleading information, including information about the identity of the sender or about the precautions taken against sending unwanted e-mail.

2. The message should not be overly verbose or so heavily formatted that it takes up large amounts of data storage space on the recipient's computer.

3. The message must have viable provisions for recipients to remove their names from the sender's mailing list at no cost to them. Thus, a "click here to be removed" hyperlink would not be acceptable because recipients at their own cost must actually be logged onto the Internet in order for such a thing to be effective. A telephone number that costs the recipient to dial is similarly unacceptable, as is a postal address that requires the recipient to use a postage stamp. The only acceptable name removal provision would be an e-mail address or perhaps a toll-free telephone number available 24 hours per day. Note that having name removal provisions is not

sufficient; the name must actually be removed from the mailing list when the recipient uses the option.

4. The mailing list used by the spammer must be screened. There are a number of Web sites that filter a prospective spammer's e-mail list; use them

5. The entrepreneur who uses a professional spammer (sometimes known as a "spamhaus") to send its electronic mail runs the risk of being sucked into litigation on account of the spamhaus's errors, omissions, or misdeeds, so check it out carefully first.

Notwithstanding these precautions, be aware that there are those who advocate a total ban on unsolicited commercial e-mail, and that their numbers and strength are growing. It's entirely possible that the entrepreneur who chooses to advertise via electronic mail might soon have the burden of proving that the recipient in fact solicited the e-mail or that there was a prior business relationship. Be sure to maintain documentation of consents or of prior business relationships.

Conclusion

Commercial laws have already begun to accommodate the Internet. They have already followed the practices of trailblazing Internet entrepreneurs when such practices are reasonable and conducive to good faith.

A vast opportunity awaits those who possess the prudence, foresight, and fortitude to properly deal with the uncertainty and risk inherent in the technical and legal environment of e-commerce. The savvy entrepreneur who is mindful of the legal issues in e-commerce stands to gain by the prudent exploitation of these business opportunities.

Chapter 10
TAXATION OF
E-COMMERCE

Tax policy will be a major factor in the success of e-commerce. If new taxes are imposed and regulations increase, the benefits and potential of e-commerce may be curtailed. This chapter considers the tax implications of e-commerce, with particular attention to the Internet Tax Freedom Act.

Because of the enormous commercial potential, state and local governments are examining ways to tax both ISPs and transactions occurring in cyberspace. At present, the federal government has chosen not to enact federal taxes, but some state and local governments are taxing Internet commerce. State tax officials are examining current laws to determine how goods and services bought across state borders should be taxed.

The area of taxing e-commerce is ambiguous, confusing, and unsettled. Because Internet commerce is intangible, there are presently no tax rules. When taxation of e-commerce varies by state, ascertaining what's taxable and who's responsible for paying those taxes becomes complex. Depending on the state you're in, e-commerce may be taxed as a telecommunications service, an information service, a computer service, or some combination. Confusing and overlapping tax laws may cause double taxation as well as multiple reporting and compliance problems. Many businesses may not even know if they are even subject to sales and transaction taxes for what they sell over the Internet.

The Internet Tax Freedom Act

The Internet Tax Freedom Act says that cyberspace will be a tax-free zone for most transactions for the three-year period after the act is enacted, giving state and local governments time to come up with a consistent set of rules concerning Internet taxation.

235

The purpose of the Act is to have neutral tax treatment of economic activity, electronic or otherwise. There will be tax-free Internet access. The act provides for a review panel and a moratorium on new state and local Internet taxes. It treats sales of merchandise on the Internet like phone or mail order transactions.

The act blocks taxes on information, but eight states (Connecticut, Iowa, Ohio, New Mexico, South Dakota, North Dakota, Wisconsin, and Tennessee) that already tax Internet access could have those taxes grandfathered if the states affirm within a year their intent to tax Internet access. But "bit taxes" representing fees on e-commerce tied to the volume of digital information transmitted would be barred.

Supporters of the act believe that tax exemption is essential to the growth of e-commerce. They feel that multiple taxes imposed on some customers by local governments will inhibit technology growth.

Even if a category of services is taxable in a state, a specific type of transaction may be exempt from the sales/use tax. Some exemptions that may apply to otherwise taxable transaction are the component services exemption, sales of financial transactions, sales to an individual customer, sale for resale, and personalized data. Even though certain states may exempt electronic services from taxation, such services may be taxable when the customer receives tangible personal property as part of the transaction. An example is the downloading of magazines coupled with the print version being sent. Also note that exemptions may be less available for inputs bought to provide taxable electronic services.

The Internet Tax Freedom Act makes no discrimination for Internet use. It protects against new tax liabilities for sellers or buyers in e-commerce transactions. This includes the imposition of taxes on out-of-state vendors based on "nexus."

Nexus means the seller has a significant physical presence in the jurisdiction where the buyer takes delivery. Under the due process clause of the Constitution, there must be a minimum connection between a state and the person, property, or transaction it wants to tax. Under the commerce clause, a tax is legal only if it applies to an activity with substantial nexus with the state imposing the tax. The physical presence of the taxpayer or its agents, employees, or property will usually mean a taxable connection with the state. The Supreme Court has ruled that some type of physical presence is required for nexus.

States are expanding their nexus claims. To establish nexus, the rules require activities like owning, leasing, using, or maintaining real or tangible personal property in a jurisdiction, or having employees in the state.

But some states have stretched their interpretations of these rules to include such factors as interest in intangible property (e.g., software license), use of a collection agency, use of the public telephone system, etc.

It would be very difficult and tricky to establish nexus in transactions over the Internet. The seller may not know the buyer' location, and therefore whether sales tax is due. Further, the seller may be located anywhere in the world, so the taxing jurisdiction of the seller may be difficult to determine.

A possible scenario illustrating the difficulty might be the following: A seller is located in California. The software product is stored on a computer server in Illinois. The customer lives in Virginia but is accessing the information while in New York. While many states identify the sale of services as where the customer uses the service, that locality may not be easily ascertainable by the seller. Further, the apportionment of sales may be difficult because sales taxes are transaction-oriented rather than income-oriented.

Internet access cannot be taxed as an information service. However, information provided over the Internet would still be susceptible to sales taxes if the service provider has a significant physical presence in the taxing locality. "Significant presence" includes having many sales representatives physically in the locality to obtain new customers or provide personal services.

The act prohibits Internet access services being treated and taxed as a telecommunications service. However, it does not affect taxes on the phone service between either the user's home and the local switch or on the phone lines leased by the ISP to enable Internet usage. Internet services are considered distinct from traditional voice phone services.

Various kinds of taxes are not affected by the Internet Tax Freedom Act, among them the usual business income taxes assessed by state and local governments, rationally allocated license taxes, local property taxes, franchise charges assessed against local cable TV firms, taxes on telecommunications common carriers, sales taxes that are not discriminatory, and taxes assessed against ISPs acting as consumers of merchandise. Telecommunications via local telephone, cellular phone, satellite transmission, or cable transmission are subject to tax in most jurisdictions. In general, states taxing telecommunications services are charging for transmission only, not for the information content itself. However, some states like Ohio treat the electronic transmission of information content as a taxable service.

There is confusion as to what is a "transmission." Telephone calls and cellular communications are clearly transmissions, but are enhanced services like Internet access, e-mail, bulletin boards, packet switching, and ATM transactions considered transmissions that would be subject to the sales tax? These enhanced services involve some additional linkage or value-added aspects, such as temporary storage of messages on a computer server. In the many states that do not have a clear position, businesses must guess whether value-added services are included within the definition of telecommunications.

Under federal regulatory definitions, a basic transmission service is a transmission between or among points without change in the form or content of the information sent and received. Examples include local and long distance phone calls. But an "enhanced" service is one offered over a telecommunications network in which computers process and manipulate data. Under the narrow definition of telecommunications, some states impose a sales or use tax on basic transmission services only. However, jurisdictions like Florida and New York are trying to expand this into a broader definition of telecommunications so as to tax a wider range of value-added or enhanced information services.

Merchandise taxable in a retail store or in a catalog would still be taxable on the Internet. The bill is designed to prohibit discrimination against the Internet, not to give it a tax preference.

The act takes the position that free trade on the Internet is global. The United States therefore takes a strong position that foreign countries should have a similar policy of Internet free taxes, unrestricted trade barriers, and no tariffs.

Information about the tax aspects of e-commerce may be obtained by accessing *http://www.taxweb.com.*

In summary, the act will prohibit state and local taxes that discriminate against the Internet. It does not prohibit all sales and use taxes on e-commerce, but state and local taxes may be assessed only if the tax is similar to that imposed on traditional transactions such as through mail order or phone. For example, an out-of-state vendor who would be constitutionally protected against a sale or use tax on a traditional sale is similarly protected for sales over the Internet. Under the act state and local government will continue to collect normal business and property taxes from retailers and ISPs.

Even if a transaction is subject to a sales or use tax, the seller who has no nexus (contacts or connections) with the taxing jurisdiction has no obligation to collect or forward the tax. Typically, a state can impose taxes on interstate transaction only if the seller has sufficient nexus.

In conclusion, the act would help businesses cut costs and be able to reach a wider market.

Most states have a tax on income obtained from business activities, including e-commerce, but states vary in determining where the corporate income is earned. Most states have an apportionment formula based on some rational allocation such as property, sales, or payroll. The sales factor is the one usually most relevant for e-commerce purposes.

Some online services such as America Online do not collect state and local taxes on subscriber fees because they are of the opinion that they are not legally required to do so. However, they do collect such taxes in foreign countries to protect themselves. Some online services advise subscribers that they may be responsible for all charges incurred, including taxes. For obvious reasons, all ISPs are actively supporting the ban on taxes we have discussed.

Chapter 11
ASSURANCE SERVICES

Consumers are very concerned about privacy and protection of personal information such as credit card numbers, social security numbers, and prior buying history. Assurance services establish criteria for independent verification of e-commerce transactions. Standards established by the American Institute of CPAs' CPA Web Trust, eTrust, and the Better Business Bureau (BBB) Online relate to the company and its business practices. These services assess the controls in place to assure the reliability and accuracy of transactions, determining whether data is secure and protected from misuse.

CPA Web Trust

The CPA (or CA) Web Trust evaluates commercial Web sites to determine if they satisfy standards set by the American Institute of CPAs (AICPA) in the United States and the Canadian Institute of Chartered Accountants (CICA) in Canada. CPAs and chartered accountants are licensed and treated the same way for the purposes of this assurance service.

The number one priority with consumers is security of their personal and financial information when they buy goods or services online. The CPA Web Trust informs prospective customers that a CPA has appraised a Web site's policies and controls and that the site conforms to standard practices. Key factors are examined for consistency, quality, and appropriateness.

The major areas examined by The CPA Web Trust are:

241

- *The protection and security of data.* Does the Web site operator have workable policies and controls to assure that consumer information is protected from misuse? Privacy protection is enhanced when the business entity's servers use up-to-date technology to encrypt customer information. However, reports do not always reflect the workings of the server. The CPA must assess for each site its encryption process, digital IDs, and socket securing. Is the system secure? Content integrity is crucial, particularly because of viruses and software counterfeiting.

- *The integrity of transactions.* Does the Web site operator use effective controls for customer orders? Are orders processed fully and correctly? Are the terms of sale and amount billed correct? Transactions must be accurate, validated, complete, identified, and timely. It's positive, for instance, when the seller sends a customer a confirming e-mail after the order is placed. Web Trust helps to minimize fraud on the Internet.

- *Disclosure of business practices.* Does the Web site operator appropriately disclose its business policies for handling transactions? Are e-commerce transactions with customers executed in accordance with those policies? How good is customer service? How long does it take to fill an order? The site should list its shipping and problem resolution policies. In effect, the site must specify how it will handle online transactions. The CPA does not assess the products or services themselves, the return policy, or any warranties. Some sites that businesses use to provide e-commerce are hosted elsewhere. The corporate policies of virtual servers hosting the site must be verified.

To protect online and other information dealing with e-commerce, here is what you can do:

- Keep an environment conducive to meaningful control to protect customer data.

- Constantly monitor your procedures to make sure they're working. If your business is deviating from the procedures or policies you've set, take immediate corrective action.

- Keep control of transmissions of private customer information over the Internet to prevent their reaching unexpected or unintended recipients.

- Prevent unauthorized outsider access to restricted areas and their contents. A customer who accesses the Web page should be restricted to customary activities, such as making inquiries, executing transactions, and obtaining information about transactions.
- Do not disclose private customer information to parties unrelated to your business unless the customer has given permission or has been notified when giving the information that such disclosure would be made.
- Prevent improper access to the customer's computer and its content. Do not modify, store, or copy data on a customer's computer without express permission.
- Do not allow your employees to use confidential customer information unrelated to their duties.
- Install safeguards to assure that viruses are not transmitted to a customer's computer.

The following are ways to protect against misuse of customer information in e-commerce:

- Protect data once it reaches your business.
- Properly store, modify, and copy data on the customer's computer.
- Get the express permission of customers to use information for purposes other than those for which it was given.
- Encrypt and guard private customer data like credit card numbers.

The CPA Web Trust seal of the AICPA and the CICA is an assurance of quality and appropriateness for e-commerce. CPAs and CAs have a reputation for integrity, trust, and objectivity. The seal assures consumers that those Web sites to which the seal is granted are reliable, accurate, and honest, and keep consumer information confidential. To display the seal, the Web site must satisfy all CPA Web Trust Criteria. Web Trust engagements fall under AICPA statements on standards for attestation engagements. Web Trust is an international program.

Veri Sign, a provider of digital authentication services including certificates, manufactured the CPA Web Trust seal to be hard to forge and revocable if the entity does not maintain its standards. (Veri Sign is discussed in detail below.)

Veri Sign digital identification shows Web users that sites are representing themselves properly. Consumers who want to make sure a site is certified can click on the seal and access a Veri Sign Web page to confirm the entity's status. By clicking on the seal the consumer may also access the CPA's report and the CPA Web Trust principles and criteria.

A digital signature on content distribution also assures users of the quality of downloaded content. Veri Sign will issue for a site a Secure Server ID for the Web Trust Program. There are about 35,000 Veri Sign Secure Server IDs for Web Commerce.

Web Trust officials are extending their standards to conform with privacy protection guidelines formulated by the Online Privacy Alliance (OPA), a coalition of American businesses established to promote safeguards and support self-regulation, and the European Union (EU). The EU has its own privacy protection rules, which may limit e-commerce between Europe and non-complying U.S. companies. OPA and EU guidelines require businesses to post notices on their Web sites of the types of personal information they are gathering electronically, and how the information will be used.

Only CPAs who have been licensed to perform Web Trust examinations may do so. You can find a list of licensed CPAs at *www.cpaWebtrust.org*. To provide this attestation service, a CPA must:

- Be a member of the AICPA.
- Be licensed to do this service.
- Attend a special seminar.
- Be subject to quality inspection.

To become certified, the CPA should be competent in such areas as firewalls, communication protocols, hardware security devices, and server technology. They should also have proper malpractice insurance coverage.

To get the seal, the business must be able to show that for at least two months and usually more:

- Its controls have been operational and effective.
- It has maintained an environment with effective controls in place.
- The site is monitored framework to assure that business practices are kept current.
- It has been executing transactions in conformity with its disclosed e-commerce business practices.

At a minimum, to verify that standards are being maintained, the CPA must examine each site quarterly, and dynamic Web sites more often.

The CPA may facilitate his review by giving the company a self-assessment questionnaire so it can evaluate its online system, including the control environment, and how it processes orders. CPAs working with Web Trust can also get assistance from ISPs.

The electronic Web Trust Seal of Assurance attached to the Web site provides a level of assurance but is not a guarantee. If the Web site has satisfied Trust criteria, the CPA issues a report that it is in compliance. The report (see Exhibit 11.1) clarifies what is or is not covered. To get the seal, the report must be unqualified. The business must post the online auditor's report.

Exhibit 11.1: Independent Accountant's Web Trust Report

To The Management of ABC Company:

We have examined the assertion by the management of ABC Company (ABC) on its Web site for electronic commerce (at www.ABC.com) during the period January 1, 2000 through March 31, 2000, ABC:

- disclosed its business practices for EC transactions and executed transactions in accordance with its disclosed business practices,

- maintained effective controls to ensure that customers' orders placed using EC were completed and billed as agreed, and

- maintained effective controls to ensure that private customer information was protected from uses not related to ABC's business in conformity with the AICPA/CICA Web Trust Criteria (hot link)." ABC's management is responsible for its assertion (hot link to management's assertion). Our responsibility is to express an opinion on management's assertion based on our examination.

Our examination was made in conformity with standards set by the AICPA. Those standards require that we plan and conduct our examination to obtain reasonable assurance that management's assertion is not materially misstated. Our examination included (1) obtaining an understanding of ABC Company's EC business practices and its controls over the processing of EC transactions and the protection of related private customer information, (2) selectively testing transactions executed in accordance with disclosed business practices, (3) testing and appraising the operating effectiveness of the controls, and (4) performing such other procedures as we considered necessary in the circumstances. We believe that our examination provides a reasonable basis for our opinion.

Because of inherent limitations in controls, errors or fraud may exist and not be detected. Further, projections of any evaluation of controls to future periods are subject to the risks that controls may become inadequate due to changes in conditions or that the effectiveness of such controls may deteriorate.

In our opinion, ABC management's assertion for the period January 1, 2000 through March 31, 2000 is fairly stated, in all material respects, in conformity with the AICPA/CICA Web Trust Criteria.

The CPA Web Trust seal of assurance on ABC's Web site for EC constitutes a symbolic representation of the contents of this report and it is not intended, nor should it be construed, to update this report or provide any additional assurance.

XYZ CPA Firm   _____
Address   _____
Date   _____

Thus the CPA's report should at a minimum:

- State to whom the report is directed.
- Set out management's assertion.
- Enumerate the purpose of the engagement, the subject matter, and the time period covered.
- Discuss the responsibilities of management and the CPA.
- Cite the relevant standards.
- Make a conclusion about the work performed, including any reservations.
- Indicate the period covered and the date of the report.
- Provide the name and address of the CPA firm.

Each CPA Web Trust site is linked to a directory of all sites having the seal of approval. The public can access the criteria and principles set forth by the CPA Web Trust as well as the reports issued. For more information about the Web Trust, access *http://wwwaicpa.org/Webtrust/*

index.htm or *http://www.cpaWebtrust.org* or e-mail to Web-
Trust@aicpa.org (see Exhibit 11.2).

If the CPA later believes that the seal should be withdrawn from a
Web site, the CPA will so instruct the business and Veri Sign and will send
Veri Sign a seal display authorization removal notification. In any case
the seal cannot be displayed past its expiration date.

A business that wants to see if its Web site meets Trust criteria for
business controls and practices can call in a consultant to evaluate the site
before asking for a Trust appraisal.

Veri Sign

Veri Sign provides technical support and helps to secure online transactions and Internet, Intranet, and Extranet applications. Veri Sign specializes in digital encryption.

Among the electronic credentials Veri Sign provides are:

- Personal IDs to secure e-mail and Web site access.

- Server IDs to secure e-commerce and communications.

- Code signing and developer toolkits.

- Enterprise solutions for corporate or government services.

Veri Sign and Microsoft together provide digital signatures and IDs
to validate the origin and integrity of downloaded applications and to digitally authenticate products and services. Content signing using digital
IDs and digital signatures helps prevent security breaks caused by downloaded software, including viruses, attacks, and counterfeit publishing.

A digital certificate issued by Veri Sign or another trusted third party
is issued only after background checks of the business or individual.
Public-key cryptography is used to bind the owner's unique digital key
into a record that is digitally signed by the issuing agent.

Veri Sign has four assurance levels of digital IDs for business people
and consumers wanting secure transactions and communications plus an
assurance level for secure Web Servers.

Exhibit 11.2: Online Information for CPA Web-Trust

E-Commerce Will Be More Trustworthy

- Consumer and Developer Site for CPA WebTrust
- AICPA Launches Electronic Commerce Seal - 9/16/97 Press Release
- Streaming Video Overview of WebTrust as Presented to the Press on 9/16/97
- WebTrust Principles and Criteria (HTML Version)
- Download WebTrust Principles and Criteria
  (Please allow 1 minute to download entire file with a 28.8 kbps modem.)
- CPA WebTrust Fact Sheet
- Attitudes Toward Web Research (Yankelovich Partners Research)
  This information can also be viewed as a slide show. First, download the Microsoft
  Powerpoint Animation Publisher and begin the slide show.

- Register Now for WebTrust Seminars
- Discuss WebTrust Online in our Assurance Services Forum
- Complete Report from the AICPA Special Committee on Assurance Services
- Questions?: E-mail webtrust@aicpa.org
- Frequently Asked Questions (FAQs)
  - General FAQs
  - Practitioner FAQs
  - Client FAQs

Press Contacts

AICPA
Dave Dasgupta 212/596-6111
Dan Mucisko 212/596-6110

Ruder Finn
Joanne Jordan 212/715-1627
Yin Chang 212/593-6305

WebTrust in Action

View sample Web pages
with the *WebTrust* seal.

AICPA

The AICPA is the national professional organization of CPAs with more than 331,000 members in public
practice, business and industry, government and education.

Exhibit 11.2: Online Information for CPA Web-Trust , *Cont'd*

LINKS IN THE WEBTRUST SUB-SITE:

- WebTrust Main Page
  - WebTrust Fact Sheet
  - WebTrust Principles and Criteria
    - Business Practices Disclosure
    - Transaction Integrity
    - Information Protection
  - WebTrust Demonstration Site
  - Client FAQ About WebTrust
  - General FAQ About WebTrust
  - The WebTrust Certification Seal

  NEWS RELEASES:

  - Bennett Gold News Release
  - CICA News Release
  - Internet Casino Announcement

More about WebTrust...

- American Institute of CPA's WebTrust Program
  AICPA detailed Information from their Website
- WebTrust Principles and Criteria
- WebTrust in Action View sample Web pages with the WebTrust seal.
- The CPA Connection - Small business advice, tax information and how
  to find a CPA.

The company has two new digital IDs for software publishers, one for individual publishers and one for commercial publishers. Both types check the publisher's identity through a third party and require the publisher to attest that it will not knowingly publish malicious code. The commercial digital ID further attests that the publisher is financially sound. Veri Sign also has digital signing services for developers interested in the turn-key method to secure signing.

For more information, call (650) 961-7500 or browse *http://www.verisign.com/*.

eTrust

eTrust certifies that merchants like online retailers on the Internet may be trusted by consumers. eTrust issues digital certificates and signatures for those merchants meeting its criteria standards. This assurance standard is supported by Ernst and Young because the firm believes it is more focused on privacy; it has been installed on about 300 business sites.

The Better Business Bureau (BBB)

Better Business Bureaus (BBB) are private nonprofit entities supported mostly by membership fees paid by businesses and professional groups in a given geographic area. There are about 130 BBBs in the United States and about 20 in Canada.

BBBs keep files on many businesses in their areas and some outside. BBB service areas can be found by entering a ZIP code online. The Web page for the nearest BBB will be displayed. BBB Online is being promoted by Hewlett-Packard. *www.hp.com.*

The objectives of a BBB are usually to assure that members provide quality products and services, promote customer education, engage in ethical activities, are reliable and honest, and regulate themselves.

Membership in a BBB has the following benefits:

- BBB decal, plaque, and certificate evidencing membership, giving the business greater credibility with consumers
- Customer referrals through a BBB service line or its literature.
- A "hotline" about companies, products/services provided, and professional advice. However, the BBB does not endorse any specific company, product, or service.

- Alternative dispute resolution (ADR) for responding to complaints and fostering customer goodwill.
- Listing on the Internet at reduced rates.
- Tax-deductible membership fees.

For BBB membership your company must:

- Pay the fees.
- Provide background data about the business and its principals.
- Furnish information about your business activities, reliability, and reporting.
- Have been in business for at least six months unless one of the principals previously operated a business with a satisfactory record, the business is a branch of a company that has met BBB standards, or the business has made a Pledge to Arbitrate or set up an ADR pre-commitment program with the Bureau and is not in a business that has had many complaints against it.
- Sign the membership application.
- Have outstanding against it no government actions related to consumer fraud or poor customer relations.
- Conform to BBB standards for advertising, promotion, and sales.
- Comply with any BBB arbitration findings.
- Cooperate with any voluntary self-regulation within your industry.
- Attempt to eliminate the causes of customer complaints.
- Meet federal and local licensing and bonding requirements.
- Respond quickly to any complaints forwarded by the Bureau.
- Make a reasonable effort to resolve customer complaints consistent with good business practice.
- Update information with the BBB annually.
- Do not use the logo of the BBB improperly, as for sales, advertising, or commercial purposes, without prior approval.

Some regional BBBs may have additional requirements.

BBB reports are issued on all businesses, members or nonmembers, that receive a lot of consumer inquiries or complaints; if there is no BBB report on a particular company it means one or more of the following:

- Business activities have been minimal.
- Complaints against the business are non-existent or minimal.
- It's a new business.

Information in BBB reports, which typically cover three years of business activity, include:

- Nature and type of business.
- How long the company has been in business.
- How many years the BBB has been evaluating the business.
- Whether the company has a dispute resolution program.
- Frequency, nature, and pattern of complaints, if any.
- Whether federal or local government agencies have taken any actions against the company and their results. (For example, has the company been fined by the Federal Trade Commission or a state Attorney General?)
- Whether the company is a member of the BBB.

Two BBBs make their reports available in separate databases online, the one covering Eastern Massachusetts, Maine, and Vermont, and the one serving the Metropolitan New York, Mid Hudson, and Long Island Regions.

Conclusion

The Web Trust evaluates the security, privacy, and sound business practices of Web sites, providing independent third party verification. Participants in the Web Trust Program are entitled to display the seal on their sites with a digital identification and expiration date. There is a link from the Web site to the Trust's report. The Web Trust seal assures consumers that they are "safe" online. The seal is revocable if the business at any time stops complying with Web Trust criteria. Federal Trade Commission guidelines may also apply.

Veri Sign helps to authenticate downloaded applications and content. The company concentrates on digital authentication products and services. Its digital certificates promote secure software distribution over the Internet.

ETrust is particularly popular with online retailers.

A Better Business Bureau report is issued on many businesses. As a consumer you should look at the report on a company before doing business with it.

In general, eTrust and BBB Online are less costly and faster to obtain for most businesses than WebTrust.

Chapter 12*
ESTABLISHING A PRESENCE ON THE WEB

Domain Names

A domain name is the part of the Internet address that is unique to you. It identifies your business and is used by others to access your web site. As an example, if the Internet address is "*http://www.yourcompany.com*," the portion that follows the "www." is the domain. The suffix ".com" stands for "commercial"; it denotes that the address belongs to a business or industry. Other suffixes found in North American domain names are:

- .edu—for degree-granting colleges and universities.

- .gov—for agencies and branches of the U.S. government.

- .us—used for state and local governments in the United States.

- .net—for entities that are part of the Internet's infrastructure. Intended for use by network information centers (NICs), network operations centers (NOCs), administrative computers, and network node computers. The .net suffix is used worldwide.

- .org—for nonprofit organizations.

---

*This chapter was authored by David Erlach, Ph.D., J.D., computer consultant and assistant professor of accounting and information systems at Queens College.

International Domains

Domain names for entities located outside North America generally do not end with .com, .edu, or .gov. The domain names for these organizations end with a two-letter suffix identifying the country of origin. For example, the Internet address *http://www.mycompany.ca* indicates that the site owner is based in Canada. Other international suffixes include:

Argentina	.ar		Israel	.il
Australia	.au		Italy	.it
Austria	.at		Japan	.jp
Bolivia	.bo		Liberia	.lr
Chad	.td		Netherlands	.nl
China	.cn		Nigeria	.ng
Finland	.fi		Pakistan	.pk
France	.fr		Russia	.ru
Greece	.gr		Spain	.es
Hong Kong	.hk		Switzerland	.ch
Iceland	.is		Trinidad/Tobago	.tt
India	.in		United Kingdom	.uk
Indonesia	.id		Vietnam	.vk
Ireland	.ie		Western Sahara	.eh

Registering the Name

InterNIC is the domain registrar, offering registration services and maintaining a central database of all Internet addresses and their registrants. InterNIC services are performed by Network Solutions Inc., in Herndon, Virginia (*http://www.internic.net*). InterNIC works with domain administrators, network coordinators, ISPs and a variety of other users.

Network Solutions registers names and generates domain zone files for the Internet community. Network Solutions also helps users with policy and monitors the status of their registration requests.

Before registering a domain name, you need to see if that name has already been appropriated. This is where the WHOIS searchable database maintained by Network Solutions comes into play. Among other information, WHOIS lists domain names and the contacts associated with them for the .com, .edu, .net, and .org domains. You can use WHOIS not only to ascertain whether the name you want is available but also to find out who owns other names.

Domains are registered online on the web site or via an FTP archive. New registration data is installed into the Domain Name System (DNS) root servers daily. Users not previously registered are given records in the WHOIS registry of applicants. (See Exhibit 12.1.)

Exhibit 12.1: The InterNIC Registration Process

1. Registrant fills out application.
2. Registrant e-mails application to hostmaster at InterNIC.
3. Request is acknowledged and assigned a tracking number.
4. Application is checked for errors.
5. InterNIC checks the WHOIS database to verify that the requested domain is available.
6. Application is processed and the registrant is notified via e-mail.
7. Information for the new domain is added to InterNIC's WHOIS database.
8. InterNIC bills registrant for the domain registration.
9. Registrant pays invoice.
10. InterNIC sends registrant a renewal notice 60 days before the two-year anniversary of the initial registration.

However, for the typical business owner, domain registration directly with InterNIC is *not* possible because it requires a primary and a secondary server system. The requirement for this technology precludes most business owners from direct registration with InterNIC.

Using an ISP for Registration

You must therefore use an ISP to register a domain name. This is quite simple. The ISP site will have a search form that allows you to verify that the name you want is available, and you will typically be asked to provide:

1. Full name of contact.
2. Company name

3. Company description

4. Address

5. Telephone contact

6. Fax contact

7. Valid e-mail address

8. Web site password

9. Credit card information

10. Electronic signature of a licensing agreement.

The ISP will tell you what it will charge you for its domain registration service and should clearly inform you that you will get a bill directly from InterNIC in the amount of $70 for the first two years of domain registration.

Chapter 13*
WEB SERVERS

A Web server is a program housed in a remote computer that processes information requests for pages on the Web. Every page on the Web is stored on a server that is connected to the Internet 24 hours a day. A server has special software that allows pages to be "served" to the Internet user when the user types in the URL, the address of the document on the Web. This has three basic steps:

1. The user enters the Web address to which access is desired.

2. The Web browser connects the user to a particular computer on the Internet, and asks that computer's Web server for the selected site.

3. The server sends the requested documents to the user's computer using HTTP.

If you rent space on someone else's server, you must acquaint yourself with the search tools it makes available to clients. If you set up your own server, a variety of software packages allows you to control your Web site's capabilities.

Netscape FastTrack Server 3.01

The Netscape FastTrack Server 3.01 is easy to use. It allows you to set up a Web presence quickly, regardless of the level of sophistication of your Web site. Because FastTrack Server 3.01 is bundled with Netscape Communicator 4.0 or Netscape Navigator Gold, it's simple to create Web content and publish it (send it to a remote server) with the One Button

---

*This Chapter was authored by David Erlach, Ph.D., J.D., computer consultant and assistant professor of accounting and information systems at Queens College.

Publish feature without having to relinquish performance, security, or hardware choice. FastTrack Server 3.01 is built for individuals or small businesses that need an easy way of creating and publishing Internet documents.

FastTrack Server 3.01 provides automatic installation so you can get started in minutes. It allows point-and-click creation of HTML documents, and drag-and-drop insertions of multimedia documents. FastTrack Server 3.01 also provides document templates for the first time user.

Integrated log analysis tools provide-one click access to reports such as total hits, most popular pages, total bytes transferred, and source of HTTP requests, as well as summary analysis of the user agent and referrer fields.

Exhibit 13.1: Security Features in FastTrack Server 3.01

1. Restricted access to data stored on the server.
2. Encrypted information transfer between server and Web client.
3. Access control to directories, documents, and applications via authentication based on user name/password pairs.
4. Secure Sockets Layer (SSL) 3.0 Internet channel security.
5. Client authentication.
6. Support for 40-bit encryption.

Netscape Enterprise Server: A Step above FastTrack

Netscape Enterprise Server allows organizations to be more productive by letting them manage, process, locate, and share information over the Web. Because users manage their own content, the information systems department traffic jam for obtaining Web information is significantly reduced.

Companies building Web sites and Web-based business applications can use the strengths of Enterprise Server, which can develop and maintain intricate content.

Enterprise Server is designed for businesses running complex Web installations. Users of FastTrack Server should consider upgrading to Enterprise Server whenever:

1. Multiple users publish to the same server.
2. End users desire search capabilities on the server.

3. End users need a way to manage content.

4. It's necessary to administer multiple servers centrally.

5. The server must process distributed high performance database applications.

The following features can be found in Enterprise Server but not in FastTrack Server:

End User Content Management

- Netshare Web publishing, revision control, access control, agent services, and link management
- Search capabilities
- Custom views

Centralized Administration

- Cluster management (simultaneous management of multiple servers)
- SNMP-based monitoring

Advanced Information Management Application Services

- Native database connectivity to Informix, Oracle, Sybase, and IBM DB2 (Fast Track provides ODBC connectivity only)
- Object database connectivity (ODBC), a standard that enables Web browsers to communicate with a variety of database applications
- Java servlets
- CORBA and IIOP-based applications

Microsoft Windows Internet Information Server

The Microsoft Windows 2000 Server provides Web services via its Internet Information Server (IIS), which has Active Server Pages that can combine HTML, scripts, and reusable ActiveX server components to create Web-based business solutions. Microsoft FrontPage and full-text searching are fully integrated into the operating system. Crystal Reports, included with IIS, let you create presentation-quality reports and integrate them into database applications. It can be used to create high-quality Web sites, administer your network, increase system scalability, and maintain comprehensive security. IIS offers: (1) application services, (2) Web services, and (3) network services.

Application Services

• Crash Protection allows users to run multiple applications reliably on the Web server, even if a particular application crashes. The failed application will restart with the next request.
• Transactional Active Server Pages (ASP) allows applications with components and scripts to perform multiple actions, with all actions engaged together, or none at all. This is crucial for database applications.
• Script Debugging makes it easier to develop ASP applications.
• Integrated Message Queuing provides an easy way for applications to send and receive messages over a network.
• Support for Java includes a set of Java classes to build server-side components.

Web Services

• Total Content Control can configure the Web server on a per server, per site, per subdirectory, per virtual directory, or per file basis for maximum flexibility.

• Content Management and Site Analysis features custom error messaging, PIC ratings, basic log file, and content analysis, to monitor usage patterns and visualize site structures.

• Multiple Web Sites supported on a single IP address lets organizations provide hosting services to multiple Internet sites.

• Internet Standards incorporates HTTP 1.1 for increased Internet performance, issuing and managing X.509 digital certificated, and sending messages to standard NNTP news and SMTP mail servers.

• Automated Management Support lets you write scripts and execute them at the command line using objects, so you can coordinate various management tasks. Sample scripts are included; they can be customized.

Network Services

By integrating the Web server with the base operating system, Windows 2000 Server and IIS provides businesses with a solid platform for managing Web and application services.

- Setup is easy; you have a choice of components you may wish to install. Unattended installation capability lets you install IIS on multiple servers without having to monitor the installations.

- Management administration tools include a Windows-based management console, enhanced browser-based administration, command line scripting, and programmable interfaces for building customized management tools. Configuration rollback functionality lets you bring a server back to previously saved configurations.

- Security integrates a certificate server with the Windows 2000 Server security model, letting you issue and manage Internet standard X.509 digital certificates. Also, using Server Gated Crypto Technology, international banks can offer the strongest encryption (128 bit) for online transactions.

- The Search Engine lets you develop custom search forms with Active Server Pages, ActiveX Data Objects, and SQL queries to search for data on the Web server.

Chapter 14*
A REVIEW OF HTML EDITORS

Hypertext Markup Language (HTML) is the computer language used to create electronic documents on the World Wide Web. HTML uses coding tags to structure a Web page. The following is a review of selected HTML editing software.

Adobe Pagemill

Main Features

WYSIWYG (what you see is what you get) Interface. Common functions occur on a button bar or by pull-down menus. WYSIWYG lets you see your Web page the way visitors to your site will see it.

Drag-and-Drop Feature. Web pages can be created either by typing in text or by dragging and dropping contents from other software applications. Animation, movies, and sounds can be added.

Tables. PageMill lets you use tables that include images, text, and video; you can also cut and paste spreadsheets from other software applications. Table support lets you select and control table and cell heights and specify alignment, border, spacing, width, and padding.

Adobe PhotoShop LE image editing software is included with PageMill. Use Photoshop to correct colors, create logos, apply filters for special effects, icons, buttons, and background textures.

---

*This Chapter was authored by David Erlach, Ph.D., J.D., computer consultant and assistant professor of accounting and information systems at Queens College.

265

Ready-to-Use Elements. PageMill includes thousands of Web-ready images, animations, and customizable templates.

Managing Your Site with PageMill

Site Overview. View your Web site's resources at a glance in a Windows Explorer or Mac OS Finder display. Links are automatically updated when files are renamed or rearranged.

Errors Directory. When you load your site, PageMill will automatically analyze it and report errors in an "errors" directory, allowing you to correct references.

Built-in HTML Editor. PageMill provides an integrated source code editor so you can add and format HTML directly.

Built-In Uploader. When you're ready to post your site, you can transfer it directly to the Web with the built-in FTP Uploader, which will also changes, to any Web server.

E-commerce. With a built-in link, Open Market ShopSite Express software secures e-commerce transactions from your Web site. ShopSite Express creates a shopping cart for your customers on your site.

How to Get It

PageMill is available for Mac or Windows for US$99 in the United States and Canada. Call 1-800-411-8657 to locate the store nearest you or check the Adobe Web site, *www.adobe.com.* If you have an earlier version, the upgrade is priced at US$49.

Microsoft FrontPage 2000

Tools for Creating Web Sites

Pre-Designed Themes. Choose from over 60 new pre-designed business-ready Themes to provide a consistent look for a page or an entire Web site. Custom Themes can be used for logos, colors, graphics, and bullets.

Cross-Browser HTML Animation Effects. The Web page animation effects are designed to work seamlessly with Netscape Navigator 4.0 and Microsoft Internet Explorer 4.0.

Color Tools. Choose Web-safe colors for graphics and text or custom colors from a color picker.

Pixel Precise Positioning and Layering. Page elements can be placed anywhere with absolute and relative positioning.

HTML Editing

HTML Source Preservation. HTML created in other tools can be brought into FrontPage without modifying the code, tag and comment order, or capitalization.

Personalized HTML Formatting. You decide how you want your code indented, what colors the tags will appear in, when to capitalize, and when to use optional tags.

Reveal Tags in WYSIWYG View. You can see which HTML tags create which effects by selecting Reveal Tags in a page while still in Normal (WYSIWYG) View.

Database Integration

Database Publishing. Create and update a Microsoft Access database that FrontPage automatically creates.

Database Results Wizard. Even if you have no database experience, you can incorporate database queries directly into your pages.

Web Technology

Pre-Built Web Components. Insert advanced functionality into your Web pages through the Category Component and Office Web Components.

Microsoft Script Editor. Edit and debug scripts including JavaScript and VBScript.

Automatic Hyperlink Fix-Up. When you rename or move a page in a FrontPage-based Web site, hyperlinks are automatically adjusted.

Publishing Features

Page-Level Control. You can decide which pages are to be uploaded to the server by making pages as "do not publish," or by publishing only pages that have changed.

Create Web Pages Anywhere. You do not need access to a Web server to create Web content. Your site can be created on your hard drive or on a Personal Web Server and then published to a server when ready.

Publish Anywhere. Publish to a server using the built-in FrontPage

FTP whether or not the server has FrontPage Server extensions installed.

Progress Indicator. This feature makes it easier to monitor the publishing process as it's happening.

Collaboration Features

Nested Sub-Webs. You can set rights to the Web as a whole and set specific rights to subgroups so you have total control of subsites.

Check In/Check Out. Use this feature to reserve a file in the FrontPage-based Web so that no one else can edit it.

Multi-User and Remote Authoring and Management. All members of a team can add content to FrontPage-based Web sites at the same time.

Pricing and Availability

More information can be found at www.microsoft.com. The street price for FrontPage 2000 is US$149/CD$239. If you live elsewhere, consult your country's Office Web site for availability and pricing information.

Net Objects Fusion 4.0

Basic Characteristics

NetObjects Fusion (NOF) API. With API you get an expanded Java application programming interface; the introduction of NetObjects or third-party components or feature sets is seamless.

Database Access. NOF wizards can be used to design applications that connect to databases or application servers without programming. A drag-and-drop feature can also be used to place components for live database connectivity.

E-commerce Components. Elements that connect to an iCat Commerce Online server can be dragged and dropped onto the NOF layout editor.

Site Structure Editor

Site Import. NOF supports a wide array of HTML table tags. The layout of any Web site that you import is kept consistent with the original site.

International Character Sets. The requisite character set for a page or a series of pages can be specified in Site view.

Layout Editor

Table Tools. Tables can be created any way you want. Merge and split cells; resize cells, rows, and columns; apply font and other attributes; and enter custom HTML for a cell, a row, or a column.

JavaBean Tool. This tool lets you place JavaBeans on the page, access their parameters, and attach actions to them.

Go Menu Component. You can add a drop-down menu with items that are dynamically linked to other pages in the site without JavaScript coding. Site visitors will select from the drop-down menu to go to the linked page.

Ad Banner Component. Display advertisements and other graphics on your Web pages without any JavaScript coding. You pick the images, transitions, rotation times, and the URLs; NOF does the rest.

Rich Text Format Conversion. NOF supports pasting or dragging and dropping RTF files, especially those containing tables.

International Features. Besides character sets you can specify time, date, and number formats; spelling dictionary; and character set guidelines for importing HTML pages.

HTML Publishing Control

Additional HTML Output Methods. The HTML generated by NOF can be tailored for a specific browser. You can also choose either tables or Cascading Style Sheet Positioning (CSSP) and Layers for cross-browser compatibility.

Control over Generated HTML. There's ample user control over the look and content of generated HTML. You can place specific information in the HTML, including custom Meta tag information and descriptive comments.

Incremental Publishing. You can publish all or part of a page instead of republishing the entire site each time a change is made.

Prices and Availability

NetObjects Fusion 4.0 is available worldwide; check the *Purchase* section of the Web site, *www.netobjects.com*. You can also get NetObjects Fusion 3.0i International in French, German, Italian, Spanish, and Brazilian Portuguese; check the *International* section of the Web site.

In the United States NOF 4.0 costs US$299.95. Registered North American users of NOF 2.0 and 3.0 can upgrade for US$99. The estimated price for NOF 4.0 for international customers is US$335.

Home Site 4.0

Features and Benefits

Three-Way Development. You can switch from coding HTML, DHTML, SMIL, and JavaScript (Edit View) to working in a higher-level visual development environment (Design View) to checking the site in an internal browser (Browse View).

Create and Edit HTML. You can access features like Tag Insight, Tag Completion, pre-built templates, Tag Inspector, Tag Tree, Tag Snippets, thumbnail image preview, and color coding. Wizards are included for Frames, Tables, Projects, JavaScript, etc. Style Editor creates and edits Cascading Style Sheets.

Search and Replace. This includes support for both wild cards and regular expressions.

Site Visualization. The Site View feature gives you a hierarchical view of the full Web site, and integrates the link verification and document weighing quality control features.

"Pure HTML"

Code Preservation. HomeSite maintains the integrity and formatting of HTML pages; it does not add code to the HTML page other than what is necessary for display through a browser. When you open existing Web pages, HomeSite will not re-write any of the HTML code.

Quality Control Tools. These include link verification, spell checking, document weighting, and HTML validation.

One-Step Deployment System

Integrated FTP. FTP is built into HomeSite for uploading and download-ing site files.

Project Management. HomeSite lets you import entire Web sites, centralize file management, and publish incrementally where only new files and files that have changed are uploaded to the server.

Prices and Availability

HomeSite 4.0 Electronic is US$89; HomeSite 4.0 Packaged is US$99 (the Packaged version includes a CD-ROM and printed User Guide; the electronic version includes a User Guide in HTML). The electronic upgrade is $US29; the CD-Rom is US$39. For more information, visit www.allaire.com

Other Products

Other software products for HTML and other Web applications include:

Product	Information
Symantec Visual Page 2.0	*www.symantec.com*
GoLive CyberStudio	*www.golive.com*
ImageStyler	*www.adobe.com*
Macromedia Dreamweaver 2	*www.macromedia.com*
SilverStream 2.0	*www.silverstream.com*
Splash! Web Author	*www.gosplash.com*
Chili!ASP	*www.chilisoft.com*
IBM WebSphere Studio	*www.ibm.com*
Macromedia Flash 3	*www.macromedia.com*
ColdFusion 4.0	*www.allaire.com*

Chapter 15*
WEB SITE HOSTING SERVICES

Hosting is the provision of Internet services so that the user need not maintain sophisticated computer hardware with a line to the Internet. A host is a company that provides a user desiring a web presence with computer space along with other web services.

This section reviews a sampling of ISPs that host web sites.

Dynamic Web Internet Services
www.dynamicweb.ca/hosting
1-888-WEB-HOST
1-416-362-5550
(Prices in US dollars)

	Liteweb	Corpweb	Proweb
Monthly	$24.95	$49.95	$99.95
Memory	40mb	100mb	250mb
Hits	unlimited	unlimited	unlimited

Other Features

FrontPage extensions, real audio/video, shopping cart, e-mail, toll-free telephone support, SSL encryption.

Range

International (any country suffix).

---

*This Chapter was authored by David Erlach, Ph.D., J.D., computer consultant and assistant professor of accounting and information systems at Queens College.

273

E-commerce features

1. Secure, on-line, real-time processing of credit card purchases
2. RT/OL delivery of electronic receipt and authorization to customer.
3. Delivery of consumer orders for merchant fulfillment.
4. Draft capture and settlement of Visa and MasterCard transactions.
5. Electronic funds transfer to merchant bank and other accounts.

RapidSite United Kingdom
www.rapidsite.co.uk/features.html
The Quadrangle
44 Atalanta Street
London SW6 6TU
sales@rapidsite.co.uk 011-44-171-610-3992
(Prices in UK pounds)

	Pers.	Pro.	Corp.	Comm.	Enterp.
Monthly fee	17.95	24.95	47.95	74.95	179.95
1 time set-up	19.95	19.95	29.95	29.95	49.95
Data transfer	600mb	2000mb	3000mb	4000mb	5500mb
Disk storage	20mb	30mb	50mb	75mb	100mb
POP3 accounts	5	10	20	30	40
E-mail options	10	20	30	40	50
Domain registr.	*	*	*	*	*
Unlim. e-mail	*	*	*	*	*
Unlim. FTP updates	*	*	*	*	*
Control panel	*	*	*	*	*
Web stats	*	*	*	*	*
Raw log file access	*	*	*	*	*
FrontPage ext.	*	*	*	*	*
CGI-local directory	-	*	*	*	*
Anonymous FTP	-	*	*	*	*
Excite! search	-	*	*	*	*
True Speech server	*	*	*	*	*
Volcano chat	-	*	*	*	*
MSQL dBASE sup.	-	-	*	*	*
Shopping cart	-	-	*	*	*
SSL secure server	-	-	*	*	*

Crusoe Internet Services
Cherry Tree House, 7 Dean Street
Marlow, Bucks
2L7 3AA, United Kingdom
www.crusoe.com/uk/web/hosting.htm
(Prices are in UK pounds and do not include VAT)

Web Space Accounts
(*www.crusoe.com/yourname*)

	Monthly	Quarterly	Annually
1mb	5.45	16.35	58.86
5mb	7.95	23.85	85.86
10mb	10.95	32.85	118.26
20mb	13.45	40.35	145.26

Virtual Domain Accounts
(*www.yourname.com*)

	Monthly	Quarterly	Annually
5mb (Unix-based only)	19.95	59.85	215.46
20mb (Unix or NT-based)	26.95	80.85	291.06

Additional items:

	Monthly	Quarterly	Annually
20 mb web space	9.95	29.85	107.46
E-mail box	2.95	8.85	31.86
User account (TELNET & FTP)	2.95	8.85	31.86
Real Audio (5 streams)	13.45	40.35	145.26

Web World Ireland
20 Knocklyan Heights
Templeogue
Dublin 16, Ireland
011-353-1-495-1112
sales@webworld.ie
(Prices are in Irish pounds)

All plans include unlimited traffic and unlimited e-mail forwarding.
Plan A 10 mb hosting space   15.00/month
   1 e-mail account

Plan B 25 mb hosting space   20.00/month
    1 e-mail account
Plan C 50 mb hosting space   25.00/month
    1 e-mail account
Plan D 250 mb hosting space   30.00/month
    3 e-mail accounts
Plan E Unlimited hosting space   35.00/month
    5 e-mail accounts
    Web site marketing

LFC Hosting
3126 Assiniboine Avenue
Regina, Saskatchewan S4S 1E3
Canada
http://lfchosting.com
support@loosefoot.com
306-584-3968
(Prices are in US dollars)

Loose Foot Computing describes itself as a web hosting service for small businesses that includes everything necessary to conduct secure electronic commerce. There is no minimum contract.

Services include

Private or parked domains Microsoft Windows NT
SSL secure service access 24 hour TelNet access
24 hour FTP access   Web page stats
CGI-BIN w/perl 5.x installed FrontPage extensions
10 POP3 e-mail accounts Raw log file access
Shopping cart software CGI scripts

Prices

20mb	$18/month
50mb	$25/month
100mb	$30/month
200mb	$40/month

Webnet Advertising Services
Suite 4, Level 3
379-383 Pitt Street,
Sydney P.O. Box 682
Rozelle NSW
Australia 2039
http://virtual.inta.net.au
(Prices are in Australian dollars)

Basic Plan: 10MB
Set-up: $59   Monthly: $25   Annually: $275
Unlimited data transfer   POP e-mail accounts
2 Auto responders Unlimited e-mail aliases
24-hour CGI-BIN access   24-hour TelNet access
Free CGI scripts OC3 connection
FrontPage (optional) Dedicated IP address
Real Audio/Video (optional)
Netscape Compatible Encription/SSL (optional)

Developer Plan: 25MB
Set-up: $59   Monthly: $45   Annually: $495
Plan includes all features of Basic Plan but with 3 POP e-mail
accounts, and 3 Auto Responders.

Developer Plus Plan: 50MB
Set-up: $59   Monthly: $65   Annually: $715
Plan includes all features of Developer Plan with more space.

Professional Package: 75MB
Set-up: $89   Monthly: $89   Annually: $979
Plan includes all features of Developer Plus Plan but with 5 POP
e-mail accounts, 5 Auto Responders, and more space.

WebMaster Package: 100MB
Set-up: $159   Monthly: $149   Annually: $1639
Plan includes all features of the Professional Package but with:
Unlimited POP e-mail
Unlimited Auto Responders

Unlimited e-mail aliases
1 Page SSL Secure Server
Real Audio/Video Set-up

CYBERARTS/swissart
Im Grund 21
CH-8424
Embrach, Switzerland
www.cyberarts.ch
Tel: 011-41-1-865-0853
Fax: 011-41-1-865-0869
info@cyberarts.ch
(All prices are in Swiss francs)

CYBERARTS offers web hosting services in English and German. The minimum contract is for three months. Services other than those listed are available.

	Individual	Professional	Commercial	Industrial
Monthly fee	45	75	125	150
Set-up fee	100	100	100	100
Space	20mb	30mb	50mb	75mb
Data transfer				
(MB/month)	600	2000	3000	4000
E-mail address	10	20	30	40
POP3 accounts	6	11	21	31
Domain name				
registration	*	*	*	*
FTP updates	*	*	*	*
Web stats	*	*	*	*
Raw log access	*	*	*	*
FrontPage support	*	*	*	*
Guest book		*	*	*
CGI script support	-	*	*	*
Anonymous FTP control	*	*	*	*
Volcano chat	-	*	*	*
Real Audio	-	-	*	*
Real Video	-	-	*	*
SSL secure server	-	-	*	*
Shopping cart	-	-	*	*

Virtualis Systems, Inc.
11288 Ventura Blvd., Suite 717
Studio City, California 91604
U.S.A.
Tel: 818-766-7976
Fax: 818-985-3833
www.virtualisys.com
virtuali@virtualisys.com
(Prices are in US dollars)

VS Mini Plan

15mb total space	$36/month	$96 set-up fee
Private domain	24-hour free tech support	
T3 access Full FTP/Telnet access		
1 POP e-mail address	Standard stats reporting	
3 custom e-mail aliases	Full FTP/Telnet access	
1 GIG daily transfer	On-line order form	
Fully automated Guest Book	SSL (option)	

FrontPage server extensions available
Search engine registration support
Unlimited use of forms and CGI scripts

VS Midi Plan

30mb total space	$56/month	$96 set-up fee

This plan includes all the VS Mini options plus:
"Dump account" e-mail feature Unlimited e-mail aliases

Unlimited POP accounts	VS Stats Gold reporting
Full support Real Audio	Bulletin board feature

VSA Web Site Security utility VSA Web Page spell check

VS Mega Plan

60mb total space	$96/month	$96 set-up fee

This plan includes all of the options of the VS Midi Plan plus:

Virtual hosting support	Unlimited auto responders
VSA search engine	VSA Post Office
VSA Auto Response Manager	Anonymous FTP upload
Web stats e-mailed daily	Anonymous FTP download

VS Meta Plan

150mb total space $176/month $96 set-up fee
This plan includes all VS Mega options plus:
5mb SSL secure server for e-commerce
Multi-FTP software
Chat room software
Web site installation of mSQL database engine

AdvanTech Consulting Corporation
Tel: 860-668-0044
Fax: 860-668-7471
http://www.atconsult.com
info@atconsult.com
(Prices are in US dollars)

All plans include:

Unlimited traffic   FrontPage support
Unlimited e-mail tech support   Private domain
CGI options including hit counters and e-mail forms
Multiple high-speed DS3 connections to the Internet

All plans entail registration of your domain name for a one-time fee of $70. This includes the first 2 years of use. There is a one-time server set-up charge of $75.00. Extra disk space for each plan is $1.50 per MB per month.

Option 1: Basic Web Site
$29.95/month

Included are:
5MB total space   10 e-mail aliases
Updates via FTP or through AdvanTech Consulting

Option 2: Web Site Plus
$64.95/month

This plan includes everything in Option 1 plus :
25MB total space   Unlimited e-mail aliases

Support for mSQL database   Shell Unix account
Extras available:
Netscape Compatible Encryption Support: $75. One-time fee, not
   including fee for annual digit certificate from VeriSign.
Real Audio: $75 set-up fee plus $10 per stream per month.

Option 3 Fully Functional Server
$99.95/month
This plan includes everything offered in Option 2 plus:
75MB total space   Creation of POP e-mail accounts
Unlimited e-mail aliases   FTP access to your site
Extras available:
Netscape Compatible Encryption Support and Real Audio as priced
   in Option 2.

TaylorFX Web Services
P.O. Box 31
Whitelaw, WI 54247
920-732-3448
www.taylorfx.com
admin@taylorfx.com
(Prices in US dollars)

	Personal	**Commercial**
Monthly fee/account	$29.95	$59.95
One time set-up fee	$40.00	$40.00
Storage space	10MB	20MB
Multiple T1 connection	*	*
Telnet access/24 hour	*	*
FTP access/24 hour	*	*
Unlimited monthly Web transfers	*	*
Extra storage space	....available...	
Daily usage stats	-	*
Unlimited e-mail support	*	*
Online user's manual	*	*
Private domain and IP number	-	*
1 POP e-mail box	*	*
Unlimited e-mail aliases	-	*
E-mail forwarding	-	*
Unlimited mail redirection	*	*

Additional POP mailboxes	...available...	
Imagemaps	*	*
Private CGI-BIN	-	*
Anonymous FTP (by request)	-	*
Password-protected pages	-	*
Autoresponders (unlimited)	-	*
Listserv/mailing list (majordomo)	-	*
Apache SSL secure server	-	*
24-hour system monitoring	*	*
System backups every 2 days	*	*
Counter Script	*	*
WWWBoard generator	-	*
Guestbook generator	-	*
Chat room generator	-	*
HTML script	*	*
mSQL database software	-	*
PGP (encryption)	-	*
HTGREP (site search)	-	*
CGI e-mail forms	-	*
PHP2	-	*
CGI WRAP	-	*
Meta-HTML (by request)	*	*
Parked domains	...available...	

GLOSSARY

A

Address Resolution Protocol—helps network equipment and devices to ascertain an Internet protocol address.

Asymmetrical Digital Subscriber Line—a protocol facilitating delivery of substantial amounts of information over copper telephone lines.

Asymmetric Cryptography—the means by which decryption and encryption occur using different keys.

Automated Clearing House (ACH)—an electronic funds transfer system used in the United States to clear electronic payments for participating banks.

B

Back-End Processes—computing of information on mainframe systems or services.

Blind Signatures—DigiCash system that delivers e-cash from a financial institution without revealing the name of the person authorizing the delivery.

C

Cable Modem—a modem providing information transmission bandwidths of up to 30 Mbps using cable TV wiring.

Certificate Authority—an independent entity issuing and maintaining digital certificates for those on the Web who qualify.

Certificate Revocation List—the listing of participants on the Web who no longer qualify for digital certificates.

Common Gateway Interface (CGI) Script—the scripting process for HTTP Web servers. The script typically allows for information to be exchanged between databases and a Web server. The coding language is Pearl.

Cipher—the procedure to be followed in translating information into a code, such as for security purposes. The encoded message is referred to as cipher text.

Common Data Security Architecture (CDSA)—a cross-platform applications programming interface developed by Intel that acts at the system level. It enables performance of cryptographic activities, including algorithms of encryption, using a uniform interface. Many companies are active in this area of use, including VeriSign, Netscape, and Datakey.

Crypto API—an application-oriented programming interface developed by Microsoft that allows for cryptographic functions. Its modular nature provides for substitution in cryptographic algorithms. It can also be used with digital certificates.

Cryptographic Algorithm—the mathematical derivation integrating text with a series of digits (a "key") to generate unintelligible cipher text.

D

Data Encryption Standard—an algorithm or block cipher developed by IBM that has a 56-bit key plus functions in a 64-bit block, is an expeditious way to encrypt voluminous data.

Diffie-Hellman—an approach enabling two people to share a key to exchange messages. The drawback to this system is that it cannot be used with digital signatures or encryption.

Digital Cash—cash in electronic form.

Digital Certificate—a document in electronic form issued by a trusted third party to substantiate the reliability of an Internet vendor or to state a business entity's identity by substantiating its public key.

Digital Signature—unique signing of electronic correspondence through encryption of a message along with the private key of the sender.

Distributed Computing Environment Protocols—protocols for the storage of software modules and their use on a network. It is typically used for authentication and for common interface applications.

Domain Naming Service—a service to networks for translating numeric IP addresses to text-based names.

E

Electronic Data Interchange (EDI)—standardized electronic exchange of documents among the computers of different business entities. Documents exchanged include sales invoices, purchase orders, quotes, credit memos for damaged or returned goods, and shipping reports. EDI transactions are usually between a buying company and a supplier company.

Electronic Fund Transfer (EFT)—a mechanism facilitating electronic payments such as remittance advices among banks and direct deposits of salaries into the bank accounts of workers.

Extranet—the connection of the Intranets of two or more businesses. The Extranet is a bridge between the public Internet and private Intranets; it allows connection of multiple companies such as suppliers, distributors, contractors, customers, and trusted others behind virtual firewalls. Extranets enable commerce through the Web at a very low cost and allow companies to maintain one-to-one relationships with their customers, members, staff, and others. Information on the Extranet may be restricted to the collaborators or may be public. Because Extranets are flexible, scaleable, portable, and extensible, they significantly reduce barriers to cross-organizational networking.

F

Fiber Distributed Data Interface—a standard used in transmissions over fiber optic networks.

File Transfer Protocol (FTP)—a protocol associated with the transfer of information on the Internet between client computers and file servers. Files may be transferred, downloaded, and uploaded individually or in batch form.

Financial EDI—EDI between businesses and their banks, enabling banks to receive money from companies and release money to pay suppliers, payees, utilities, etc.

Firewalls—security controls for information transferred over a network between two parties providing protection against misuse of data. A firewall prevents protocols or databases from being compromised. However, firewalls cannot protect against viruses or assure authentication or privacy.

Front-End Processes—computer applications using client computers attached to mainframes or servers.

G

Gateway—software that enables two networks to transfer data between them even though they are different protocols.

H

Hypertext Markup Language (HTML)—uniform coding for defining Web documents. The browser examines the HTML to ascertain how to display graphics, text, and other multimedia components. HTML is easier to program than Window environments like Motif or Microsoft Windows. HTML is a good tool for integrating database applications and information systems. It facilitates the use of hyperlinks and search engines, enabling the easy sharing of identical information among different segments of the company. Intranet data usually goes from back-end sources (e.g., mainframe host) to the Web server to users (e.g., customers) in HTML format.

Hypertext Transfer Protocol—the protocol that determines how an HTML file is transmitted from server to client on the Web.

I

Integrated Services Digital Network (ISDN)—a global, totally digital, communications network using telephone lines. It has a lot of bandwidth.

International Data Encryption Algorithm—an encryption algorithm with a 128-bit key.

Internet Mail Access Protocol—a recent protocol for processing messages.

Internet Protocol—a protocol providing address space for directing packets over an network.

Internet Service Provider (ISP)—a company such as Prodigy, CompuServe, and America Online in business to service customers so they may access the Internet.

Intranet—a private network within a company. Intranet users can access the Internet, but firewalls keep outsiders from accessing confidential data. Making use of the infrastructure and standards of the Internet and the Web, Intranets use low-cost Internet tools, are easy to install, and are flexible. They have already been established by at least two-thirds of Fortune 500 companies and many other organizations. Quick response times require that the Intranet have a direct connection to the server. Employees in different divisions of the company and in different geographic areas can use centralized as well as scattered information. The major element in an Intranet is the Web server software running on a central computer that serves as a clearinghouse for all information. Intranet applications are scaleable: They can begin small and grow. This feature allows many businesses to "try out" an Intranet pilot, publishing a limited amount of content on a single platform and evaluating the results. If the pilot succeeds, additional content can be migrated to the server. Intranets also provide access to external information resources, including group access to mailing lists, threaded discussion groups, and stock/bond quotes.

IP Address—identification of a computer in the network by a numeric address.

K

Key—a sequence of digits that, coupled with a cryptographic algorithm, results in cipher text.

M

Market Space—the market in which e-commerce is carried out.

Microcash—digital tokens of small denomination.

Micromerchants—businesses on the Internet providing goods or services and receiving payment in digital cash or e-cash.

Microtransactions—real-time transactions with microcash.

Middleware—software that processes transactions for a customer who is accessing many company databases.

Multimedia Internet Mail Extensions—a protocol attached to e-mail messages comprised of two or more multimedia parts, such as sound, video, and graphics.

N

Network Access Points—on-ramps to the Internet, such as that kept by Sprint.

O

One-Way Hash Function—the process for translating a message into a message digest (string of digits). A key is not needed.

P

Packet—information grouped for transfer on a digital network. The packet is comprised of a bit sequence that combines actual data with control data to assure proper transmissions.

Personal Digital Assistant—a small portable device for electronic computing.

Points-of-Presence—in a domestic or global communications network, the local access points. A local call will access the network. For example, a user of America Online dials a local telephone number to access a global network of information.

Point-to-Point Protocol—a protocol for transmission using serial modems.

Post Office Protocol—a protocol for e-mail on the Internet that facilitates message retrieval.

Pretty Good Privacy—control of and security for e-mail transmission on the Internet. Encryption standards are used for a particular operating system. The message may be encrypted before e-mail software is used.

Privacy-Enhanced Mail—the safeguarding of e-mail via symmetric or public keys. However, this standard cannot be used with multimedia Internet mail extensions.

Private Key—a key for encrypting messages; the originator does not know what it is.

Protocol—the guidelines and principles associated with the workings of a network; the rules for data and electrical signals on the network, how information is transmitted, accessing the network, and processing applications on the network.

Proxy Server—used to safeguard key information and applications related to a network. Proxy servers close out an incoming connection and initiate a second connection to the destination to assure that an incoming user has to use information asked for from the destination before the information is transferred to the user.

Public Key—the key a receiver uses to decrypt a message, made public to interested parties as required.

Public Key Cryptography—an encryption approach using both a private and a public key. Encoded messages can be decoded with either key.

R

RC—an algorithm of RSA Data Security Inc. that uses ciphers for quick bulk encryption applications; faster than the Data Encryption Standard.

RSA—a public key encryption algorithm of RSA Data Security Inc. involving encryption of a variable key length and blocksize text. The text block is smaller than the key length, which is customarily 512 bits.

S

Secured Electronic Transaction (SET)—a protocol used both for other applications (e.g., Web browser) and as a standard to process credit card transactions over the Web.

Secure Hypertext Transfer Protocol—a protocol supporting the hypertext transfer protocol that fosters security, privacy, and authentication for data communications between a browser and a Web server.

Secure Multimedia Internet Mail Extensions (S/MIME)—a more recent standard of RSA Data Security Inc. using cryptographic algorithms to provide authentication from a certificate authority for digital certificates.

Secure Sockets Layer (SSL)—a protocol giving authentication, confidentiality, and information integrity when communicating. SSL security applies between the application layer and the transport and network layers. While SSL may be applied to transactions outside the Web, it does not provide authentication at the document or application level.

Secure Wide-Area Network—a protocol for authentication and encryption of packets, including the management and exchange of keys. The protocol fosters interoperability between firewall vendors and router.

Simple Mail Transport Protocol—an Internet protocol important in transmitting e-mail messages between servers.

Simple Network Management Protocol—a protocol to manage network equipment, including switching hubs, bridges, and routers.

Smart Card—a small plastic card resembling a credit card that is uniquely embedded with an integrated circuit for electronic data. It provides security on who uses it, how it is used, and what data is stored on it.

Spoufing—an individual pretending to be someone else on the Web; otherwise, any improper electronic transfer of information.

Symmetric Encryption—a method wherein receiver and sender of electronic data use the identical key so either may encrypt or decrypt information.

T

TCP/IP Protocol—a protocol explaining the subdivision of information into packets for transmission and how applications transmit e-mail and files.

TelNet—an Internet standard applying to remote host access and terminal emulation.

Tokens—strings of digits representing an amount of a particular currency. Each token is digitally stamped by a bank for authentication purposes.

Trading Partner Agreements—the terms acceptable to two or more parties to a business transaction that stipulate the type of data to be exchanged electronically.

Transactional Commerce—customer transactions in real time with data contained in corporate databases.

Transmission Control Protocol—a protocol determining the highest packet size and other attributes of the transmission. This protocol is designated if the objective is to have perfect transmission.

Triple DES—encrypting a grouping of data three times, each time with a different key.

U

Uniform Resource Locator (URL)—a method of identifying and describing a resource on the Internet. A URL starts with the protocol name to obtain the data from the server, followed by the text name of the resource or IP address.

User Datagram Protocol—a protocol defining the maximum packet (transmission) size as well as improving the transmission. If perfect transmission is not needed, this may be the way to go.

V

Value Added Network—a private network for electronic transfer of information among business partners.

Virtual Corporation—a company having employees in many different geographic localities who communicate with each other totally or mostly in electronic form.

Virtual Private Network—a private network that uses the Internet to save on costly leased telephone lines.

W

Wallet—an aid to a Web browser in which an encrypted credit card number is passed between buyer and seller. It remains on the server of the credit card company (e.g., Cyber Cash) for approval after authentication has been made.

Web Browser—software that enables one to hook up with network servers to obtain HTML documents and Web pages, linking pages and documents. The physical server may be on the Internet or on a private network. The browser may contain "help" applications for special files.

Web Server—software that manages information at the Web site. The program enables responses to be made to requests for information from Web browsers.

Index

I

X

Y